印度

中国

CHINA
AND
INDIA

चीन

LEARNING FROM
EACH OTHER

Reforms and Policies
for Sustained Growth

भारत

Production: IMF Multimedia Services Division
Cover design: Noel Albizo
Typesetting: Michelle Martin

Cataloging-in-Publication Data

China and India : learning from each other : refoms and policies for sustained growth/
[editors: Jahangir Aziz, Steven Dunaway, and Eswar Prasad] — [Washington, D.C.:
International Monetary Fund, c2006]
   p. cm.
  ISBN 1–58906–519–0
  Includes bibliographical references.
   1. Banks and banking — China. 2. Banks and banking — India. 3. Securities
industry — China. 4. Securities industry — India. 5. China — Foreign economic
relations — India.
I. Aziz, Jahangir. II. Dunaway, Steven. III. Prasad, Eswar. IV. International Monetary
Fund.

HG3334.C35 2006

Price: $35.00

Please send orders to:
International Monetary Fund, Publication Services
700 19th Street, NW
Washington, DC 20431 USA
Telephone: (202) 623-7430   Telefax: (202) 623-7201
E-mail:publications@imf.org
Internet: http://www.imf.org

recycled paper

Contents

Foreword
Governor Zhou v

Preface. ix

Acknowledgements xv

Part I. Financial Sector Reforms: Banking

1. Banking Sector Reform in India
    Nachiket Mor, R. Chandrasekar, and Diviya Wahi. 3

2. Reforming China's Banking System: How Much Can Foreign
    Strategic Investment Help?
    Nicholas Hope and Fred Hu. 33

3. The Banking System Structure in China and India
    Luo Ping. 84

Part II. Financial Sector Reforms: Securities Markets

4. Development of the Securities Market in India
    G.N. Bajpai 93

5. Development of Securities Markets: The Indian Experience
    Narendra Jadhav. 114

6. Accelerating the External and Internal Opening Up of China's
    Securities Industry
    Xinghai Fang, Ti Liu, and Donghui Shi 135

Part III. Financial Integration

7. Domestic Financial Liberalization and International Financial Integration: An Indian Perspective
    Suman Bery and Kanhaiya Singh 145

8. Putting the Cart Before the Horse? Capital Account Liberalization and Exchange Rate Flexibility in China
    Eswar Prasad, Thomas Rumbaugh, and Qing Wang 181

Part IV. Other Policies for Sustaining Growth

9. Some Apparent Puzzles for Contemporary Monetary Policy
    Rakesh Mohan 203

10. Fiscal Policy in China
    Steven Dunaway and Annalisa Fedelino 231

11. Labor Mobility in China and India: The Role of Hukou, Caste, and Community
    Arvinder Singh 241

Part V. Indo-China Economic Cooperation

12. Indian Economic Development and India-China Cooperation
    Nalin Surie 263

13. India-China Economic Cooperation
    Arvind Virmani 270

Foreword

On October 27 and 28, 2005, the international seminar *Changing Economic Structures in China and India: Domestic and Regional Implications* jointly organized by the International Monetary Fund, the China Society for Finance and Banking, and the Stanford Center for International Development was held in Beijing. Representatives from central banks and monetary authorities as well as research institutions in China, India, Japan, Korea, Singapore, and China's Hong Kong Special Administrative Region attended the Seminar and discussed the subject from six perspectives, that is, banking sector reform, securities market development, domestic financial liberalization and international financial integration, fiscal dimensions of sustaining high growth, Sino-India economic cooperation, and the implications of China and India's emergence for the regional and international financial system.

It is a pleasure to know that the IMF has compiled the presentations and discussions of the seminar into this book. I would like to take this opportunity to offer my own views on the subject, especially the changing economic structure in China.

Since the inception of reform and opening up in 1978, the Chinese economy has been growing in a steady and rapid manner, with GDP growth averaging 9.4 percent annually. However, like many other countries in the world, the prospect of sustainable economic development hinges on its economic structure. At the moment, the structural problems are mainly reflected in the excessive investment growth on the one hand and slow growth of consumption (both domestic consumption and imports) on the other; economic growth relies heavily on manufacturing while service industry is relatively underdeveloped; the inequality of income distribution has somewhat deteriorated. Consequently, these structural problems caused over-consumption of energy and raw materials, excess capacity and associated excessive competition in investment goods, induced export, external account imbalance, and rapid build up of foreign exchange reserves.

Having acknowledged these problems, the Chinese government has adopted structural adjustment measures. The direction of such adjustment is clearly explained in the *Outline of the Eleventh Five-Year Plan* adopted at the Fourth Session of the Tenth National People's Congress. We are going to build a harmonious society and, in particular, a socialist new countryside, in order to solve the problems facing agriculture, rural areas, and farmers with preferential fiscal policies to improve and build rural infrastructure; we also advocate a principle of giving priority to efficiency while attaching importance to equality in income distribution; and we have taken measures to lower the domestic saving rate and increase consumption by boosting domestic demand. Unlike other countries, China can not depend on short-term investment to raise domestic demand. Rather, we need to encourage household consumption. According to statistics, household consumption accounted for only 40 percent of China's GDP. There is a large potential for further expansion. However, due to limited land and energy resources, adjustment of consumption structure will have to rely on service sector growth. It is worth mentioning that as a populous country, China's labor market is very flexible, because a large number of farmers look for jobs in cities and coastal areas. China has benefited a lot from such flexibility of the labor market.

Despite statistical factors, compared with India, Russia, and Brazil, China's service industry still has much room for further growth. For example, the share of China's service output in GDP was only 40.7 percent in 2004. In contrast, India's service industry made up more than 50 percent of its GDP in 2003. Take the film industry as an example. The output of Bollywood might be about 20 times that of the Chinese film industry. After allowing for culture, language, and other factors, we ought to reflect on the reasons behind such a difference, and find out why and how the service industry in China is lagging behind.

While some countries have called for greater liberalization of the service industry and some news magazines are also busy discussing the possibilities to further grow the global service trade with the support of the increased transportation capacity and advanced technology like the Internet, it should be recognized that even liberalization of the service industry could only play a limited role in fixing the imbalances in goods trade. For example, the service industries including travel, catering, and hotel and entertainment are mostly concentrated in the fields of culture and arts, which carry a strong local flavor, thus are on most occasions classified as domestic trade. Except by international sea and air transport, domestic shipments are hard to deliver across the border. Some sensitive sectors such as the telecommunication industry are yet to be liberalized completely for competition. Even with enforced protection of intellectual property rights, the transaction volume of service trade between China and the United States is limited to tens of millions of dollars, with barely any significant impact on the Sino-U.S. trade.

Take the financial industry as an example. With the pace quickened to open the domestic financial sector to foreign competition, China has started allowing foreign investors to buy stakes in domestic financial institutions and become participants in the domestic financial market. These include the Bank of America's equity investment in the China Construction Bank, the Royal Bank of Scotland's investment in the Bank of China, New Bridge's equity taking in Shenzhen Development Bank, and the introduction of qualified foreign institutional investors in the domestic market. These foreign investors usually send a few people only to hold key positions in risk control and business management in the invested companies while leaving all other responsibilities to the staff from the Chinese side. Based on rough calculations, we could see there is only a fairly limited amount of service trade in these transactions. Even in terms of the insurance industry, which takes a relatively large proportion of the financial service trade, only a bit more than US$6 billion of deficits was recorded in China's balance of payments in 2005. Intermediary services like the accounting service display some similarities to the financial sector. All in all, the financial sector usually does not account for a large proportion of the total service trade, and its role particularly needed in certain countries to compensate for the deficits in goods trade is even more limited.

According to relevant reports, commercial banks are developing soundly in India with low NPL ratios, proper order, and a good legal environment. In terms of capital market development, India also has relatively advanced stock and equity markets. Despite the fact that China has a high saving rate and the Chinese financial sector maintains a comparatively high liability ratio (with broad money supply accounting for 180 percent of the GDP), there exists a great potential for growth of the financial industry. Compared with India, what are the reasons behind some of the weaknesses that have emerged in the course of financial development in China? The answers, according to our own studies, may lie first in the "financial eco-system" of China. "Financial eco-system" comprises not only environment at the macro level such as the legal, supervisory, regulatory, and government intervention policies, but also micro conditions related to efficiencies of the financial institutions' business operation. Besides, the centralized planning economic system adopted in the past has consequently resulted in low efficiencies of the financial sector in many aspects as well as some mistakes in the building of institutions, policy framework, management framework, and the regulatory system. These mistakes need to be corrected continuously in the ongoing reform process.

China and India are both large developing countries and we face similar challenges in developing our respective economies. In this regard, the experiences and lessons gained by our two countries are worth learning from each other. I believe frequent exchange and cooperation between our two countries will help to strengthen mutual understandings and economic growth in the region, thus benefiting people of both countries.

DR. ZHOU XIAOCHUAN
Governor of the People's Bank of China

Preface

Over the last 15 years, China and India have added more than US$2¼ trillion to global GDP, 120 million in employment in China alone, and have pulled 220 million people out of poverty. These are large numbers: like adding a country with the economic size of Greece to the world each year; creating as many new jobs in a year as Australia's total employment; and completely eradicating poverty in Ethiopia, Nigeria, Tanzania, and Zambia combined. It is, therefore, not surprising that the international community has paid a lot of attention to economic developments in China and India. This surge in attention has resulted in a large number conferences on the countries in the last few years. More often than not, the focus of these conferences has been on what the rise of China and India as economic powerhouses means for the world. This is an important question.

Another, equally important, question is: what can the two countries learn from each other's experiences? With this in mind, the IMF and India's National Council of Applied Economic Research (NCAER) organized the first China-India conference in New Delhi in November 2003, bringing together policymakers, officials, and academics from the two countries to share their experiences.[1] That conference stimulated lively and productive discussions, and encouraged us to organize a follow-up meeting two years later; this time in Beijing in October 2005, with the help of the China Society for Finance and Banking (CSFB) and the Stanford Center for International Development (SCID).

This book is a compilation of selected papers presented at that conference. Its unique contribution is that a majority of the chapters are written by policymakers and practitioners, rather than just academics. For instance, Reserve Bank of India Deputy Governor Rakesh Mohan discusses how the forces of globalization can complicate the challenges facing monetary policymakers in emerging economies, such as China and India. In his contribution, People's Bank of China Governor Zhou Xiaochuan contrasts the growth of the services sector, including financial

---

[1]Papers from that conference were published in Tseng and Cowen (2005).

services, in China and India and discusses the importance (and difficulties) of developing this sector in China. Other contributions bring to bear perspectives from the financial sector, banking regulators, securities regulators, stock exchange officials, planning commissions, and think-tanks closely affiliated with decision makers. Thus, the analytical discussions in this book are all infused with a sense of pragmatism and policy relevance.

Financial Sector Reforms: Banking

Financial sector reforms are a key component of the economic reform strategies of both China and India. The important role of the banking sector in financial intermediation in these countries has focused particular attention on this aspect of financial reforms.

Nachiket Mor, R. Chandrasekhar, and Divya Wahi provide a brief history of bank regulation in India and then review the main banking reforms since the early 1990s. They note that banking sector performance has improved in many dimensions and may have contributed to improved growth performance over the last decade. They argue, however, that further reforms are needed, including improvements in the financial services infrastructure, reductions in the cost of intermediation, and scaling up of banking services to provide broader access to financial services, especially in rural areas.

Reform of the Chinese banking system was pushed into high gear earlier in the current decade. While some progress has been achieved, however, Nicholas Hope and Fred Hu contend that the core problems of the banking system remain unresolved. Their paper enumerates the priorities for banking reform and provides an assessment of the role that foreign strategic investors could play in the reform process. They conclude that foreign investors could catalyze improvements in corporate governance, disclosure standards, and asset quality, but they also caution that these very issues could pose risks and obstacles for foreign investors.

Luo Ping compares the structure and robustness of the Chinese and Indian banking systems as well as the effectiveness of their banking supervisory systems. He observes that both countries have accomplished a great deal in reforming and improving their banking industries in recent years. But the Indian banking system has, by virtue of India's earlier start in the reform process, attained greater improvements in asset quality, capital adequacy, and quality of supervision. He notes that the Indian experience may provide some useful lessons for Chinese policymakers.

Financial Sector Reforms: Securities Markets

A well-rounded financial sector that does not rely solely on banks is important for effective financial intermediation. In their papers, G.N. Bajpai and Narendra Jadhav describe the importance of securities market development. Bajpai provides an overview of the steps that India has taken to build a well-supervised world-class infrastructure for trading securities, and discusses how this has been associated with improvements in corporate governance among listed companies. Jadhav traces the development of specific securities markets in India—equities, corporate debt, and government securities—and discusses how policy reforms have contributed to these outcomes. Bajpai and Jadhav concur that, despite all of the progress that has been made, deepening of the corporate debt market and some refinements in regulation of securities markets are still needed in India.

Xinghai Fang, Ti Liu, and Donghui Shi argue that opening the Chinese securities industry to both internal and external competition could play a crucial role in enhancing its efficiency. They argue forcefully that fears that foreign competition could overwhelm the domestic securities industry are misplaced and that, in the absence of innovation and discipline stimulated by increased competition, development of the securities industry could in fact be greatly hampered.

Financial Integration

Suman Bery and Kanhaiya Singh provide an overview of the literature on the costs and benefits of integration with international capital markets, and how the cost-benefit tradeoff is related to domestic financial liberalization. They then trace the evolution of India's financial liberalization and financial integration processes, including the relationship between policy reforms and outcomes in terms of the nature and level of liberalization and integration, respectively. Bery and Singh conclude that, while one cannot ignore the risks of international financial integration, further integration could have significant benefits for India in terms of stimulating financial sector development and improving macroeconomic policy discipline.

Eswar Prasad, Thomas Rumbaugh, and Qing Wang contend that, while capital account liberalization could play an important role in China's economic development, undertaking further liberalization *before* allowing for greater exchange rate flexibility could pose some risks. They note that the Chinese banking sector has limited net foreign exchange exposure and could withstand fluctuations in the exchange rate. But banking system weaknesses could make premature capital account liberalization risky. Exchange rate flexibility would provide room for an independent monetary policy oriented to domestic objectives, which would help foster macroeconomic and financial stability.

Other Policies for Sustaining Growth

Rakesh Mohan provides a sweeping overview of some challenges facing modern monetary policymakers. He sets the stage by providing an analytical characterization of a number of contemporary "puzzles," including the strength of the U.S. dollar despite soaring twin deficits in the United States, low consumer price inflation in major economies despite abundant global liquidity, and continued strong global growth despite the surge in oil prices and low investment rates. He contends that rising globalization may make traditional monetary policy instruments less potent, and uses the examples of China and India to illustrate that this point is particularly relevant for developing economies.

Steven Dunaway and Annalisa Fedelino discuss fiscal policy in China. Chinese fiscal policy has been prudent in recent years, with low levels of fiscal deficits and debt (relative to GDP), especially compared to many other emerging market economies. These authors note that fiscal policy has been guided largely by the government's medium-term focus on fiscal consolidation to make room for financing contingent liabilities, including in the state-owned banking system, and rising spending pressures as the population ages. They argue that, to make greater use of fiscal policy for demand management, broader and better coverage of fiscal accounts, an improved budget classification system, and better cash management to facilitate coordination of fiscal and monetary policies are needed.

Arvinder Singh examines the factors behind, and the implications of, labor mobility in China and India. He notes that, unlike the *hukou* system in China that restricts movement of labor from rural to urban areas and across provinces, there are few legal restrictions on labor mobility in India. Nevertheless, in both economies, cultural and social factors play important roles in determining the levels and patterns of labor mobility.

Indo-China Economic Cooperation

Arvind Virmani examines the rising trade linkages between China and India. While the level of bilateral trade has grown in recent years, it remains low in absolute terms. Virmani argues that the bilateral trade potential is very high, given the size and dynamism of the two economies and their complementary production and trading patterns. He discusses the main barriers to realizing the full potential of China-India trade—including customs rules and procedures, certification and regulatory practices, nontariff barriers, and rules of origin—and makes some specific recommendations to reduce these barriers. Virmani also makes the case for a comprehensive economic cooperation agreement between the two economies.

Nalin Surie describes how, despite following different reform trajectories, both China and India have now moved on to high growth paths. He compares and contrasts the two development models, picking out some important lessons from each country's experience. In India, stable financial markets have facilitated an efficient allocation of resources, but public sector inefficiencies and an underdeveloped infrastructure have held back growth. China's rapid integration into the global economy, especially through rising trade linkages, has boosted its growth, but the underdeveloped financial sector remains a weak spot. Surie notes that both countries face similar socio-economic challenges—unemployment, rural-urban inequality, environmental and water problems, needed improvements in health and education, the status of women, etc. He concludes that China-India development cooperation is not a zero-sum game and that effective cooperation between the two countries could have broader benefits for the Asia-Pacific region and the global economy.

Jahangir Aziz, Steven Dunaway, and Eswar Prasad

Acknowledgments

This volume is a compilation of selected papers and presentations from a conference held in Beijing in October 2005. The co-sponsors with the IMF of this conference were the China Society for Finance and Banking (CSFB) and the Stanford Center for International Development (SCID).

We are very grateful to David Burton, Director of the IMF's Asia and Pacific Department, for his constant support of and encouragement for this project. We thank Akira Ariyoshi, Director of the IMF's Office of the Asia and Pacific, for sponsoring this conference. Li Yang of the CSFB and Nicholas Hope and Roger Noll of the SCID helped organize the program, with valuable guidance from the People's Bank of China.

Carolina Klein did an outstanding job managing the logistics of the conference and also prepared the manuscript. Li Jing and Belinda Ruch provided excellent administrative support. Sean Culhane edited the manuscript and managed the production process with his customary efficiency.

The Editors

PART I

FINANCIAL SECTOR REFORMS: BANKING

1

Banking Sector Reform in India

Nachiket Mor, R. Chandrasekar, and Diviya Wahi*

It is widely believed[1] that the reforms of 1991, both in the industrial sector and the financial sector, released a variety of forces that propelled India into a new growth trajectory.[2] In this paper, we are going to assess the role that the banks played in making this growth happen and the impact that these reforms had on banks.

We start with a brief history of banking regulation in India. We then move on to outline some of the principal reforms that were implemented in the 1990s and their impact on the banking sector. Although this section does present some data in support of its arguments, it is by no means a rigorous analysis of the issues at hand. It seeks instead to present ideas and hypotheses based principally on the insights gained by the authors through observing these developments as participants in the system. We suggest that this period created certain problems for the banking system, the sources of which remain largely unresolved. We propose that unless

---

*Nachiket Mor is an Executive Director with the Industrial Credit and Investment Corporation of India (ICICI) Bank, India, and is the Chairman of the Managing Committee of the Institute for Financial Management and Research (IFMR), Chennai, India. R. Chandrasekar is a faculty member at IFMR and is the founder of the Centre for Advanced Financial Studies at IFMR. Diviya Wahi is a Manager with ICICI Bank. An earlier version of this paper was presented by Nachiket Mor at an India policy conference organized by Stanford University's Center for International Development on June 1–3, 2005. The current version is a substantially revised one. The authors thank Lakshmi Kumar of IFMR for providing very able research assistance.

[1]See DeLong (2003) and Clark and Wolcott (2003) for an alternate point of view.

[2]See, for example, Mohan (2005).

the unique set of circumstances[3] that existed during the past decade manifest themselves in this decade, there is a possibility that the future could see the Indian banking system facing difficulties. We conclude by suggesting some reform strategies that could equip the financial sector to better address the challenges that lie ahead.

History of Bank Regulation in India

The financial sector in any country acts as an intermediary between suppliers of funds and borrowers. In many countries, banks have traditionally taken center stage among financial intermediaries. The banking regulatory framework that was put into place in many countries following the Great Depression of the 1930s had two broad goals. The wave of bank failures and the subsequent move by surviving banks into "safe haven" investments (typically government bonds) meant that credit availability shrank dramatically, exacerbating the economic downturn. Hence, one goal of the United States Federal Reserve Board was to prevent this scenario from recurring. The resulting regulations were formulated with the objective of reducing the risks inherent in banking. Regulation Q[4] controlled the cost of deposits, and several restrictions were placed on how banks operated.[5] Many central banks, including the Reserve Bank of India (RBI), followed these regulations. The second broad regulatory goal was to protect depositors from bank failures. By providing assurances of safety to depositors, the regulator could ensure that the supply of savings was not affected. In the United States, this took the form of a formal deposit insurance scheme by the Federal Deposit Insurance Corporation (FDIC), which was initiated in 1934. Diamond and Dybvig (1983) and Holmstrom and Tirole (1997) suggest that aggregate liquidity shortages provided the rationale for deposit insurance. These two regulatory goals were complementary in that both helped ensure the flow of credit, and the deposit insurance scheme was in a sense guaranteed by the regulated borrowing and lending rates. Implicit in this model of regulation was the notion that the failure of a bank could cause a run (Diamond and Rajan, 2001), which could spread to other banks and create a generalized credit shortage that could have severe adverse economic consequences.

---

[3]Specifically, a decline in interest rates and a rapid growth in the balance sheet size.

[4]The ceiling stipulated in Regulation Q became binding in the 1960s and was extended to all depository institutions after 1966.

[5]See, for example, Fabozzi and others (2002) for a description of regulations governing financial intermediaries and the changes that have taken place.

In India, neither externality was of consequence, given the practice of monetizing the budget deficit,[6] the prevalence of directed credit, and the fact that the system of industrial licensing that was in force in India until 1991 served to provide significant "credit insurance" to banks, by protecting borrowers from meaningful economic competition.[7] And even the possibility of a run was remote because the nationalization of the bulk of the banking sector in 1969 meant that an implicit guarantee from the government applied to deposits in certain categories of banks.[8] Banking regulation in India, nonetheless, continued to follow the "classical" pattern and in practice meant the following:

- The regulator specified detailed procedural guidelines on each aspect of the banking business.
- The principal focus of inspection and supervision was ensuring that procedures were followed.
- There were fixed borrowing and lending rates, and a completely fixed set of interest rates and slowly moving exchange rates in the larger economy.
- Lending was directed toward certain "priority" sectors (such as agriculture and small-scale industries) and a specified class of "weaker" borrowers.
- There was a very tight separation between banks and nonbanks.[9] Banks[10] could offer checking and savings accounts to the general public but were constrained to maintain very high liquidity ratios and engage only in "safe" working capital finance. The nonbanks—which included the development finance institutions (DFIs), such

---

[6]This practice meant that an independent monetary policy was impossible (Reddy, 2002).

[7]As the paper later argues, the removal of this form of "credit insurance" in 1991 led to a significant buildup of nonperforming assets in the banking system, because banks lacked the capability to properly assess the enhanced level of credit risk.

[8]This has been further reinforced by the repeated injections of capital by the government into poorly performing government-owned banks and financial institutions, even in the past decade. Even the private sector banks have largely been free from the fear of failing owing to the government's guarantee of taking over uncovered liabilities of the bank, whether private or nationalized, in the event of a failure. See Banerjee, Cole, and Duflo (2004).

[9]India, while very particular about this separation for a variety of reasons, does not seem to have toyed with implementing Glass-Steagall type regulation.

[10]Unfortunately, even though the regulatory intent may have been to let only highly regulated and well-capitalized institutions into this "club," whether by design or by accident, relatively poorly capitalized and poorly regulated entities, such as cooperative banks and regional rural banks, were also permitted entry.

as the Industrial Development Bank of India (IDBI), the Industrial Finance Corporation of India (IFCI), and the Industrial Credit and Investment Corporation of India (ICICI), and a large group of non-bank finance companies (NBFCs)—were given a much wider latitude in their lending operations but were allowed to borrow only from wholesale sources and capital markets. By offering term deposits to retail individuals (not checking or savings accounts), they were not allowed to participate in the interbank market or clearing.

Essentially, the banking process became the focus of regulation and supervision. Consequently, the delivery of credit and the risks assumed by the banking sector received very little attention from the regulator. Although it is possible that there were large economic costs paid by the country of this process-driven approach, it is generally believed that the system held together, albeit with periodic blowouts ("scams"). In this paper, we attempt to show that the reforms of the 1990s not only failed to address the basic philosophical underpinnings of the regulatory process but also removed some of the key "safeguards" that kept the structure broadly intact, and that it is fortuitous that we are not in a major banking crisis today.

Reforms of the 1990s

Although there is some debate on whether the reforms of 1991 were the single point of departure for the reforms process within India (see Clark and Wolcott, 2003), there is no doubt that the measures that were announced then (and shortly thereafter) had a profound impact. Because the details of the full reform process are easily available elsewhere (see Mohan, 2005), the following paragraphs discuss only a few of these measures.

Industrial licensing was effectively dismantled and entrepreneurs were essentially free to set up any capacity, subject only to obtaining some minimal clearances (Rajaraman, 1993). However, because there were very few business houses and even they had very little capital, the only real constraint became the availability of finance from the DFIs. Given the manner in which banks and DFIs were being regulated, as described earlier, industrial licensing combined with fixed interest rates was the most important form of implicit "credit insurance" available to the financial system. The removal of this safeguard, given the shallow project finance competencies that DFIs had built by then, was significant.[11] The sections

---

[11]Neither the industrialists nor the bankers had any real experience dealing with risk (credit risk and market risk) implications of free markets. They therefore financed proj-

below on drivers of post-liberalization growth of the Indian economy, the rapid buildup of gross nonperforming assets of banks and nonbanks, and the annexed case study on the steel industry show that many decisions taken by the banking system after this liberalization were consistent with the hypothesis of a serious lack of competency. The commercial banks were historically permitted to participate only in working capital finance.[12] They were therefore largely insulated from the vicissitudes of the Indian economy, because they always enjoyed the protection of equity from the promoter and the capital markets, and long-term debt from the project financier. The reforms of the 1990s permitted them entry into project and other long-term financing. To that extent, the removal of this "safeguard" affected them directly. Even in their core business of working capital finance, they experienced a similar consequence—they did not have as much "protection" from equity and long-term debt—in the case of small and medium enterprises and priority-sector lending.

Pricing of Some Financial Assets Determined by Market Forces

In particular on the lending side for nonpriority sector debt, commercial banks and DFIs were given complete freedom to lend money at rates of interest that they could freely determine (Reddy, 2002). As there were no market benchmarks and very little liquidity in either the government of India securities market or the corporate bond market, this effectively meant that each lender was free to determine its own methodologies for arriving at these prices. However, it was this partial deregulation that created a high level of distortion in the interest rate market because, very importantly, the rates of interest on the savings and current accounts were kept

---

ects in a mechanical manner and at historically fixed rates of interest, despite multiyear drawdowns. For example, published information for ICICI shows that there was a swing of more than 2 percent in the net interest margin, from 5.22 percent in 1993–94 to 3.37 percent in 1995–96. This swing, in all likelihood, was entirely due to lack of experience among bankers because during this period market interest rates and therefore funding costs rose by 2 percent (see Figure 1.4). There were very few business houses, and the reform had the effect of transferring the decision-making process from a few members in the planning commission (who at least had the benefit and the incentive to look at economy-wide demand-supply gaps) to a few businessmen who had neither the incentive nor the competency to fully understand market dynamics of demand and supply in a rapidly globalizing marketplace.

[12]Working capital finance in cash-flow terms always has first charge on the borrower's cash and goes up and down with the actual sales or production of the company.

regulated[13] across the banking system, and only commercial banks (not NBFCs and DFIs) were allowed to access these low-cost funds. Because these accounts together accounted for approximately 30 percent[14] of the liabilities of the banking system, they became the strong anchors of the entire interest rate structure. The fact that short-sales were not permitted and interest rates on priority-sector loans and small loans were tightly capped further exacerbated the situation. In return for being permitted to offer savings and checking facilities, commercial banks continued to be required as a part of their statutory liquidity ratio (SLR) to maintain a high level of investment in government securities (GSecs)[15] in India and a substantial cash reserve ratio (CRR).[16] On the other hand, an additional measure that had a very negative impact on the DFIs was the removal of the SLR status of bonds issued by the DFIs, in 1991.[17]

Post-1991 Reforms: Developments in the Indian Economy and Their Impact on the Banking System

In the period since the 1991 reforms, the Indian economy and the financial system witnessed many changes. It is not clear if all of these changes

---

[13]Current accounts were permitted only to businesses and had to offer a zero rate of interest. Savings accounts were permitted only to individuals and had to offer a 3.5 percent rate of interest. (Figure 1.6 shows the savings account rate over the past decade.) A lower rate was effectively given to active account holders because of the methods used in computing the principal amount to which this rate could be applied.

[14]Calculated from RBI, Annual Accounts Data on Scheduled Commercial Banks, 1990-93.

[15]It is not clear if this was really a penal measure because almost all the government-owned commercial banks maintained a significantly higher than required proportion in these securities. These investments had a very high duration for almost all the banks, in large part as a direct consequence of the issuance of these securities by the government of India with long maturities combined with high durations. (Very little floating rate debt has to date been issued by the government of India.)

[16]This high degree of preemption may have acted as a kind of "credit risk protection" by limiting the freedom of the commercial banks to participate in the lending business.

[17]The SLR status effectively ensured that commercial banks (CBs) treated these bonds almost on par with government of India securities. A case can be made that the DFIs lost relative competitive strength when compared with CBs as the effective systemic subsidy provided to the CBs through strong interest rate controls on savings and current accounts remained high. This led to (1) a strong resistance on the part of the CBs to further interest rate deregulation and (2) an equally strong desire on the part of the DFIs for conversion to a CB despite the fact that the onerous SLR and CRR obligations would have to be met upon conversion to a bank.

Figure 1.1. Growth in GDP and Credit
(In percent)

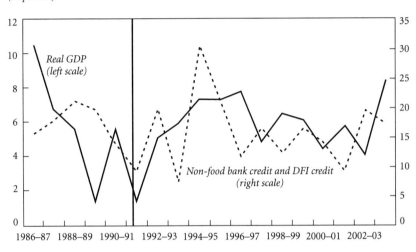

Sources: Central Statistical Organization; and Reserve Bank of India (RBI).

Note: Development Financial Institutions include Industrial Development Bank of India, Industrial Finance Corporation of India, Industrial Credit and Investment Corporation of India, Small Industries Development Bank of India, and Industrial Investment Bank of India.

were directly related to the reforms, but we address a few of the changes and explore whether the reform process could have had any bearing on them.

Acceleration of Growth Rates

After the 1991 reforms, acceleration of growth in all sectors of the Indian economy was the most visible consequence of the reforms. The break in the growth trend during 1992 is clearly discernible from Figure 1.1. However, if one looked more carefully at the sources of growth, one would possibly discover that very high, largely finance-led capacity accounted for the rapid growth rates, and that the lowering of growth rates in subsequent years was therefore not entirely an unsurprising consequence. Credit grew rapidly in the early 1990s and declined in the later years. In addition, studies suggest that the growth during the 1990s was unaccompanied by any growth in total factor productivity (TFP). Goldar (2003) finds a decline in the productivity growth rate in the 1990s relative to 1980s; although TFP growth accounted for 7 percent of the manufacturing growth during the 1980s, it accounted for almost nothing of the manufacturing growth during the 1990s.

Figure 1.2. Excess Capacity in Industries After Reforms
(In percent)

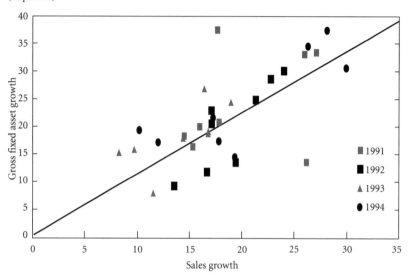

Source: Prowess Database, Centre for Monitoring Indian Economy.
Note: Industries covered: textiles, food and beverages, chemicals, machinery, metal and metal products, nonmetallic mineral products, transport equipment, and miscellaneous manufacturing.

Very High Levels of Capacity Creation in Almost Every Industry

In part led by the consortium financing system, but largely because neither industrialists nor bankers had any experience operating in liberalized environments, almost every project that was submitted for financing was accepted. As a consequence, the system created capacity (which is quite possibly what showed up as growth numbers) in industry after industry—steel, man-made fiber, paper, cement, textiles, hotels, and automobiles received a major share of the large loans given principally by the DFIs and partly by the CBs. Figure 1.2 shows excess capacities created in the manufacturing sector, particularly textiles, chemicals, food and beverages, and metals industries, which is reflected by the excess of growth of fixed assets over growth of sales in these industries.

High Buildup of Gross Nonperforming Assets in the Banking System

As can be seen from Figure 1.3, there was a rapid buildup of nonperforming assets (NPAs) in the banking system. These mounting NPAs, together with excess capacity, suggest a strong possibility that these two

Figure 1.3. Gross and Net Nonperforming Assets (NPAs) of Commercial Banks, End-March

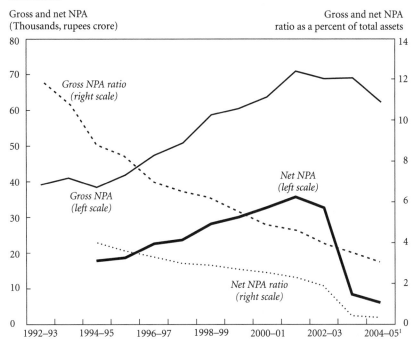

Sources: RBI, Report on Trend and Progress of Banking in India, Handbook of Statistics on Indian Economy; and Centre for Monitoring Indian Economy.

[1]Data for 2003–04 and 2004–05 pertain to Centre for Monitoring Indian Economy sample.

developments were linked to each other in a causal fashion. Almost four in five projects experienced large delays in implementation, and a few celebrated cases could not complete financial closure because of the collapse of equity markets. Three of the five major financial institutions— Unit Trust of India, IFCI, and IDBI—had to be given large infusions of capital by the government of India. One major institution, ICICI, entered the retail finance business and between itself and its subsidiary, ICICI Bank, raised about US$2 billion from international and domestic sources. Despite staying largely out of the project finance business, the CBs also experienced a great deal of stress, with the net worth of three government-owned CBs turning negative. All industrial investment largely came to a halt with all players experiencing a "knee-jerk" reaction to these developments in the financial system. The Appendix presents a case study of the steel industry, which gives a more detailed insight into how these capaci-

Figure 1.4. Trends in Yield on 10-Year Government Securities (GSecs)
(In percent)

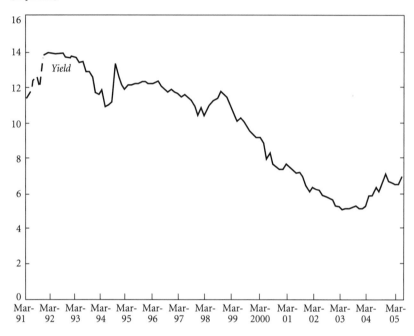

Sources: Various publications of RBI; Bloomberg; and ICICI Bank Research.
Note: Year: (a) Mar-91 to Mar-96—Approximate yearly average 10-year GSec yield; (b) Mar-97 to Mar-05—Monthly 10-year GSec yield series.

ties, NPAs, restructured assets, and high levels of provisioning came about for one major industry in India. RBI for the first time issued guidelines, in 1994, for the classification of assets and recognition and provisioning of non-performing assets using exclusively a days-overdue criterion and allowed a great deal of time before even unsecured defaulting loans had to be fully provided for. To date, this very heavily lagging indicator, remains the sole benchmark of asset quality.

Secular Decline in Interest Rates From 1996 to 2004

The yield on 10-year government of India securities fell from 13.93 percent in April 1996 to a low of 5.15 percent in April 2004 (Figure 1.4). Banks continued to invest heavily in GSecs during this entire period, with the proportion of incremental deposits invested in these securities rising to as high as 100 percent for some banks. Figure 1.5 shows that the differential between annual increments in GSec holding and demand

Figure 1.5. Yearly Change in Demand Deposits and Government of India Security (GSec) Holding of Commercial Banks
(In thousands of rupees crore)

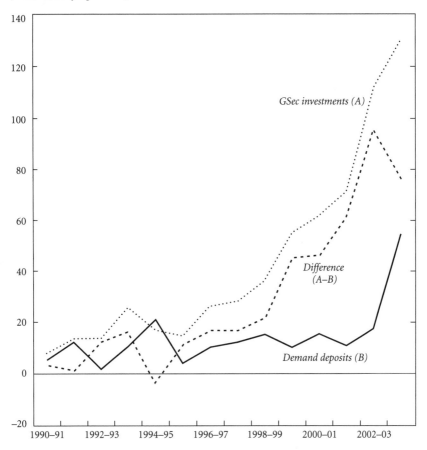

Source: RBI, Handbook of Statistics.

deposits was positive (except in 1994–95) during the 1990s, and that the gap continued to widen towards the end of that decade. And even though interest rates on these securities fell steadily (because interest rates on savings accounts and current accounts were tightly regulated and kept well below the "risk-free" rate, as can be seen from Figure 1.6),[18] they

_____

[18]Unavailability of sufficient data does not permit precise comparisons in Figure 1.6; however, it does reflect to some extent the argument made here about the higher Indian gap (Indian 10-year GSec yield vis-à-vis savings rate) as compared to the U.S. gap).

Figure 1.6. Deposit Rate vis-à-vis 10-Year Government of India Security (GSec) Yield in India and the United States
(In percent)

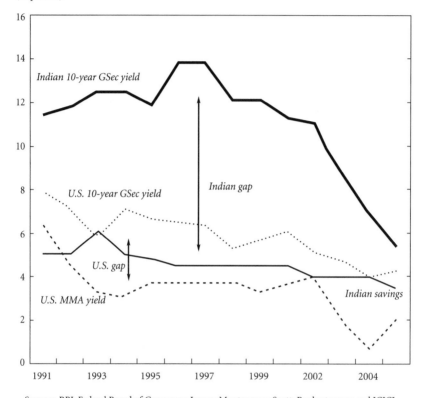

Sources: RBI; Federal Board of Governors; Janney Montgomery Scott; Bankrate.com; and ICICI Bank Research.

Note: Indian GSec yields and savings rate pertain to the fiscal year. U.S. GSec yields pertain to the calendar years.

MMA: 1991–2000: approximate MMA rate of a sample bank in Janney Montgomery Scott's Asset/Liability Report plots yields for the month of March for that year. 2001–04: approximate MMA national averages sourced from Bankrate.com plots yields for the month of March for that year.

imposed a substantial implied tax on depositors. Commercial banks were permitted to retain the entire benefit of this implied tax, which in effect amounted to a large-scale recapitalization of the banks.[19] Although it is possible that the interest rate developments were entirely the consequence

---

[19]The government largely owned these banks, which presents an interesting conundrum when examining the fiscal deficit of the government of India.

Figure 1.7. Yield on 10-Year Government Securities of Select Nations
(In percent)

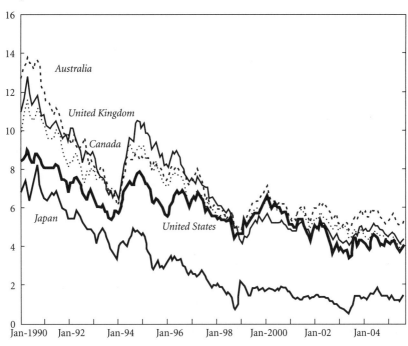

Source: Bloomberg.

of similar trends elsewhere in the world (Figure 1.7), these developments are important because in our view, they are the most important reasons the system remains broadly solvent.

This is because banks maintained a very high level of investment in government of India securities (Patnaik and Shah, 2002), not only in terms of the total quantum invested but also relative to the maturity profile of their deposits (Figure 1.8). These high levels of investments mismatched in amounts and in maturity profile were the direct consequence of the very same poor understanding of risk management within the system that produced excess capacity, outlined above. In addition, the banks' net income from these sources relative to other sources of income become a dominant part of their income streams. These two factors alone produced a net transfer from the government and the depositor to the banking system of an average of approximately Rs. 106 billion a year between 1990–91 and 1999–2000.

Figure 1.8. Investment in Government of India Security vis-à-vis Maturity Pattern of Term Deposits, End-March
(In thousands of rupees crore)

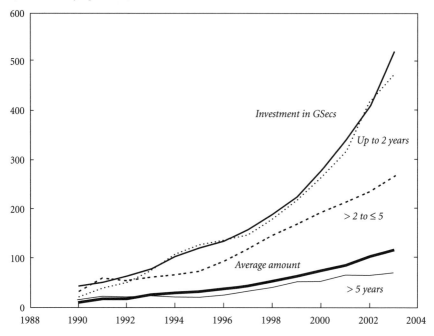

Source: RBI, Handbook of Statistics.

To summarize, four factors are therefore principally responsible for the current "healthy" state of the banking system. Three of these produced incremental profits and capital that was used toward very high levels of incremental provisioning.

1. The implied government guarantee ensured that the public never lost confidence in the banks. For instance, despite the fact that Indian Bank's net worth turned negative in 1995–96, the bank has continued to maintain an average growth in deposits of more than 10 percent (1995–96 to 2003–04).[20]

---

[20]This is one of the key risks of "premature" privatization. If the process of privatization precedes an improvement in the manner in which these banks are run and managed, the recurrence of such an event could lead to a large run on these banks and/or a sharp increase in their cost of funds.

Figure 1.9. Commodity Price Index (1967 = 100)

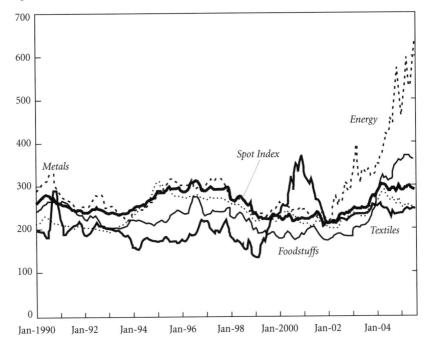

Sources: Commodity Research Bureau and Reuters.
Note: Spot Index for 22 main commodities.

2. The large and persistent difference between the cost of demand deposits (current and savings) and the rate of return on the government of India securities (risk-free rate) helped banks to post some profit.

3. The secular fall in the interest rates on government of India securities, the very long-duration issuance and purchase by public sector banks, and the very high level of duration mismatch between assets and liabilities of banks allowed banks to book profits in their trading books at will by simply selling the older bonds and buying newly issued ones.

4. High levels of explicit capital injection into DFIs and banks helped these banks to remain liquid.

In the above sections, we have tried to argue that the removal of the two key safeguards in the economy (industrial licensing and full control of interest rates), when combined with poor regulation of and competency in risk management, government ownership, and fresh injections of capital in a few cases, produced effects that served to cancel each other out as interest rates declined rapidly.

There have been some additional developments from the late 1990s to the present that have allowed imbalances in the financial system to persist without revealing the true extent of the underlying problems. Some of these are mentioned below.

Rapid Buildup of Retail Finance Since 1996

There has been a very strong upsurge in demand for retail loans. Unlike corporate loans—where the focus is principally on the quality of analysis and on a multistage review process that sometimes goes all the way to the chair and managing director of the bank, which (presumably) ensures that all of the talent of the bank is brought to bear on the exposure—retail loans, given their inherently small value but very high volume, need to be dealt with differently. Unless very tight process disciplines are maintained and a fair degree of centralized control is exercised through the use of technology and formalized protocols, underlying risk levels, in part linked to a rising incidence of fraud, can quickly start to produce very high levels of nonperforming assets.

Increase in Commodity Prices Since 2000

Thanks largely to Chinese demand and the domestic retail financing boom, prices in several key sectors are at all-time highs (Figure 1.9). As a consequence, except in a few cases, after some deep restructuring most of the NPAs have now started to generate an adequate level of cash to service their obligations.

Impact of SARFESI, DRTs, CDR, and ARCIL

Facilitative regulation and the development of asset reconstruction companies have made it somewhat easier to recover at least some money from bad loans.

Likely Developments in the Economy After 2005 and the Impact on the Banking System

Enhanced Levels of Volatility in Financial Asset Prices

Commercial banks (which now include even the former DFIs—ICICI and IDBI—that have converted themselves into banks) continue to have on their books very long-duration government of India securities, with some holding as much as 45 percent of their assets in these securities (Patnaik and Shah, 2004). Interest rates have started to rise, with 10-year government of India securities increasing from 5.11 percent in October 2003 to 6.99 percent in April 2005 (and trading at 7.19 percent on May 16, 2005). Although there is clearly a strong desire to hold high-quality assets, given the virtually complete absence of transfer pricing methodologies in operation, there is no link between the cost of funds and the rates that are offered on loans.[21]

Enhanced Levels of Volatility in Commodity Prices Accompanied by Fundamental Shifts in Sector Shares

As the economies become more globally integrated, it becomes harder to keep them insulated from global shocks. Increasing volatility has more pronounced adverse effects, especially on developing economies, which rely on undiversified export baskets or the risk of unfavorable terms of trade. Because it is neither feasible nor sustainable for the government to interfere in market mechanisms to overcome global price volatilities accompanied in some cases by sectoral shifts, it is imperative for the key players to develop tools and capabilities to mitigate such risks by factoring them in early in business proposals.

Increased Demand for Credit from Manufacturing, Infrastructure, and Agriculture

A strong demand for project finance is emerging. Given the complete absence of risk quantification and capital attribution methodologies[22] actually being by banks, it is not clear if the banks and DFIs will be able to correctly assess the risks inherent in these projects and meet the required demand in a manner that is substantially different from their behavior in the early 1990s.

Enhanced Levels of Competition from Insurance Companies and Asset Management Companies for Bank Deposits

Historically, banks have acted as prime intermediaries by channeling financial flows from the surplus to the deficit sectors. However, opening

---

[21]It is very difficult to find any direct relationship between rates of interest that are charged by the banks and the credit risk or market risk that these rates imply.

[22]Although many banks will claim that they have these in place, even if they do have a formal risk department and risk policy in place, it would be important to see what the relationship between the pricing of specific loans is relative to the underlying rating, capital attribution, and the bank's target return on equity numbers.

up the mutual fund and insurance sectors to private players in 1993 and 2001, respectively, has freed up avenues for such flows across the economy. This ongoing relaxation has put pressure on bank-assured sources of funds.

Suggestions for the Reform Process

The earlier sections attempted to make the argument that even though a number of changes have been made to the manner in which banks are regulated, the basic philosophical underpinnings of regulation have not changed.

It is our view that there is a need to fundamentally shift the focus of regulation from adherence to procedures for each bank to banking outcomes for the banking system as a whole.[23] It is our belief that privatization of banks is neither a necessary nor a sufficient condition for these reforms to take root and show results. In fact, "premature" transfer of ownership to an overly activist management or, worse, a corrupt management, in the absence of these changes runs the risk of serious bank failure and loss of confidence in the banking system.[24] The above-mentioned shift in focus and some additional reform suggestions are discussed in greater detail below.

Shift from a Focus on Detailed Processes that Banks Use to a Monitoring of Outcomes

This constitutes a shift at the most fundamental level in the basic philosophy with which banks are regulated. In practical terms this means that the banking regulator will not specify procedures that banks must follow, but will allow each bank to design them internally[25] and will specify only the desired outcomes in the broadest possible terms. The focus of regula-

---

[23]Perhaps an outcome-oriented mission statement for the regulator for which it is responsible, such as universal access to financial services and increased depth of financial markets, may be useful to explore as well.

[24]It is important to remember that even if the capital base supporting a bank is supplied by the private sector, even under very conservative capital adequacy regimes no more than 6 to 8 percent of Tier 1 capital is required (compared with close to 25 to 30 percent even in the most leveraged industries). It is not very difficult to erode that level of capital (and under current regulation, without even being aware that this has happened) unless the bank is managed very tightly.

[25]The most recently issued technical paper on banking correspondents is a good example of what needs to stop.

tion will then shift from assessing adherence to standardized procedures[26] to qualitatively assessing the basic competencies of bank managements to develop and execute consistent strategies and business models.

For this to work, however, the outcomes will need to be specified and measured very carefully, and then will have to be publicly[27] disclosed with reasonably high frequency. Thus, such meaningful disclosures will result in (1) market disciplining of the bank by altering the availability and price of capital, (2) signaling potential weaknesses to both customers and regulators, (3) allowing the regulator to focus on issues relating to the accuracy and timeliness of disclosures rather than on processes, and (4) focusing of regulation on outcomes (both systemic and institution specific) rather than on processes. One of the most important outcomes and one that has been the basis of much of the work in the Basel Accord of 2004 (commonly referred to as Basel II) is the manner in which the capital base of the bank is linked to the risks that the bank takes and the returns that it earns on them. Fortunately, even though there is not a complete consensus on the models that should be used to compute capital consumption for each risk class, there is a sense that most modern models (even those completely internally developed by a bank), if adequately tested historically and applied consistently going forward, have the power to provide a reasonably accurate estimate of actual capital usage. Clearly the most important piece of disclosure for a bank would be to report and for the auditor to certify, at least once every quarter, (1) a detailed analysis of the consumption of capital at an aggregate level[28] and by each

---

[26]A "regulation-by-circular" approach runs the very real risk of attempting to develop mechanical processes to try to manage the complexity that is faced at every level in a bank. This is not only an impossible task within a bank but also an enhancement to the systemic risks faced by the banking system because every single bank takes an identical approach to each problem.

[27]Even a partial listing in the stock market (even as low as 1 percent) with an active minority shareholder base and suitable securities regulation that supports class action suits, for example, would render this a very effective tool. High frequency of public disclosure of outcomes is the principal reason the asset management industry continues to perform in an orderly manner, despite the largest asset manager being owned directly by the government of India and several others by very activist private sector managements.

[28]Some observers may argue that under Basel II, although segment reporting is not a requirement, at an aggregate level this reporting and adherence will become mandatory. However, the guidelines give the local regulator a great deal of flexibility in interpreting and applying the rules. For example, even under the proposed Basel II norms, large asset classes (such as fully committed but undrawn cash-credit lines) are excluded from assignment of capital. In addition, market risk capital is to be examined only on the traded book, not on the entire balance sheet. Further, under the standardized approach (which many

customer segment (urban individuals, rural individuals, manufacturing companies, financial market participants, and so forth) and by each line of business (credit cards, mortgages, corporate loans, financial markets, and so forth), and (2) an analysis of the return on that capital for each of these segments. Major banks in the United States, to a fair degree of detail, report by segment. Bank of America's annual report provides a good illustration of such reporting (Table 1.1). Furthermore, the reports should also satisfy a "readability" requirement for better understanding by lay investors and depositors.[29] Methodologies must also be developed to evaluate the impact on the bank of important prespecified shocks, such as movements in commodity prices, interest rates, and exchange rates.[30]

The focus of inspection can then shift to qualitative issues such as specific competencies of the bank staff and management (and boards) to measure and manage these outcomes. Mor and Maheshwari (2004) and Mor and Sharma (2002) argue that the very basic competencies that a bank needs to function effectively are (1) funds transfer pricing, (2) activity-based costing, and (3) risk quantification methodologies. It is indeed very surprising how few banks (if any) have these competencies.[31] However, we believe that once detailed public disclosure requirements are imposed, banks will have no choice but to rapidly develop them.[32]

The key to avoid the problems mentioned earlier is to ensure that bank managements have an incentive to develop the competencies required to consistently manage their day-to-day operations. Merely the requirement of full disclosure as specified above, combined with minority shareholdings, can substantially reform the current state of affairs.

Develop Essential Financial Services Infrastructure

Adequate infrastructure is indispensable for a well-functioning banking sector. The explicit government guarantee for bank deposits is one of the more obvious sources of moral hazard in the Indian banking system.

---

banks may choose to follow), unrated paper has 100 percent risk weight, creating a strong incentive for banks to choose this approach because lower grade ratings require higher risk weights. Such anomalies need to be addressed comprehensively.

[29]See the U.S. Securities and Exchange Commission handbook on how to create disclosure documents, www.sec.gov/pdf/plaine.pdf.

[30]See Mor (2005) for a listing of some of the unasked questions.

[31]Loans priced without any reference to the current interest rate environment, a quantified level of credit risk, and the implied operating cost are the norm within most private and public sector banks.

[32]Methodologies to do this are well within the reach of every bank.

Table 1.1 Segment-Wise Income, SVA, and ROE: Bank of America

(In millions of U.S. dollars)

Segment	Net Income		SVA[1]		ROE[2]	
	2003	2004	2003	2004	2003	2004
Global consumer and small business banking	5,706	6,548	4,367	3,390	42.25	19.89
Global business and financial services	1,471	2,833	846	884	25.01	15.34
Global capital markets and investment banking	1,794	1,950	893	891	21.35	19.46
Global wealth and investment management	1,234	1,584	854	782	33.94	20.17
All other	605	1,228	−1,339	36		
Total	10,810	14,143	5,621	5,983		

Source: Bank of America, Annual Report, 2004.

[1]SVA: Shareholders' Value Added (cash basis earnings on an operating basis less a charge for the use of capital, i.e., equity).

[2]ROE: Return on Average Equity (net income divided by allocated equity).

If indeed large and small bank failures become a real possibility, it will become important to ensure that systems such as the Real Time Gross Settlement are universalized.[33]

Lower the Cost of Intermediation

The cost of intermediation is very high in India, possibly among the highest in the world. A McKinsey study (Bekier and Nickless, 1998) shows that very heavy use of cash is responsible for this high cost of intermediation (something that is generally known to be true also for India). To gradually reduce these costs and the associated error rates (and therefore additional costs on account of these errors), there is an urgent need to increase the penetration of electronic payments on a nationwide basis by (1) immediately extending the electronic credit system to approximately 2,000 locations; (2) moving toward national settlement in payment systems with two entities, one each in physical and electronic settlement, respectively; and (3) allowing cash dispensation by debit to a credit/debit/ smart card at nonbranch/non–automated teller machine locations.[34] If, however, cash must be used, then there is a need to strengthen cash-

---

[33]See Mor (2005) for a discussion of some of the basic financial market infrastructure that would be needed.

[34]This last issue is likely to be addressed with the introduction of the Banking Correspondent Regulation.

handling capabilities nationwide while simultaneously providing strong incentives for switching to card-based or electronic transactions. The national cost savings, as well as the consequent reduction in the size of the parallel economy, could more than pay for the tax loss.

Improve Access to Financial Services

In over 600,000 villages in the country (and a far larger number of hamlets), the total number of rural bank branches of scheduled commercial banks (SCBs) does not exceed 30,000. The distance from a bank branch can be many kilometers for some residents. Even the total number of banks in India (284 SCBs in 2005) is significantly lower than that of the United States (7,630 FDIC-insured commercial banks in 2004), where community banks and national banks both work (and compete) to serve communities. In India, over 500 million people do not have bank accounts—against an estimated annual demand of Rs. 45,000 ($10 billion), the supply from the formal system is less than Rs. 2,000 ($400 million), and SMEs are not receiving adequate funds from banks. The formal rural financial sector is deeply troubled. Both regional rural banks (RRBs) and cooperative credit institutions suffer from poor access for customers, low levels of capitalization, and high default rates. The solutions being attempted even at this stage are minor modifications of earlier solutions; they do not appear to offer any real hope of solving the problems of either access or asset quality.[35] The "semi-formal" institutions (such as micro-finance institutions (MFIs) that are rapidly building outreach to (previously unserved) poor households are often hampered by implicit price caps, in the case of credit. Without a regulatory framework for correspondent banking arrangements, banks are unable to leverage

---

[35]There is also the added problem of specific institutional bias in favor of government-owned or -managed institutions, which urgently needs to be addressed. For example, while an RRB (RRB Act 1976, RBI Act 1934, Banking Regulation Act 1949) is able to operate as a full-service bank with only Rs. 10 million of capital, a microfinance institution is not permitted even NBFC (RBI Act 1934, Companies Act 1956) status with even Rs. 20 million of capital. A cooperative bank (Cooperative Societies Act, RBI Act 1934, BR Act 1949) can be set up with almost no capital but is permitted to deal with only apex cooperative banks and primary agricultural societies (state legislation). Short-term refinance support from National Bank for Agriculture and Rural Development is provided only to cooperative institutions and not to any other rural financial institution, no matter how much more effective and better performing it is in terms of indicators. It is also possible that the presence of this type of refinance support is delaying the creation of markets (and through that an implicit disciplining mechanism) for this class of assets.

the outreach built by MFIs to extend saving facilities. Thus, if the banking system is to scale up to meet this demand either directly or indirectly,[36] a lot more effort is required to put in place financial sector infrastructure and conducive regulation. This is critical if this scale-up is to happen, and if systemic risk is to be avoided as the system scales up. There is also an urgent need to build basic retail information infrastructure that comprises, among other things, (1) biometric identity cards for every adult with a unique national identity number, (2) a rural credit bureau, (3) universal Internet connectivity,[37] and (4) rural electronic weather stations (for index-based weather insurance).

Allow Innovative Approaches

Banks need to be provided with a great deal of leeway in terms of building outreach models (franchisee, branch, correspondent), with a focus on outcomes and not on uniform processes across banks. For instance, as opposed to the mandatory branch licensing approach in India, the banking correspondent model has been implemented to a fair degree of success in South Africa and Brazil. In Brazil, banking correspondents offer plain vanilla banking services from stand-alone kiosks and retail outlets located at superstores, drugstores, and petrol stations. These services usually include deposits and withdrawals, bill payment services, and insurance products, with formally licensed banks taking full responsibility for their correspondents' business conduct.

Appendix

Case Study: The Indian Steel Industry After Reforms

The Indian steel sector was one of the first core sectors to be freed from the licensing regime and the pricing and distribution controls during the reforms of the 1990s. Immediately after the reforms, the steel industry received a spate of investments. Appendix Figure 1.A.1 shows the cross-sector investment in plants and machinery since 1990. The figure clearly reveals that steel, despite having a relatively large asset base (even at the

---

[36]Through banking correspondents.
[37]See http://www.dotindia.com/uso/usoindex.htm. Current USO guidelines continue to emphasize voice over data.

Figure 1.A.1. Investment in Plants and Machinery in Select Industries during the 1990s

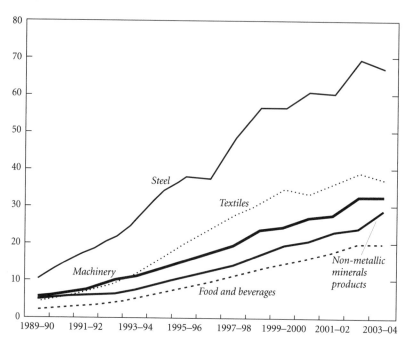

Source: Prowess Database, Centre for Monitoring Indian Economy.

beginning of the decade), continued to invest in assets, so that the gap between steel and other sectors widened considerably.

These investments were made with very little systematic analysis. Steel companies anticipated a large growth in demand from user industries after de-reservation. However, the expected demand on both domestic and global fronts failed to materialize. There were many reasons. Domestically, for example, investments in infrastructure fell short of expectations. Because of this and other factors, estimates reveal that against a projected demand of 31.0 mtpa (million tons per annum) in 2001–02, only 27.0 mtpa[38] materialized. The domestic steel industry also lost protection from competition, which resulted in depressed steel prices. Data suggest that the customs duty on HR (hot-rolled) coils was reduced in successive phases from 40 percent in 1994–95 to 27 percent in 1997–98.

---

[38]Data are from the Ministry of Steel.

Figure 1.A.2. International and Domestic Prices: Hot-Rolled Coils

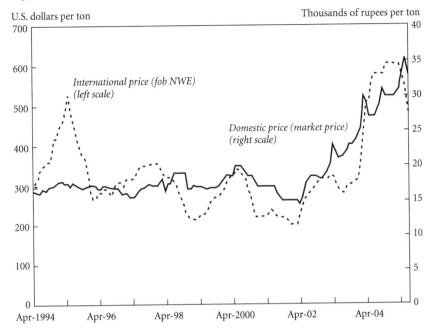

Source: CRIS INFAC Industry Information Service.

On the export side, the disintegration of the Soviet Union led to a glut in the markets as Commonwealth of Independent States countries began dumping steel. The lowering of customs duties and the excess supply in the global and local markets both exerted a lot of pressure on the steel prices in India (Appendix Figure 1.A.2).

Moreover, nontariff barriers imposed by major steel importing nations, particularly the United States and the European Union, also made conditions more difficult for exporters. Canada levied antidumping duties ranging from 16 to 96 percent on HR products imported from India in 2001 (Iyer and Wahi, 2004). The United States also initiated its preliminary antidumping investigations and imposed Section-201 in 2002. Other nations, worried that their markets would now be freely accessible to the steel diverted from these restricted markets, imposed a spate of similar barriers on Indian steel. The global economy also experienced the meltdown of South Asian markets in 1997–99 and the devaluation of the ruble that accompanied the 1999 Russian crisis. All these factors put tremendous pressure on steel prices worldwide (Appendix Figure 1.A.2).

Figure 1.A.3. Trends in Select Parameters of Steel Industry from the 1990s to the Present
(In thousands of rupees crore)

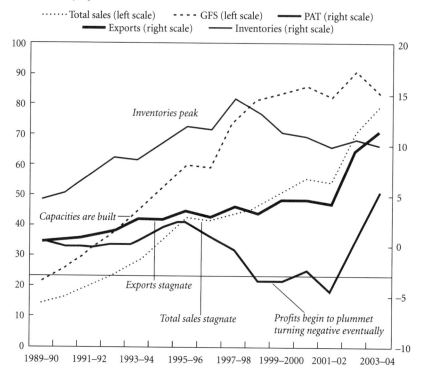

Source: Prowess Database, Centre for Monitoring Indian Economy.

Steel players in India faced a situation wherein excess capacity creation domestically coincided with domestic and global downturns. Appendix Figure 1.A.3 shows how the some of the key parameters behaved in the 1990s. It shows that after reforms, large investments in capacity creation were reflected in high gross fixed asset numbers. The events in the domestic economy and international economy, as mentioned above, created conditions during the mid-1990s in which inventories started to build, exports stagnated, and profits plummeted and eventually turned negative.

However, besides these external environmental factors, an analysis at the micro level (company by company) reveals that there were several internal factors as well that led to such a dismal performance by the steel sector. Evidence suggests that some of the promoters were first-generation entrepreneurs in

Figure 1.A.4. Credit Extended to Iron and Steel Industry

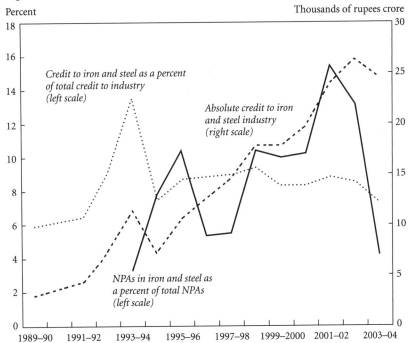

Source: Money and Banking, Centre for Monitoring Indian Economy.
Note: NPAs of one of the largest banks in India.

steelmaking who lacked the requisite experience to handle a downturn in this cyclical sector. This inexperience sometimes led to a multiplicity of objectives and business interests, and to midway modifications in project scope, a reflection of poor management skills. Poor vertical linkages and inability to grade the products also made production inflexible. In addition, most players lacked the ability to forecast the price and demand scenario. Because the import barriers came down faster than expected, the Indian steel industry was exposed to severe global competition in adverse economic conditions when both domestic and global markets were showing a downturn.

There was also a mismatch between some of the projects that were being implemented and the existing balance sheets of the companies, which were already facing inadequate internal accruals and high leverage. Companies sought to alleviate these constraints on internal resources through the capital markets. However, this solution was difficult because of high volatility in stock prices and several scandals, which shook the stock markets in the early 1990s and kept investors away. For example, a fixed income and equity market scandal in 1992 led to the crash of the stock markets in April 1992, just after the SENSEX (Bombay Stock Exchange, sensitive index) had reached its all-time high. Tax authorities froze shares of various big companies that belonged to proxy holders involved in the scandal. Similarly, owing to a ban on badla (forward) transactions, trading thinned after the Sensex had reached an all-time high in September 1994. As a consequence, the steel industry had to rely on debt as a primary means of finance during a period when interest rates were at record highs. In certain cases, projects were implemented without fully tying up the means of finance, which led to delays in project implementation as some of the anticipated sources of funds (such as capital markets) failed to deliver. Meanwhile, the interest burden continued to mount on the money that was borrowed to start the project.

The financial intermediaries who could have had a disciplining influence on all these companies and promoters were completely inexperienced themselves. The combination of inexperienced players acting in concert had a grave affect on the banking sector's level of nonperforming assets (NPAs). Appendix Figure 1.A.4 shows that there was a clear surge in credit extended to the iron and steel industry, both as a percent of total credit to the industry after the reforms of the 1990s, and in absolute terms showing a jump of 70 percent in the year 1992–93. Quite unsurprisingly, as a direct consequence of this profligacy, with a lag of a few years (because of the manner in which the NPA norms are defined) the share of NPAs of the iron and steel sector as a percentage of total NPAs of one of the largest banks in the country also shows a rising trend.

Bibliography

Ananth, Bindu, and Nachiket Mor, 2005, "Regulatory Aspects of Universalising Financial Services Access," Working Paper (Chennai, India: Centre for Micro Finance Research, Institute for Financial Management and Research). Available via the Internet: http://www.ifmr.ac.in/cmfr

Banerjee, Abhijit, Shawn Cole, and Esther Duflo, 2004, "Banking Reform in India," Department of Economics Working Paper (Cambridge, Massachusetts: Massachusetts Institute of Technology). Available via the Internet: http://econ-www.mit.edu/faculty/?prof_id=banerjee&type=paper

Bekier, Matthias M., and Sam Nickless, 1998, "Banks Need Fewer Checks, Not Fewer Branches," *McKinsey Quarterly*, No. 1.

Berger, Allen, Richard Herring, and Giorgio Szegö, 1995, "The Role of Capital in Financial Institutions," *Journal of Banking and Finance*, Vol. 19 (June), pp. 393–430.

Calomiris, Charles W., 1999, "Building an Incentive-Compatible Safety Net," *Journal of Banking and Finance*, Vol. 23 (October), pp. 1499–1519.

Clark, Gregory, and Susan Wolcott, 2003, "One Polity, Many Countries: Economic Growth in India, 1873–2000," in *In Search of Prosperity: Analytic Narratives on Economic Growth*, ed. by Dani Rodrik (Princeton, New Jersey: Princeton University Press).

Dasgupta, Susmita, 2002, "Non-Performing Assets of the Steel Industry—A General Economic Concern," Joint Plant Committee.

DeLong, J. Bradford, 2003, "India Since Independence: An Analytic Growth Narrative," in *In Search of Prosperity: Analytic Narratives on Economic Growth*, ed. by Dani Rodrik (Princeton, New Jersey: Princeton University Press).

Diamond, Douglas W., 1984, "Financial Intermediation and Delegated Monitoring," *Review of Economic Studies*, Vol. 51 (July), 393–414.

———, 1996, "Financial Intermediation as Delegated Monitoring: A Simple Example," Federal Reserve Bank of Richmond *Economic Quarterly*, Vol. 82 (Summer), pp. 51–66.

———, and Philip H. Dybvig, 1983, "Bank Runs, Deposit Insurance, and Liquidity," *Journal of Political Economy*, Vol. 91 (June), pp. 401–19.

Diamond, Douglas W., and Raghuram G. Rajan, 2000, "A Theory of Bank Capital," *Journal of Finance*, Vol. 55 (December), pp. 2431–64.

———, 2001, "Liquidity Risk, Liquidity Creation and Financial Fragility: A Theory of Banking," *Journal of Political Economy*, Vol. 109 (April), pp. 287–327.

Fabozzi, Frank J., Franco Modigliani, Frank J. Jones, and Michael G. Ferri, 2002, *Foundations of Financial Institutions and Markets* (Pearson Education Asia). Available via the Internet: http://www.asiansecurityweb.com/modules. php?name=Amazon&asin=0130180793

Goldar, B.N., 2003, "Productivity Trends in Indian Manufacturing in the Pre- and Post-Reform Periods," ICRIER Working Paper No. 137 (New Delhi: Indian Council for Research on International Economic Relations).

Gropp, Reint, and Jukka Vesala, 2004, "Deposit Insurance, Moral Hazard and Market Monitoring," Working Paper No. 302 (Frankfurt am Main, Germany: European Central Bank).

Holmstrom, Bengt, and Jean Tirole, 1997, "Financial Intermediation, Loanable Funds and the Real Sector," *Quarterly Journal of Economics*, Vol. 52 (August), pp. 663–92.

Iyer, Prahalathan and Diviya Wahi, 2004, "Export Potential of Indian Steel," Working Paper No. 6 (Mumbai, India: Export-Import Bank of India, February).

Jorion, Philippe, 2000, "Risk Management Lessons from Long-Term Capital Management," *European Financial Management,* Vol. 6 (September), pp. 277–300.

Knight, Malcolm, 2004, "Banking and Insurance Regulation and Supervision: Greater Convergence, Common Challenges," speech delivered at the International Conference of Banking Supervisors, Madrid, September 22–23. Available via the Internet: http://www.bis.org/speeches/sp040927.htm

Mohan, Rakesh, 2005, "Financial Sector Reforms in India: Policies and Performance Analysis," *Economic and Political Weekly,* Vol. 40 (March 19), pp. 1106–21.

Mor, Nachiket, 2005, "Expanding Access to Financial Services: Where Do We Go from Here?" *Economic and Political Weekly,* Vol. 40 (March 19), pp. 1122–27.

———, and Basant Maheshwari, 2004, "Evaluation and Supervision of Banks in Deregulated Real and Financial Markets" (Chennai, India: ICICI Research Centre, Institute for Financial Management and Research, July).

Mor, Nachiket, and Rupa Rege Nitsure, 2001, "Organisation of Regulatory Function— A Single Regulator?" (Chennai, India, December). Available via the Internet: http://www.ICICIresearchcentre.org

Mor, Nachiket, and Bhavna Sharma, 2002, "Rooting Out Nonperforming Assets" (Chennai, India: ICICI Research Centre, Institute for Financial Management and Research, October).

Nakada, Peter, and John Kapitan, 2004, "How Small Banks Are Using Economic Capital to Compete More Effectively," *RMA Journal,* Vol. 86 (March), pp. 32–37.

Patnaik, Illa, and Shah Ajay, 2004, "Interest Rate Volatility and Risk in Indian Banking," IMF Working Paper 04/17 (Washington: International Monetary Fund).

Pethe, Abhay, and Rupa Rege Nitsure, 2005, "Imperfections in Indian Regulation as Measured by the Subsidy Dependence Index: A Case Study of Banks and Financial Institutions," in *Regulation of Financial Intermediaries in Emerging Markets,* ed. by T.T. Ram Mohan and others (New Delhi: Sage Publications India Private Ltd).

Rajaraman, Indira, 1993, "Recent Economic Reforms in India," *Swords & Ploughshares,* Vol. 7 (Spring).

Reddy, Y. V., 2002, "Monetary and Financial Sector Reforms in India: A Practitioner's Perspective," paper presented at the Indian Economy Conference, sponsored by the Program on Comparative Economic Development, Cornell University, Ithaca, New York, April 19–20.

Visaria, Sujata, 2005, "Legal Reform and Loan Repayment: The Microeconomic Impact of Debt Recovery Tribunals in India" (Ph.D. dissertation; New York: Columbia University).

2

Reforming China's Banking System: How Much Can Foreign Strategic Investment Help?

NICHOLAS HOPE AND FRED HU*

The problems of the Chinese financial system, and particularly of its banks, have been well known. Since the reform era began in 1978, steady progress has been made in transforming the financial system, despite which some core problems of the financial system remain unresolved:[1]

- *The financial system is unbalanced and underdeveloped.* The securities markets are dwarfed by a banking system that is large measured against Chinese GDP, and deep—by the same measure—even when compared with developed economies. The banking system dominates the financial system, even under circumstances and during periods in which technically bankrupt banks might have been lending to inherently more creditworthy companies. In addition, state-owned agencies control both the financial and capital markets.

*Nicholas Hope is Deputy Director, Stanford Center for International Development, and Fred Hu is Managing Director, Goldman Sachs, and Professor of Economics, Tsinghua University. The authors acknowledge outstanding research assistance from Liming Huang of Goldman Sachs, Junga Kim, and Anita Alves Pena, as well as assistance with data from Dr. L.H. Cook of Econdata. Insightful comments from Steven Barnett, Pieter Bottelier, Luo Ping, Eswar Prasad, Yingyi Qian, Charan Singh, Jesse Wang, Bingxun Zhang, and an anonymous referee are acknowledged gratefully. Remaining deficiencies are attributable to the authors.

[1]Appendix I provides a chronology of reform from 1978.

- *The financial system is under-supported.* Institutional structures that provide support, such as rating agencies, accounting and audit bodies, credit and collateral registries, information systems and associated information technology, and the legal system are in their infancy. The institutions supporting the financial system have yet to develop sufficiently to provide an adequate framework for efficient and effective financial intermediation. The support provided by the legal system remains especially problematic, with particular concerns about contract enforcement, recovery of collateral, adequate standards of disclosure, and the vexed issues associated with bankruptcy and creditors' rights.
- *The banking system is inefficient.* In terms of both cost and allocation efficiency the performance of banks leave much to be desired. The banks are hugely over-staffed, and their overly extensive branch networks contribute heavily to their high operating costs. Their portfolios owe little to market-based assessments of the creditworthiness of their borrowers, and the result of the largely policy-based direction of their lending is very high levels of nonperforming loans (NPLs).
- *The banking system is potentially fragile.* As a legacy of central planning, the state-owned commercial banks (SCBs) are burdened with massive NPLs, which, if measured rigorously, imply that the SCBs are technically bankrupt, though that concept might have little meaning in a system in which the banks and most of their clients are state owned. Moreover, under no feasible assumptions could the SCBs reconstitute their ca pital by growing their way out of trouble. And further, even if freed from the obligation to prop up shaky state-owned enterprises (SOEs), there is every reason to question whether the four SCBs could rapidly reduce loan losses to acceptable levels, because of both a dearth of banking skills and the lack of a credit culture that emphasizes timely servicing of bank loans and supports efforts to recover collateral or other assets in cases of default.

These problems are generally attributable to the policies of the government and the lack of financial expertise residing in domestic financial institutions. But considerable efforts have been made in recent years to reduce the impact of all of the deficiencies outlined above; compared with any past year, the situation in 2005 shows general, across-the-board improvement.[2] And what has become evi-

---

[2]The next section and Appendix I describe some of the main accomplishments of financial reform to date.

dent, especially since China acceded to the World Trade Organization (WTO), is that the government has become increasingly willing both to amend its policies and to entertain (at least) partial foreign ownership of Chinese banks in order to improve their performance and competitive position. In some cases, policy changes seem to have as their main objective the encouragement of foreign investment in the Chinese banking sector. The Chinese government and foreign investors seem to agree that engaging the expertise of international strategic partners has the potential to improve virtually every dimension of Chinese banks' performance—overall governance; control and management of operations; introduction and marketing of new products; enhancement of asset quality; comprehensive, timely and accurate compilation of management information; better management of risk; stronger capital positions and better returns on equity; and rehabilitation of the banks' reputations.

In 2004–05, with the WTO deadline less than a year and a half away, much government focus and foreign investment interest developed around three of the four major SCBs, as well as several of the smaller banks. The introduction of foreign strategic investment holds tremendous promise for the on-going reform of the Chinese banking system, and both international investors and Chinese banks can potentially forge a mutually beneficial partnership. Nevertheless, the expectations of the foreign investors, of the broad spectrum of Chinese banks, of the Chinese government, and of its regulators might diverge. Moreover, a number of factors such as regulatory restrictions that limit foreign ownership to a minority interest, foreign investors' inability to gain meaningful control and influence over the Chinese banks, and possible cultural clashes increase the likelihood of initially uneasy partnerships, which could take some years to deliver the results that all parties hope to achieve.

Table 2.1 outlines the pros and cons of investment in Chinese banks from the viewpoint of the foreign investor. Even if the foreign investor is committed to entering the Chinese banking sector via a minority equity investment in a local bank, three distinct strategic possibilities present themselves depending on whether the investor wants to begin with a clean slate in a "greenfield" bank; take advantage of the huge distribution networks of the big four SCBs, despite their dubious asset quality and governance practices; or adopt an intermediate approach. Each option has advantages and disadvantages. However, if the Chinese concern is to enable the indigenous banking industry quickly to become competitive, stimulating foreign participation in the big banks seems to be the

Table 2.1. Potential Targets of Foreign Investors

Investment Target	Pros	Cons
Greenfield banks (e.g., Bohai Bank)	Clean slate Easy to infuse international best practices Attractive upside potential	Need time to build Inability to own more than 20 percent; difficulties in finding compatible domestic partners
Smaller banks (e.g., joint-stock banks; city commercial banks)	Fewer legacy assets Smaller capital commitment Faster growth Better governance and transparency Potential flexibility in sharing management control	Limited franchise and distribution network Complex shareholder structure and often more difficult decision-making processes Often unrealistically high price expectations and tougher negotiation positions
Big Four SCBs	Immediate access to extensive nationwide distribution systems Meaningful strategic cooperation in attractive business segments (e.g., credit and other cards, consumer finance) Significantly escalate investor's position in China through a single investment	Massive legacies in asset quality and operational systems Large capital commitment required for meaningful stake and associated uncertainties about ability to influence management decisions High political sensitivities regarding deal terms/face issues in relation to foreign players' share of national franchise

most attractive option.[3] The issue is how to make that also an attractive option from the viewpoint of the strategic investor. (Table 2.2 highlights strategic investment in Chinese banks to date.)

China's Banking System: Progress in and Priorities for Reform

The two most striking features of the Chinese financial system are the extraordinary size of monetary assets relative to GDP and the comparative lack of development of the securities markets when compared with the size of the banks. By the end of 2004, the ratio of money and quasi-

---

[3]Appendix Table 2.A2.1 shows that very rapid growth in the assets of foreign-funded banks in China during the past three years (2002–05) has raised their share in the assets of financial institutions only from 1.5 to 1.9 percent. After all restrictions on the foreign banks' activities are eliminated in December 2006, their market share might be expected to grow somewhat faster. Nevertheless, improved performance of the banking system as a whole will be a slow process if it relies solely on the growing role of foreign banks.

money (M2) to Chinese nominal GDP was 1.85,[4] a startlingly high figure even compared with those commonly found in developed economies. By then, total deposits with financial institutions were renminbi 24.1 trillion yuan, and lending by them was Y 17.8 trillion.[5] The People's Bank of China (PBC) reports that, at the end of June 2005, deposits (in both local and foreign currencies) in all financial institutions totaled Y 28.3 trillion and local currency deposits alone were Y 26.9 trillion.[6] Using comparable data from the end of 2003, deposits with financial institutions amounted to Y 20.8 trillion, compared with Y 3.4 trillion in bonds of all kinds,[7] and Y 4.2 trillion in total market value of stocks listed in the Shanghai and Shenzhen exchanges.[8] Bank lending has continued to grow rapidly in the ensuing two years, while the capital markets have dawdled.

Yang (2004, Table 2) presents data on the evolving shares of lending by financial institutions and the outstanding balance of negotiable securities. She estimates that the share of bank loans in combined assets fell from 90.4 percent in 1991 to 81.7 percent in 2001.[9] The corresponding figure for end-2003 was 77.3 percent (Y 16 trillion of a total of Y 20.7 trillion).[10] Even with the massive bond issuance of the central Government and the PBC's sterilization activities in recent years, China's debt markets still comprise predominantly bank loans, which are about five times as large as the value of outstanding bonds. Recent experiments in liberalizing lending rates for bank loans, including provisions in 2004–05 that give banks considerable freedom to adjust lending rates, have had little effect on bond yields,

---

[4]World Bank (2005) p. 8. The ratio was only 0.37 in 1980.

[5]PBC Annual Report (2004).

[6]People's Bank of China, 2005. "Financial Industry Performance Remained Stable," http://www.pbc.gov.cn/english/

[7]Data on bonds and stocks are from China Statistical Yearbook (2004); other data from PBC (2004). Bonds outstanding at end–2003 comprised 52 percent central government bonds, 35 percent financial bonds (mainly the policy banks and asset management companies), 10 percent PBC bills (issued primarily to sterilize foreign currency inflow) and 3 percent corporate bonds (almost all issued by state-controlled enterprises or entities).

[8]Only about 30 percent of listed shares are tradable; the remainder comprises government held and/or legal person shares. The Y 4.2 trillion total market capitalization for 2003 is as reported in the 2004 Statistical Yearbook. The CSRC website reported that the market capitalization of listed stocks fell to Y 3.9 trillion in August 2004, only Y 1.2 trillion of which was accounted for by tradable shares, and further to Y 3.71 trillion in December 2004 and Y 3.16 trillion in June 2005. (See http://www.csrc.gov.cn/en/statinfo/index.)

[9]Yang, Ya-Hwei, 2004, "Development and Problems in China's Financial System," Discussion Paper No. 04-E-06, Taiwan Study Center.

[10]China Statistical Yearbook 2004.

Table 2.2. Strategic Investments in Chinese Banks

Bank	Profile	Strategic Investor(s)	Date Complete	Deal Size (US$ million)	Investment as Percentage of Company	Key Terms
Ningbo Commercial Bank	City commercial bank	OCBC	Jan 2006	71	12	NA
Industrial and Commercial Bank of China	The largest commercial bank in China Assets of Y 5.59 trillion, end-2004	Goldman Sachs, Allianz, and American Express	Jan 2006	3,800	10	One board seat Extensive cooperation in corporate governance, treasury operations, risk management, asset management, and human resource training, etc.
Tianjin City Commercial Bank	City commercial bank	ANZ Banking Group	Nov 2005	120	19.9	NA
Nanjing City Commercial Bank	City commercial bank	BNP Paribas	Oct 2005	87	19.2	NA
Shenzhen Development Bank	Fourteenth largest bank	GE Consumer Finance	Oct 2005	100	7	NA
Huaxia Bank	Regional bank	Deutsche Bank	Oct 2005	325	14	NA
Bank of China	Second largest commercial bank in China Assets of Y 4.27 trillion, end-2004	Royal Bank of Scotland and coinvestors	Aug 2005	3,048	10	Various cooperation in credit card, corporate business, personal insurances, etc. One board seat
		Temasek	Aug 2005	1,524	5	Committed to acquire no less than US$500 million worth of shares during IPO One board seat

Bank	Description	Investor	Date		%	Terms
China Construction Bank	Third largest commercial bank in China Assets of Y 3.91 trillion, end-2004	Temasek	July 2005	1,466	5.1	Committed to acquire no less than US$1.0 billion worth of shares during IPO Facilitate CCB's restructuring One board seat
		Bank of America	June 2005	2,500	9.1	Cooperation includes corporate governance, risk management, information technology (IT), finance management, etc. Board seats Approximately 50 BOA employees going to CCB to provide consulting services Option to purchase additional shares in future to increase ownership up to 19.9 percent
Bo Hai Bank	Newly established bank	Standard Chartered	Sept 2005	123	19.9	Right to nominate vice chairman of board
Hangzhou City Commercial Bank	Regional bank	Commonwealth Bank of Australia	April 2005	76	19.9	Board seats Technical Assistance Agreement
Bank of Beijing	Regional bank	ING	Mar 2005	215	19.9	Two board seats Potential cooperation in retail banking
Ji'Nan City Commercial Bank	Regional bank	Commonwealth Bank of Australia	Dec 2004	17	11	One board seat
Xi'an City Commercial Bank	Regional bank	Bank of Nova Scotia	Nov 2004	7	5	Rights to increase ownership to 24.9 percent in 4 years
		IFC	Same as above	19.9	12.5	NA

Table 2.2 (*concluded*)

Bank	Profile	Strategic Investor(s)	Date Complete	Deal Size (US$ million)	Investment as Percentage of Company	Key Terms
Minsheng Bank	Only private-sector bank in China	Temasek	Oct 2004	106	4.55	None
	Tenth largest bank	IFC	Same as above	23.5	1.2	NA
		Hang Seng Bank	Same as above	NA	8	NA
Bank of Communications	Fifth largest bank	HSBC	Aug 2004	1,747	19.9	HSBC to have two board seats. Cooperation on credit cards with plan to establish credit card joint venture subject to regulatory approval
Shenzhen Development Bank	Fourteenth largest bank	Newbridge Capital	May 2004	149	17.9	Half board seats. Controlling management position
Industrial Bank	Thirteenth largest bank	Hang Seng Bank	Dec 2003	208	15.98	One board seat. Plan to explore cooperation in credit cards and consumer
Shanghai Pudong Development Bank	Ninth largest bank. Franchise concentrated in Shanghai region, China's richest city	Citibank	Dec 2002	72	5	To set up ring-fenced credit card unit, with goal to form credit card JV once regulation allows. One board seat; Citi to run credit card operation. Transfer of best practices in risk management, IT, and marketing

Nanjing City Commercial Bank	City commercial bank	IFC	2002	27	15	NA
Bank of Shanghai	Top-tier city commercial bank	HSBC	Dec 2001	62.6	8	One board seat Loose business alliance in credit card, consumer finance, and corporate finance Jointly launched co-branded credit card for HSBC customers (not profit-sharing)
		IFC	Same as above	50.3	7	NA

Sources: Federal Reserve Bank of San Francisco *Asia Focus* (July 2005); Hope/Hu presentation "Foreign Investment in Chinese Banks" (2nd NCER-SCID Conference at Tsinghua University, April 28, 2005, and 4th SCID China Conference at Stanford University, October 1, 2005); Bottelier testimony "The General Health of China's Banking System" to the United States-China Economic and Security Review Commission (August 11, 2005).

Note: Profile size rankings are based on asset size.

which are remarkably similar irrespective of maturity. Bank deposit rates as well as bond yields are still largely administered.[11]

Figure 2.1 presents an overview of the structure of China's financial system and Figure 2.2 a more detailed structure of the banking system. Although strictly speaking the asset management companies (AMCs) are nonbank financial institutions, they are included as part of the banking system, given the role that they continue to play in assisting in the resolution of the major SCBs' nonperforming assets. Appendix II provides supplementary selected data on the banking system. The numbers of actors in the financial system change frequently, but Figure 2.2 lists the main classes of banks and nonbank financial intermediaries with recent reports of their numbers.

Within the banking system, the new century has seen a decline in the dominant position of the four main SCBs. They accounted for more than 60 percent of the assets of financial institutions (excluding the People's Bank of China) in 2001, when three of them—the Industrial and Commercial Bank of China (ICBC), the Bank of China (BOC), and the China Construction Bank (CCB), in that order—were among the 50 largest global banks, and all 4 (the other being the Agricultural Bank of China, ABC) were in the top 10 banks in Asia by asset size (Solvet 2002). They continued to account for 60 percent of banking assets at the end of 2003. The SCBs, together with the state policy banks (since 1994) and the four AMCs that were set up in 1999 to deal with some of the bad loans on the books of the four main SCBs and one of the policy banks—the China Development Bank (CDB), overwhelmingly compose the core of the Chinese banking system, even allowing for the rapid recent emergence of many smaller banks and increasing activity from foreign banking interests.[12] But as a result of that emergence and the activities of the policy banks and AMCs, the share in assets of the four major SCBs fell sharply during 2004 and the first half of 2005 (Appendix Table 2.A2.1), reflecting both the very rapid growth in lending by China's smaller banks in the boom of 2003–04, and the successful efforts of the SCBs to reduce their NPLs during that period. By the middle of 2005, the

---

[11]Pieter Bottelier (2005b) has observed that a motivation for freeing lending rates was the growing extent of informal lending. Especially in Zhejiang, the practice of drawing down bank deposits to lend directly to enterprises apparently has become widespread.

[12]The policy banks (in order of asset size) are the China (State) Development Bank, the Agricultural Development Bank of China (ADBC) and the (much smaller) Export-Import Bank of China, which together have total assets less than ABC, the smallest of the major SCBs. The AMCs and their original partner banks are: Cinda–CCB and CDB; Great Wall–ABC; Huarong–ICBC; and Orient–BOC. Beginning in 2004, the AMCs have begun to compete to acquire NPLs from the banks.

Figure 2.1. Structure of the Chinese Financial System

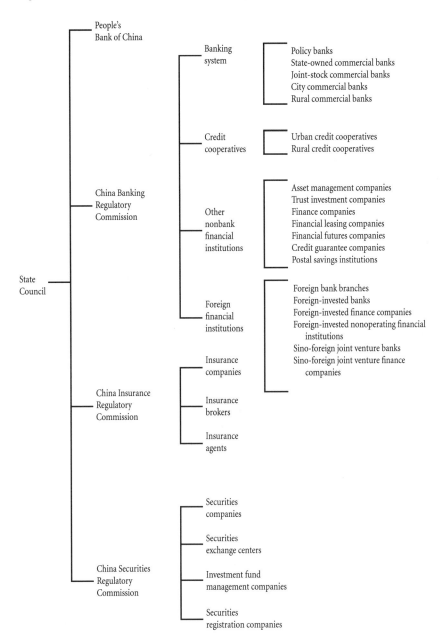

Sources: Solvet (2002) and Yang (2004).

Figure 2.2. Structure of the Chinese Financial System

State Council

Regulatory Institutions

The People's Bank of China (est. 1984) Governor: Zhou Xiaochaun	China Banking Regulatory Commission (CBRC) (est. 2003) Chairman: Liu Mingkang

Banking Institutions

Policy lending banks (3) (since 1994) Agriculture Development Bank of China Export Import Bank of China China Development Bank	"Big Four" state-owned commercial banks (SOCBs) (since 1980s) Industrial & Commercial Bank of China (ICBC) China Construction Bank (CCB) Bank of China (BOC) Agricultural Bank of China (ABC)

Other Commercial Banks

Joint-stock banks (JSCBs) (11)
China Merchants Bank (CMB)
Shanghai Pudong Develop. Bank (SPDB)
Hua Xia Bank (HXB)
Fujian Industrial Bank (FIB)
Senzhen Development Bank (SDB)
CITIC Industrial Bank (CIB)
China Everbright Bank (CEB)
Bank of Communications (BOCO)
Guangdong Development Bank (GDB)
China Minsheng Banking Group (CMBG)
Hengfeng Bank/
Yantai Housing Saving Bank (YHSB)

Rural commercial banks (3)

Foreign banking institutions (191)
(at end of 2003)
157 branches
11 sub-branches
15 subsidiaries
(incorporated locally with 8 branches)

City commercial banks (CCBs) (112) (since mid-1990s)

Luoyang	Huangshi	Hu'hehaote	Yichang	Hengyang
Changsha	Taizhou	Zibo	Jinhua	Zhenijang
Quanzhou	Nantong	Yinchuan	Jingzhou	Fuxin
Ma'anshan	Xiamen	Ningbo	Chongqing	Xianyang
Nanchong	Huzhou	Huaiyin	Cangzhou	Weihai
Fuzhou	Shenzhen	Qingdao	Liaoyang	Yantai
Luzhou	Shaoxing	Wenzhou	Zhengzhou	Wuxi
Nanjing	Tianjin	Dalian	Xiaogen	Rizhao
Hefei	Xi'an	Chendu	Shenyang	Huaibel
Daqing	Jiaxing	Shi'jiazhuang	Zhanjiang	Guangzhou
Dongguan	Kunming	Wuhan	Dandong	Langfang
Yangzhou	Guilin	Xiangtan	Foshan	Jiujiang
Beijing	Hangzhou	Nanyang	Qing'huangdao	Zigong
Wuhu	Xinxiang	Nanchang	Ganzhou	Xining
Ji'nan	Linyi	Weifang	Yingkou	Xuzhou
Baotou	Jinzhou	Lanzhou	Anshan	Shantou
Bangbu	Jiaozuo	Wanxian	Leshan	Anqing
Guiyang	Nanning	Deyang	Kaifeng	Qi'qihaer
Pan'zhihua	Yueyang	Mianyang	Changchum	Hu'ludao
Shanghai	Ha'erbin	Tangshan	Zhuzhou	Baoji
Wulumuqi	Zhunyi	Yancheng	Jilin	
Suzhou	Changzhou	Datong	Zhuhai	
Liuzhou	Lian'yungang	Taiyuan	Fushun	

Credit Coopertives

Rural credit cooperatives (RCCs) (since 1980s) 35,544	Urban credit cooperatives (UCCs) (since 1980s) 758

Nonbank Financial Institutions

Trust and investment coporations (TICs) (since 1980s) 59	Asset management companies (AMCs) (since 1999) 4 Cinda
Other nonbank institutions finance companies, financial leasing companies, financial futures companies, credit guarantee companies, postal savings institutions, etc.	Great Wall Huarong Orient

Sources: Solvet (2002); Garcia-Herrero and Santabarbara (2004); and Hefferman and Fu (2005).

Figure 2.3. Deposits and Lending Growth
(Trillion yuan)

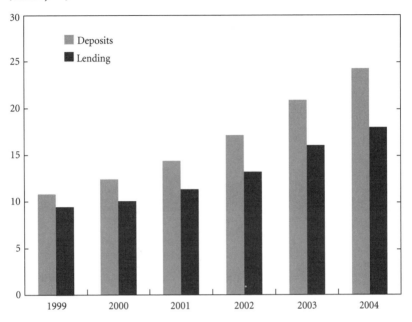

Source: PBC Annual Reports, 2003 and 2004.

share of the SCBs in total bank assets had fallen to 53 percent, though they continued to control more than 60 percent of bank deposits Bottelier (2005b).

Figure 2.3 shows how deposits in, and lending by, financial institutions have evolved over recent years and illustrates the exceptionally rapid growth in 2001–04 when deposits increased by 67 percent and lending by 59 percent. During this period, as the four major SCBs have taken a comparatively more conservative stance with respect to asset acquisition, the major increase in assets share has been attributable to the rise of "other financial institutions," mainly policy banks, trust and investment companies, securities companies, insurance companies, and AMCs, which accounted for one-seventh of total assets (as did the second-tier commercial banks) by the end of the first quarter of 2005. A noteworthy feature of loan growth during the lending boom of the past three years is that, as reported in footnote 3, the rapid growth in the assets of foreign-invested banks still left their share of system-wide assets below 2 percent at the end of March 2005. As a consequence, the ability of foreign banks

Figure 2.4. Growth of Consumer Loans
(Consumer loans as percent of total loans)

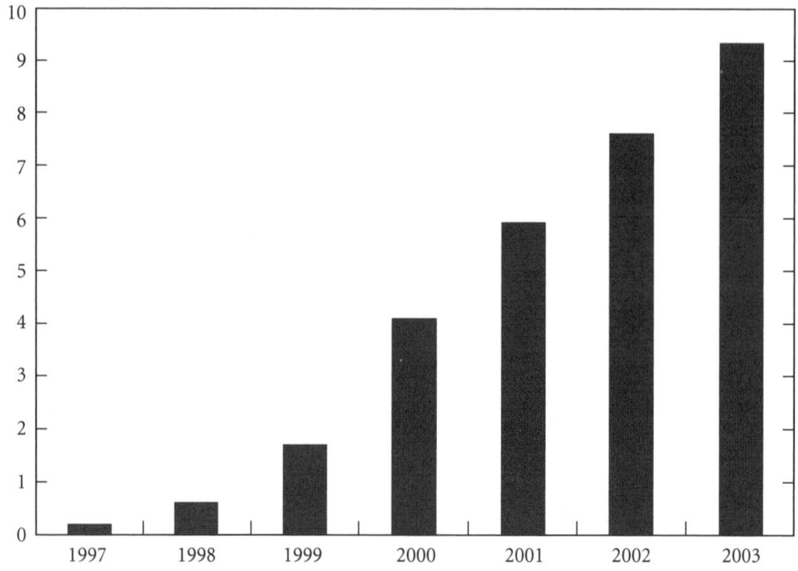

Source: PBC, brokers' research estimates.

to transform China's banking system through a rapid increase in market share appears limited compared with what might be accomplished if they could help to transform the performance of the established domestic banks, especially of the four big SCBs.

Another striking feature of the banking system over the past several years is the emergence of consumer lending, predominantly mortgage finance but also finance for purchase of consumer durables (automobiles) and credit cards. Figure 2.4 shows how rapidly the share of consumer lending in total loans has been rising: from virtually zero percent in 1997–98 to more than 9 percent in 2003. Bottelier (2005b) reports that consumer lending exceeded 11 percent of the banks' portfolios by the end of 2004 and, allowing for loans of working capital to farm households, total loans to households reached almost one-sixth of total bank lending in 2004. Nevertheless, when compared with other economies, as illustrated in Figure 2.5, China lags in the share of mortgage loans in bank assets.

The rapid growth of consumer lending has helped reduce the share of NPLs in the SCBs' portfolios, but the development is too recent to judge reliably the longer-term effects on loan performance and portfolio quality.

Figure 2.5. China's Under-Penetrated Financial Markets, 2002

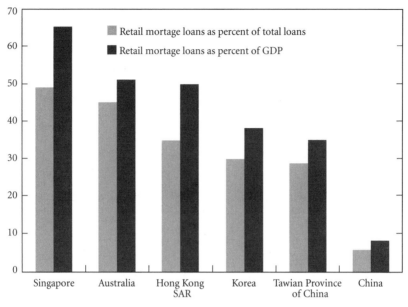

Sources: Various central banks; CEIC; brokers' research estimates.

Even after the elimination of the credit plan, the SCBs were still required to allocate the bulk of their lending to SOEs, many of which were loss-making, and used bank credit to meet current obligations to their workers and pensioners with scant concern for repayment. Until the advent of the AMCs, the SCBs remained hamstrung by the legacy of the plan and, even thereafter, NPLs were variously estimated (in 2002) to comprise one-quarter to one-half of their portfolios. The official figure generally fell at the bottom of the range; at the end of 2003, the PBC reported NPLs at Y 1.9 trillion, or one-fifth of outstanding loans of the SCBs. Solvet (2002, p. 41) put the figure at about one-third of outstanding loans, and assumed a recovery rate of about 20 percent (consistent with the experience of the AMCs) to calculate projected system-wide losses of about 30 percent of GDP in 2001.[13]

The combination of massive capital injection, transference of the NPLs of the SCBs to the balance sheets of the AMCs, and extremely fast growth

---

[13]The recovery rate is gross; after allowing for operational and other costs of the AMCs, the net rate would be considerably lower and the system-wide losses correspondingly higher.

in lending in 2002–04 has allowed the large SCBs (except the ABC) rap-idly to reduce the shares of NPLs in their portfolios. The official aggregate ratio for the SCBs' NPLs was 31 percent at end-2001, about 26 percent at end-2002, 20 percent at end-2003, and under 16 percent at end-2004.[14] Appendix II provides recent figures from the CBRC that estimate the NPLs of major commercial banks (SCBs and joint-stock commercial banks) at Y 1.16 trillion at the end of the first half of 2005, or 8.8 percent of total outstanding loans.[15] Setting aside concerns about the accuracy of the official figures (because some analysts still put the NPL ratios far higher), one might question whether banks are going about reducing their NPLs in the right way. Massive loan write-offs are unavoidable, as is the need to inject more capital to establish adequate capital bases for the SCBs, but one can question the wisdom of doing so before banks are free to make decisions based solely on commercial considerations. In addition, much of the recent improvement in banks' portfolio performance might be attrib-uted to financial restructuring measures and the youth of their portfolios rather than to fundamental improvements in their lending practices.

---

[14]Recent years have seen rapid reductions in the reported NPL ratios of the banks, despite the introduction of a more rigorous system of loan classification (see footnote 15). Barnett (2004) reports the NPL ratios for BOC, CCB, and ICBC as 16, 9, and 21 per-cent, respectively, at the end of 2003. The ratio for ABC was unavailable but known to be much higher. He notes as well the "substantial amount of special mention loans" that also threatens to become nonperforming (see Barnett, 2004, p. 48). Gilligan (2005) notes that the government's estimates of the NPL ratio for major commercial banks in China, includ-ing the four big SCBs, amounted to Y 1.7 trillion (US$240.7 billion) or 13.2 percent at the end of September 2004, down 4.6 percent from the preceding year. The BOC separately reported an NPL ratio of 4.6 percent as of October 2004, down from 5.2 percent at the end of September 2004 and 16.3 percent at the beginning of that year. The CCB reported an NPL ratio of 3.7 percent at the end of September 2004, the lowest among the four large SCBs. Bottelier (2005b, p. 9) reports similar figures and indicates that, as a result of recapi-talization and other measures, the NPL ratio for ICBC fell from 19 percent at end-2004 to 4.6 percent at mid-2005. His figure for the ABC NPL ratio is 35 percent at end-2004. Also see Appendix II, Table 2.A2.4.

[15]China's loan classification system was amended from a four- to a five-category system in 2001. Under the earlier system, criteria for recognizing loans as sub-standard, impaired, or lost were lax. The new system conforms much better to international standards (the Basel accords), but there is no way to determine how rigorously the standards are applied in practice or whether they are applied uniformly to all banks. There is little evidence to show how the system has been affected by the establishment of the CBRC to exert regulatory and supervisory oversight of the banking system; these functions had been the responsibility of the PBC. Bottelier (2005b) notes that, beginning in late 2005 or in 2006, the CBRC will require minimum provisioning requirements linked to the five-category loan classification system.

The rapid increases in consumer lending notwithstanding, both in access to bank credits and in issuance of bonds, borrowers other than the government and SOEs are severely disadvantaged. The debt markets still have far to go before they conform to the ideal of competitive markets. Lending to private enterprises has continued to be a comparatively minor activity of the SCBs, partly because of their concerns about their portfolios and partly—at least until very recently—because they have had insufficient flexibility to set interest rates at levels that would make such lending profitable when adjusted for transaction costs, monitoring costs, and risk. There are problems, too, in securing adequate information about prospective clients' credit history and loan-servicing records, and the extent to which collateral pledged to secure loans is unencumbered. Recovering collateral in the event of default is further complicated by inadequate protection of creditors' rights under the commercial law.

An unavoidable conclusion of analysis of the Chinese banking system is that system performance could be greatly enhanced if the performance of the SCBs could be improved rapidly. In that regard, one might have to accept that the SCBs are too big to fail and at the same time question whether they are also too big to reform. The government has embarked on bold steps since its announcement early in January, 2004, that it was injecting US$45 billion from the PBC's international exchange reserves as new capital to the BOC and CCB, with half of the funds going to each. A company, Central Huijin Investment Ltd., was established to hold the equity in the two banks (at that time, its only asset), and its board comprises officials from the PBC, the State Administration of Foreign Exchange, and the Ministry of Finance. A similar measure was adopted for ICBC in the first half of 2005, with Huijin providing US$15billion of new capital and the Ministry of Finance (MOF) retaining another US$ 15 billion of old equity in the bank. At the same time, ICBC's balance sheet was boosted even more by the disposal of an additional US$85 billion in NPLs to the AMCs and elsewhere.

The injection of funds has dramatically improved the SCBs' balance sheets. Many governance issues remain to be resolved, however, and even more radical solutions might be needed to improve the performance of the SCBs and permit them to compete on an equal footing with foreign banks by the second half of this decade. This is one of the key considerations behind the government initiative to seek strategic foreign partners who could inject new capital along with management and financial expertise to establish sound practices in China's commercial banks.

Progress in Reform

The remaining weaknesses of its financial system notwithstanding, over the 25 years of the reform era China has made considerable progress toward introducing a functioning financial system. In the gradual Chinese fashion, a persistent process of reform has begun to improve the structure of the system, to enhance the role of banks in resource allocation, and to build the institutions needed to underpin a modern, market-friendly financial system. Appendix I provides a selective chronology of financial sector reform, again with major emphasis on the banks; therefore the discussion here can be comparatively brief.

The main thrusts of banking reform since 1978 are:

(1) the establishment of a separate central bank—the PBC;
(2) the establishment of commercial banks independent from the monobank;
(3) the introduction of capital markets, specifically the Shanghai and Shenzhen stock exchanges;
(4) the introduction of independent regulators for the securities markets, insurance industry and banks, all of which report directly to the State Council;
(5) the introduction of policy banks to free the commercial banks from the obligation to support state priorities;
(6) the restructuring of the SCBs, including the introduction of the AMCs to deal with some of the non-performing assets of the SCBs and the policy banks;
(7) the phased introduction of market forces to allocate credit, with the abolition of the credit plan and gradual removal of controls on lending rates; and
(8) the recent preparations for competition from foreign and joint venture banks, after accepting the conditions for accession to the WTO.[16]

In none of these areas is reform complete; rather, progress continues to be made on all fronts as emphasis shifts and the timing of individual reforms has differed. The listing of reform areas conforms more or less to the chronological order in which they were initiated.

Because much of the early progress in reform is well known and well documented (see also Appendix I), comments here are limited to developments in the past few years. Since the turn of the century, the PBC, which had already been established as the central bank and relieved of

---

[16]For an alternate presentation of reforms by sub-period since 1979, see Yang (2004).

all of its commercial banking activities as well as its obligation to finance the government, has seen its responsibilities for oversight of the soundness of China's banks pass to the CBRC. As a result, the PBC now retains three chief functions: implementation of monetary policy, management of China's international reserves and exchange rate, and maintenance of stability of the entire financial system. Given that the three independent regulatory agencies report directly to the State Council, as does the PBC, how the PBC will interact with those agencies and discharge its mandate to guarantee financial system stability (with the possible exception of serving as the system-wide lender of last resort) is uncertain, though progress to date is encouraging.

Since its inception in April 2003 as the third financial regulator, the CBRC has taken action on several fronts. With an eye on the WTO deadline, the CBRC has emphasized the urgent need to restructure China's banks, especially the big four, and has encouraged foreign investment in those banks as a way to advance that objective.[17] At the same time, domestic and private investors have been urged to buy shares in the banks as part of a range of measures that should improve their governance and elevate their operational efficiency. The CBRC also has introduced measures to deal with the dysfunctional rural credit cooperatives and to develop rural (and city) commercial banks. Within a short period, the CBRC has gained considerable credibility as a modern, forward-looking regulatory body.

Impressive, too, is the rapid progress that has been made in the financial restructuring of the BOC, CCB, and ICBC. The urgency attached to this process is understandable with January 2007 looming, but the speed with which nonperforming assets have been removed from these three banks and their capital augmented is startling. The banks also have moved aggressively to reduce redundant employees and close unprofitable branches: between 2000 and 2003 the main banking institutions reduced their total employment by 8 percent and their total branches by a quarter.[18] The four big SCBs took even more aggressive action, with their total employment falling by 185,300 (11.6 percent) over the period, despite a small expansion in staffing at the ABC, and their branches by 32,418 (26.8 percent). The underlying thrust of restructuring is to equip banks to compete with foreign banks, which increasingly enjoy the freedom to challenge domestic banks across the full range of their activities. Market forces are slowly being introduced as lending rates are liberalized, though

---

[17]In this area, the CBRC clearly is taking its lead from the State Council.

[18]The data include the PBC, the big four SCBs, the policy banks and the JSCBs. See Appendix B and *China Statistical Yearbook 2001* and *2004*.

administrative control over the banks remains strong and most observers still regard credit allocation as only partly market-determined.

The policy banks essentially have failed to play the role initially envisaged for them, even though the CDB, in particular, has financed a growing share of centrally mandated infrastructure projects. The commercial banks still seem to be constrained to provide credit under government direction, and they are expected partially to finance the policy banks by buying their bonds.

Priorities in Reform

With reform moving forward on virtually every front, identifying priorities might seem somewhat arbitrary. From our viewpoint, however, the government should be concentrating on five areas to improve the performance of China's banks and of the overall financial system:

- better overall governance,
- better balance between the financial and capital markets,
- more effective regulation and supervision,
- more reliance on market forces, and
- a more supportive legal system.

The objective in improving *governance* should be to enable banks to make decisions based solely on commercial considerations and to free them from the influence of government officials and other bureaucrats. Two key required reforms are the introduction of truly independent, expert executive boards to oversee the work of the senior management of the banks, along with the freedom for boards and managers to appoint senior personnel based on merit and performance, rather than political affiliation. Just as in the reform of the enterprise system, an essential requirement for successful reform of the banks is to put them at arm's length from governments.

Better *balance between the financial and capital markets* would facilitate this objective, at the same time contributing to more robust capital markets, which would better serve the needs of long-term institutional investors and of enterprises and governments seeking access to long-term capital. Commercial banks should be under no compulsion to acquire the bonds of the government, the policy banks, or the AMCs, nor should they be obligated to make loans to the infrastructure companies organized and owned by subnational governments as a substitute for those governments' inability to raise funds through bond issuance. The development of active primary and secondary markets in corporate bonds as well as bonds of subnational governments deserves more emphasis from Chinese policymakers. A host of complementary reforms would be needed—every-thing from reputable, independent rating agencies to fiscal reforms and improved financial management at the level of provincial and municipal governments.

In its short life, the CBRC has established credibility as the *regulator and supervisor* of the banking system. Its efforts to complete the restructuring of the major SCBs have been commended previously, as has the cooperation that seems to have developed between the CBRC and the PBC. The priority for the CBRC is to train sufficient skilled bank examiners to ensure that the new classification system for asset performance is implemented effectively throughout the banking system and that banks apply the system appropriately in provisioning for bad loans and writing down their capital as losses occur. Along with the PBC, the CBRC can assist banks by developing comprehensive credit and collateral registries. In addition, the CBRC should become a strong voice in advancing the banks' rights to seniority among claimants for the assets of failed enterprises.

Increasingly, *market forces* should be allowed to determine the outcome of credit allocation and the discipline that banks and the capital markets apply to borrowers and listed companies, respectively. Currently, banks still seem somewhat reluctant to take advantage of the flexibility they have been granted to vary lending rates according to the risks and costs associated with serving different classes of borrowers. Given time, that can be expected to change, at which point limited flexibility in setting deposit rates also should be introduced.[19]

In addition, more reliance should be placed on the market to determine when enterprises, including banks themselves, should be required to exit their markets. The ultimate consequence of sustained, poor financial performance should be bankruptcy, with the assets of the failed endeavor being apportioned amongst claimants according to appropriate seniority of claims. The government and the chief financial regulators recently have seemed bent on accelerating the use of the market to dispose of NPLs. The AMCs are now allowed to compete with each other to acquire NPLs from banks that offer them, and measures were introduced in August 2005 to foster recovery of bad loans made by the PBC itself (Appendix I).

Better performance of the financial markets also will require significant improvements in the *legal system*, including both how the legal code is written (with the bankruptcy law an excellent example) and how it is enforced and implemented. At the heart of the necessary reform is the

---

[19]Newspaper reports in 2005 suggest that banks are beginning to vary lending rates according to the risk and other characteristics of borrowers.

need for China's legal system to define, protect and dispose of property rights in a cost-effective manner.[20] Without assurances that they can recover their assets in a timely way and at acceptable cost in the event of default, banks will continue to be reluctant to lend to small private enterprises. But the absence of such lending is one of the principal impediments to the sustained dynamism of private enterprise in China; its continuing absence poses a threat to fast growth over the longer term. Greater efficiency, transparency and predictability in the functioning of the legal system would be an invaluable aid to Chinese banks.

Encouraging Strategic Foreign Investment in Chinese Banks

To what extent can foreign strategic investment in China's banks promote those reform priorities? Whether because of China's entry into the WTO or for other reasons, the Chinese government has become much more receptive recently to foreign investment in China's banks and Chinese banks have actively sought strategic investment from foreign banks (see the list in Table 2.2). As emphasized above, having guaranteed that foreign banks can compete with domestic banks under identical conditions beginning in December 2006, the government apparently has decided that foreign participation in domestic banks via equity investment promises to be an effective way of enhancing their competitiveness. China seems to view foreign participation as compatible with the state's overall control of the banks and as a potentially valuable source of assistance in (1) promoting bank restructuring, (2) enhancing banking skills through business cooperation, (3) supplementing equity capital, without recourse to the fiscal budget, and (4) boosting the status of Chinese financial institutions in domestic and foreign capital markets.

Promoting Bank Restructuring

Chinese bankers and banking officials now seem to view foreign involvement as a highly cost-effective way to obtain an expert review of an individual bank's business capacity. Before taking an equity position in a Chinese bank, and as an essential part of the valuation exercise, the foreign investor will want to review the bank's financial position, the scope and nature of its operations, and how it incurs and manages the risks in its portfolio. The investor will analyze the bank's operating and funding

---

[20]This point is emphasized by Sheng, Geng, and Wang (2004).

costs, and will assess the soundness of the bank's provisioning practices and handling of problem loans. It will form a view of the expertise of the bank's officers and the extent to which the bank's performance can be improved through better training of the existing staff or by hiring people with better skills.

Armed with that knowledge, the strategic partner will then be well placed to help the management of the bank in the restructuring activities that are underway in all Chinese banks as they endeavor to improve their performance in preparation for December 2006 and thereafter. The banks can also anticipate help identifying profitable new lines of business. In particular, the strategic partner can call on its experience in international banking to help the domestic bank introduce state-of-the-art risk management systems and a management information system that provides accurate, timely information about the bank's performance. In addition, it can supply knowledge of how to measure the performance of the bank's personnel and how to structure incentives to induce and to reward better performance. Finally, if the domestic owners (still mainly governments) are willing, the foreign partner can help to set up corporate governance structures appropriate for successful banks in a market economy.

Cooperating in Business Activities

Beyond imparting the knowledge of how to restructure the Chinese bank to secure better performance, the foreign investor can contribute concretely to such a restructuring by becoming involved in the ongoing business activities of the bank. A major contribution can come through the direct secondment of skilled officers from the investor to participate in the business operations of the Chinese bank. Officers of the domestic bank can learn firsthand how an international financial institution deals with all aspects of lending, funding, containing risks, and so on. In addition, the foreign partner can supply expertise to help recommend new information systems and technology, to teach techniques for managing risk, and to train personnel.

Through participation in the business activities of the domestic bank, officers of the foreign partner will be able to transfer knowledge of, and build skills in, marketing and product development. They will be able to assess the need for specialized recruitment and training to help improve the management of the bank's human resources. And, if permitted, they can demonstrate by example how the governance structures should function in a modern, market-oriented, commercial bank.

Supplementing Equity Capital

Most East Asian governments have used offerings of stock in state-owned companies mainly as a way to secure additional capital. Better performance through improved governance of publicly listed companies has been at best an afterthought, and little concern has been shown for the interests of minority shareholders. China has been no exception to this; although in the case of strategic investors in the banks, the government appears legitimately interested in boosting performance through their involvement. However, an injection of capital still is clearly an important motivating factor in seeking a foreign partner in domestic banks, even if not to the same extent as in the proposed IPOs for the big SCBs. As shown in Table 2.2, the amounts of money injected in the acquisitions have been substantial, especially for Hongkong and Shanghai Banking Corporation's (HSBC's) acquisition of 19.9 percent of the Bank of Communications (BoCom, US$1.75 billion),[21] and Bank of America's 9.1 percent of CCB (US$3 billion). In these and the other cases, the injection of new capital substantially augments the capital bases of the recipient banks.

Wooing the Capital Markets

Last, but most definitely not least, entering into a strategic partnership with a foreign banking group can do much to enhance the public image of a Chinese bank. Despite their huge size, the four main SCBs are not well known outside China, and none would be regarded on its own as anything remotely approximating a blue-chip stock in major international capital markets. But with a stakeholder of impeccable reputation in tow, the Chinese bank can raise its credibility and its reputation markedly. The audited statements of a CCB or BoCom will have much greater authority if they have passed muster in the eyes of Bank of America or HSBC.[22] Prospective shareholders are likely to attribute more validity to disclosed information, as well as to actions taken

---

[21]Appendix D provides a case study of the HSBC investment in BoCom, with an emphasis on the progress of the transaction and the advantages it provides to both parties. Although the investments listed in Table 2.2 represent almost US$16 billion of additional capital for Chinese banks, a considerable sum, they remain small compared with the additional capital (US$60 billion) that the government has provided three of the big SCBs through Huijin.

[22]There is increasing awareness among Chinese listed firms, including the banks, of the value of reputable audits of their financial statements. Many firms have engaged the major international accounting houses to conduct audits and to certify the validity of their income statements and balance sheets.

Figure 2.6. Chinese GDP Growth

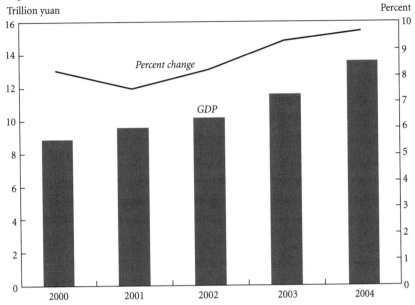

Sources: PBC Annual Reports, 2003 and 2004.

to restructure the bank and to embrace new products and new ways of doing business. All of this should pave the way for successful approaches to both domestic and foreign capital markets in future IPOs and subsequent share offerings.[23]

What Attracts Foreign Investors to Chinese Banks?

Although the attractions of the fast-growing Chinese economy are obvious, choosing to enter the Chinese market through a strategic partnership with a domestic bank is less obviously attractive. Figure 2.6 shows recent Chinese growth rates, and Figure 2.7 compares growth in the Chinese banking markets with that of other Asian economies. As shown earlier, the Chinese retail mortgage market is still in its infancy (see Figure 2.5), but the recent acceleration of consumer lending by

---

[23]As occurred in BoCom's and CCB's successful IPOs in Hong Kong SAR in June and October 2005, respectively.

Figure 2.7. Asian Banking Market Growth Comparison
Loan and Deposit Growth (1999–2003 Compound Annual Growth Rate)
(In percent)

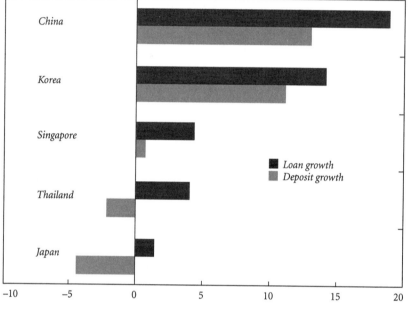

Source: Various central banks.

Chinese banks points to the vast lending opportunities that are emerging in the Chinese market, and foreign banking interests might regard the immediate access to well-developed distribution networks as more than adequate compensation for management and organizational deficiencies in their Chinese partners. Besides positioning themselves to benefit from the continuing rapid growth in bank lending, the foreign partners potentially can market their own products (for example, credit cards, fund management and trustee services, and insurance) through their partners' branch networks.

What other positives can foreign investors in the Chinese financial sector draw from the government's explicit and implicit commitments to ongoing reform of the financial system? In addition to rapid growth, there is a strong presumption that reforms will create opportunity for both banking and nonbanking financial services as the government's role in the financial system gradually recedes. In particular, the injection of strategic foreign investment followed by IPOs of the major banks should reduce the currently overwhelming influence of the state on the major SCBs (though this can be expected to be a lengthy, even if inevitable, process). The massive recapitalization of the SCBs via Huijin, as well as, in the case of CCB, via concessions from the MOF to waive dividends and taxes due, will substantially improve the capital bases and competitive positions of the SCBs. In turn, that raises the prospect of a potential financial upside for the foreign investors if they can help to engineer an effective turn-around of the efficiency and profitability of their invested banks, including the smaller ones where influence on management and operational performance might be almost immediate.

Further enhancement of the upside potential of the existing banks will derive from the nature of reform, with considerable relaxation of controls on interest rates and regulation of fees pointing toward full liberalization over time. Because nonbank financial services are growing even faster than banking services, clear potential also exists to profit from the use of the banks' well-established distribution channels to introduce "integrated financial services" business models over time. Bottelier (2005a) also points to the advantages of avoiding the need to compete for the limited local personnel with banking expertise and experience. Finally, the flurry of recent entry activity probably draws some inspiration from the example of HSBC's landmark deal for BoCom: HSBC's actual and potential competitors in the promising China market might perceive potential early-mover advantages through their acquisitions (Appendix IV).

What Comprises the Universe of Potential Strategic Investors?

Almost every type of international finance company has shown interest in penetrating the Chinese financial sector. Five broad classes of actors that have been actively seeking opportunities for strategic partnerships in China are (1) universal banks, (2) commercial banks, (3) specialty finance companies, (4) asset managers, and (5) insurers. Their interests differ, as do the pros and cons of their involvement in China's financial service industry.

- *Universal banks* refer to those engaged in a wide range of financial services, including consumer banking, commercial banking, investment banking, asset management, and insurance. From the viewpoint of Chinese banks, they offer a broad range of strategic and operational benefits and, usually, impressive financial resources. The possible downside is that conflicts of interest could arise because many of their products and services will overlap and potentially compete with those of their Chinese partners, and they will make protection of their own brand and reputation a priority. Examples of this group that have entered the Chinese market or are considering doing so are Citigroup, HSBC, and J.P. Morgan Chase.

- *Commercial banks* are primarily focused on commercial banking, with their expertise normally concentrated on corporate and consumer banking, as well as wealth management. The advantage of this group for Chinese partner banks is that its core expertise is immediately applicable to their main business lines, with particular benefits likely to be realized in the crucial areas of credit and risk management. This group of investors is likely to be culturally well attuned to its Chinese partners although it will not offer as diversified a product mix. Some members of this group are Bank of America, Banque Nationale de Paris, the Royal Bank of Scotland, and Standard Chartered Bank.

- *Specialty finance companies* focus on specific finance markets, ranging from credit cards and consumer finance to commercial finance and leasing. They bring cutting-edge expertise in selected business areas and offer innovative product and marketing capabilities. The scope of their activities is narrower than that of the banks, but their creativity and specific expertise could help their Chinese partners develop highly profitable niche products with less competitive threat to core banking business. A potential disadvantage is the possibility that multiple partners will be required to cover a range of specialty markets. Examples of companies offering these services are American Express, Commercial Investment Trust (CIT Group, Inc.), Countrywide, Ford Motor Credit, General Electric Capital, General Motors Acceptance Corporation, and MBNA Corporation.

- *Asset managers* also are seeking investment opportunities in Chinese banks to establish business development platforms. Their expertise in the asset management business complements the services available to the established customer base of major Chinese banks and is likely to be especially helpful given the current underdeveloped state of the asset management business in China. Typically, they will offer their Chinese banking partners less in the way of additional financial resources, and they have limited capacity to assist Chinese banks to restructure themselves as competitive commercial banks. Examples of companies offering these services are Capital Group, Fidelity, Franklin, and Putnam.

- *Insurers* comprise a large group of insurance companies (life and property/casualty) seeking distribution networks in China. Their primary contribution to partner Chinese banks would be through the fee-based revenues generated from distributing insurance and other wealth management products. This group probably would have little interest, as well as limited capabilities, in assisting partner banks to improve their banking performance. Examples of the large numbers of potential entrants in this category are: Aegon; Allianz; Aviva; Axa; Fortis; ING; Metlife; Munich Re; and Prudential, UK.

How Have Chinese Banks Selected Investment Partners?

In choosing among the host of interested parties offering a wide range of expertise, Chinese banks typically use a range of criteria including the following categories: profile, strategic fit, management/cultural fit, core competencies, appetite for acquisition, and ability to pay. Some illustrative criteria within these categories, along with some considerations of relevance and potential benefits, are shown in Table 2.3.

Summarizing very broadly, ideal strategic partners for Chinese banks seem to be, first and foremost, reputable financial institutions (which need not be among the world's largest) that offer proven products, refined marketing skills, and distribution expertise. The other attributes that seem particularly attractive to Chinese banks are:

(1) superior management capabilities, combined with a willingness to commit management resources to assist the Chinese partner to acquire better management skills;

(2) expertise in core competencies that add tangible benefits to the Chinese partner, while minimizing the potential for conflict and damaging competition;

(3) long-term interest in opportunities in China's rapidly growing financial services markets; and

(4) a clear strategic fit with the Chinese partner from which both parties could benefit commercially.

What Are the Main Concerns for Foreign Investors in Chinese Banks?

Up to this point, we have outlined both the attractions of China's financial sector for its prospective foreign strategic partners and the qualifications and characteristics that Chinese financial institutions might seek in potential partners. To balance the equation, and not-

Table 2.3. Criteria Commonly Used by Chinese Banks in Selecting Potential Investors

Categories	Criteria	Relevancy/Benefits
Profile	Asset size Market cap Financial strength/ credit ratings	Strong world-class profile and powerful endorsement of Chinese banks Financial strength providing long-term stability
Strategic fit	Strategic focus: product, customer, geography International revenues/profits as share of total revenues/profits China strategy and presence Expansion strategy (organic vs. mergers and acquisitions)	Strategic fit as foundation for exploring and reaping benefits Level of interest in Chinese banks Only a subset of investors with an international mindset and knowledge of Asia
Management/ cultural fit	Vision and capabilities Cohesive management culture and disciplined management system Interest in working with partners	Willingness and ability to help Chinese bank to reinvent itself by committing management resources
Core competencies	Business mix: retail banking, corporate banking, risk control, wealth management Cross-selling capabilities Infrastructure Distribution: information technology, management information system, back office, operating and financial performance	Availability of international best practices Tangible benefits to Chinese banks in its execution of strategy
Acquisition appetite	Mergers and acquisitions experience in financial services industry Experience in minority stake investments	Interest in committing to an investment in Chinese banks Willingness to negotiate reasonable terms
Ability to pay	Market cap Impacts of potential investment on capital adequacy and earnings Accounting treatment	Indication of ability to pay for an investment Impact on transaction structure (composition of investors)

withstanding the attractions of China's potential as a profitable market, the prospective investor in Chinese banks has to contend with several aspects of the Chinese environment that are less than conducive to the productive engagement of foreign interests. In weighing the decision to enter China, several types of issues should dominate an investor's deliberations, including corporate governance, control and management influence, legal and regulatory frameworks, risk management, asset quality, and liquidity and the ability to exit.[24] We consider these issues briefly.

Corporate Governance

The governance structures of Chinese banks need substantial improvement if they are to function effectively on a fully commercial basis. Currently, the board structures of the banks are not conducive to an effective system of checks and balances—there are too few independent directors and a dearth of effective key board committees, including risk and audit committees. Moreover, one can question whether internal information systems support effective governance and how well the financial statements of the banks reflect their actual financial conditions. The banks have yet to develop a culture of full disclosure, and the information that is released falls well short of international standards for best practice. In addition, the huge SCBs are encumbered with fragmented organizations that are essentially geographically based; centralized organizations are preferred with clear distinction and separation between front, middle, and back offices.

Although foreign partners potentially could do much to remedy the situation, whether they will be allowed and encouraged to do so remains in question. They presumably will have some influence on both board composition and policies; in addition, they should be represented on the key board committees as well as such key internal committees as the credit committee. The extent of their influence, however, is still very uncertain.

Control and Management Influence

The ability to influence overall governance positively will be related closely to the foreign partner's ability to exert control over the operations of its invested bank and to manage aspects of the bank's activities. By law and regulation, foreign ownership in domestic banks is restricted to 25 percent, with the holdings of any individual foreign investor to be less than 20 percent.[25] Although, in the interests of better performance, Chinese banks might cede somewhat more of their authority to their foreign partners than share ownership alone would warrant, they are at least equally likely to try to minimize the extent to which they share

---

[24]This discussion presupposes that the potential strategic investor has overcome any opposition from its shareholders to entering the Chinese market.

[25]As some Chinese banks with ownership close to the mandated limits are being prepared for IPOs, the prospects for a rise in the statutory ownership limits seem strong (Bottelier, 2005b, page 3).

decision-making power, especially in sensitive areas. For their part, the foreigners might limit their management influence to the particular niches or lines of business that are central to their interests. In the cases of Citigroup and the Shanghai Pudong Development Bank, for example, the extent of management control at the level of business units has been negotiated and agreed upon, but the operational results are as yet undetermined.[26]

Legal and Regulatory Frameworks

Great uncertainty still surrounds the legal and regulatory treatment of the banking business in China, notwithstanding the ongoing efforts to reform and the undeniable progress that has been made—at least in regard to the institutional structure, if not yet in regard to banking practice. The draft bankruptcy law, which has passed through its second reading at the National People's Congress, reportedly still subordinates the claims of the creditors, including banks, of failed enterprises to those of their current and retired workers. As long as that remains the case, banks are unlikely to lend enthusiastically to private enterprises. Even where banks could lend against collateral, pursuing claims in the event of default is expensive and time consuming and offers no guarantees of success.

Risk Management

As noted in note 15, China has recently begun a migration to a five-classification loan-grading system that aligns better with the standards under the Basel accords. The earlier four-classification system was opaque and seriously flawed, leading to endless speculation about the actual level of nonperforming assets and the extent to which loan provisioning was inadequate. Independent analysts guessed that actual NPLs were at least twice the official figures, meaning the major SCBs were seriously undercapitalized. With the huge infusion of new capital to the major SCBs and the transfer of nonperforming assets to the AMCs, the new system should overcome many of these concerns in time. To date, however, the universal acceptance and performance of the new system

---

[26]Although the text postulates a situation in which the foreign investor might have little real voice in the strategic decisions of the invested bank, Newbridge Capital and the Shenzhen Development Bank provide a contrary example. For its 18 percent share, Newbridge acquired effective management control along with the right to appoint half the board of directors (Table 2.2).

are yet to be demonstrated, as is the capacity of the CBRC to supervise its implementation.

Credit decisions are still driven by relationships, guarantees, and reliable collateral (buildings and land-use rights) when it can be obtained. The extent to which the transition can be made to international practice based on cash-flow analysis is constrained by the unreliability of the books of many enterprises. And even the biggest and most heavily scrutinized of China's banks continue to be haunted by damaging reports of scandals involving fraud and other corrupt practices. Unless the foreign partner is able to insist on more stringent and effective internal controls to curb operational risks, the likelihood is that it will confine its activity to profit making from its niche business activities, with minimal regard for the overall performance of the partner bank.

Asset Quality

The combination of poor risk management, excessive policy-directed lending, inadequate prudential norms, and under-provisioning for bad loans has burdened the banking industry with a legacy of non-performing assets. Unfortunately, more effort has been directed at the stock problem than the flow problem in the major SCBs. As a result, their reported NPLs have fallen sharply during 2000–05 (see Appendix II, and discussion on pages 54–55), but with no assurance that new lending experience will maintain loan losses at acceptably low levels. The CBRC reports that NPLs of major banks were less than 9 percent of total loans by mid-2005. For the four major SCBs, the ratio was 10.1 percent, compared with 20.4 percent at the end of 2003, and 31.1 percent at the end of 2001. If the atrocious performance of the ABC is excluded, by mid-2005 the other three SCBs had NPL ratios of 5 percent or less.

Unofficial estimates of the NPLs of the SCBs, however, have consistently exceeded officially reported levels, which seem to be conservative. Moreover, the rapid rise in lending in 2002–04 means both that at least part of the fall in the NPL ratio was due to growth in the denominator and that the performance of much of the new lending cannot yet be judged. How much of it is still directed lending to poorly performing state enterprises is unknown. And the surge in lending to households, primarily for mortgages but also for cars and credit cards, has yet to demonstrate its soundness. When combined with the continuing lack of transparency and reliability of financial statements, the foreign partners would be wise to assume that neither the flow problem nor the stock problem of the NPLs in the banking system has been laid to rest.

Liquidity and the Ability to Exit

Most foreign investors can be presumed to be taking a longer-term view of their engagement in China's financial sector, but many will still harbor concerns about their ability to extract themselves from their investment when they so desire. Once the major banks are listed, the problem will be less acute for investors in those banks as their shares will be tradable. However, the investor has to commit to holding them for some period, typically a minimum three-year lock up, which represents a substantial liquidity risk to foreign investors.

Concluding Comments

Banking sector fragility poses perhaps the single biggest threat to China's macroeconomic stability and long-term growth and the Chinese government has rightly made banking reform a top priority. In light of the sheer scale of banking problems and the enormity of the reforms required to resolve those problems, the Chinese government has wisely sought to attract foreign strategic investment to help restructure and modernize its ailing banking sector. China's decision to open the sensitive banking sector more widely to foreign investment draws from the decades-long experience in restructuring its inefficient state-owned manufacturing industry, which has transformed itself into a successful global competitor due largely to massive foreign direct investment. In the same way, the Chinese government hopes that foreign investment in the domestic banking sector will bring, along with additional equity capital, the more important contributions of modern banking practices, risk management techniques, new products and services, and international standards of governance. Foreign strategic investment appeals as a potentially effective way to foster China's ongoing banking reform and to build a healthier, more stable and more efficient modern banking system.

Foreign financial institutions, on the other hand, are attracted by China's rapid economic growth; enormous, yet-untapped market potential; and the opportunity to leverage local banks' name recognition, customer bases and distribution networks. Such alliances and partnerships formed through an equity investment can augment foreign banks' growth through their typically limited (or nonexistent) local presence in China. Equity positions in existing banks also offer foreign investors a potentially attractive financial upside if the invested banks significantly improve their operations and performance over time.

A number of obstacles could frustrate both Chinese and foreign investor's expectations. Long-standing problems with corporate governance, disclosure standards, asset quality, and internal control in Chinese banks could make foreign investors cautious and hamper business cooperation. In particular, current Chinese regulations allow for maximum foreign ownership of 25 percent jointly, and 20 percent for a single investor, thereby restricting foreign ownership of Chinese banks to a minority interest. Chinese banks' probable reluctance to cede management control and foreign investors' consequent inability to influence meaningfully their partner bank's operations raise considerable doubt about the extent to which foreign strategic investors could ultimately serve as a catalyst in improving Chinese banks' performance.

These substantial risks and obstacles notwithstanding, the remarkable fact is that China has attracted very substantial foreign direct investments into its once-highly-protected banking sector. Such leading global financial institutions as Bank of America, Goldman Sachs, HSBC, and the Royal Bank of Scotland have taken large minority positions in major Chinese banks; in 2005 alone, total foreign investment in China's banking sector exceeded US$10 billion.

We view the prospects as both promising and intriguing. If, as increasingly seems to be the case, the Chinese government is willing to mitigate some of the potential obstacles, in particular by establishing a legal system that supports banks more effectively, by limiting official intervention in the operations of the banks, and by ceding more voice to foreign strategic investors in the operations of the banks, foreign strategic investment has the potential to be a very effective way to improve China's banking system. Certainly, it promises to improve the performance of China's banks much more rapidly than simply relying on foreign banks to expand their very low current market share.

Glossary of Abbreviations

ABC	Agricultural Bank of China
ADB	Asian Development Bank
ADBC	Agricultural Development Bank of China
AMCs	asset management companies
BOC	Bank of China
BoCom	Bank of Communications
CBRC	China Banking Regulatory Commission
CCB	China Construction Bank
CDB	China Development Bank
CDC	China Government Securities Depository Trust and Clearing Co. Ltd.
CSDCC	China Securities Depository and Clearing Company
CSRC	China Securities Regulatory Commission
HSBC	Hongkong and Shanghai Banking Corporation
ICBC	Industrial and Commercial Bank of China
IPO	initial public offering
JSCBs	joint-stock commercial banks
MBNA	MBNA Corporation or its main part, MBNA America Bank
MOF	Ministry of Finance
NPLs	nonperforming loans
NSSF	National Social Security Fund
PBC	People's Bank of China
RCCs	rural credit cooperatives
RMB	Renminbi
SAEC	State Administration of Exchange Control
SAFE	State Administration of Foreign Exchange
SASAC	State-Owned Asset Supervision and Administration Commission
SCBs	state-owned commercial banks
SDB	Shenzhen Development Bank
SEZ	special economic zone
SOEs	state-owned enterprises
UCCs	urban credit cooperatives
WTO	World Trade Organization

Appendix I. A Chronology of Reform 1978–2007*

Selective Chronology of Chinese Financial Reform with Focus on Banking, 1978–2007

Date	Measures
December 1978	Communist Party Congress approved the Open Door Policy to achieve economic modernization, including measures to develop the securities markets and "special economic zones" (SEZs).
February 1979	The Agricultural Bank of China (ABC) was split from the "monobank," the People's Bank of China (PBC).
March 1979	The Bank of China (BOC) also was established separately. The State Administration of Exchange Control (SAEC, now State Administration of Foreign Exchange, SAFE) was separated from BOC and affiliated with the PBC.
1979–82	Four SEZs were created (Shenzhen, Zhuhai, Shantow, and Xiamen).
October 1979	The China Construction Bank (CCB) was transformed from a department of the Ministry of Finance (MOF) to become a bank under the State Council.
1980	The People's Republic of China assumed the Chinese seat in the IMF and the World Bank.
January 1981	China began to issue state treasury bills.
June 1981	The World Bank approved its first loan (International Bank for Reconstruction and Development (IBRD)/International Development Association (IDA) blend) to China.
December 1981	The China Investment Bank (CIB) was created to on-lend funds lent by the World Bank and (later) by the Asian Development Bank (ADB).
1982	China began to issue local enterprise bonds.
September 1983	The State Council decided to create a central bank.
1984	China opened 14 cities for foreign investments, in addition to the existing four SEZs.
1984	State-owned financial enterprises began to issue bonds and were allowed to raise funds from their shareholders.
January 1984	The PBC assumed the role of China's central bank; the Industrial and Commercial Bank of China (ICBC) was created to take over the PBC's remaining deposit-taking and lending functions.
1985	A few specialized banks were permitted to conduct foreign exchange business at their branches in three SEZs.
1986	China joined the ADB.
1986	The government first permitted state treasury bills to be openly traded in five major cities.
1987	The SAEC granted 133 new approvals for financial institutions to enter the foreign exchange market (in total, 55 branch banks and 78 trust and investment companies).
1988	China began to implement its bankruptcy law.
1988–93	Ninety securities dealers were approved and 386 trust and investment institutions were in operation.
1990	Stock exchanges were established in Shanghai and Shenzhen.
1990	China opened a total of 714 cities and about a third of the provinces for foreign investors and visitors.

Selective Chronology of Chinese Financial Reform with Focus on Banking, 1978–2007 *(continued)*

Date	Measures
1992	More than 1,000 branch banks and 145 nonbank financial institutions had been licensed to carry out foreign exchange business.
1992	Banks were given authority to write off loans of up to a half billion yuan; larger amounts still required approval from the State Council.
1994	The CIB became a commercial bank and expanded its activities to include deposit-taking and foreign exchange business.
1994	Three policy banks-Agricultural Development Bank of China, China (State) Development Bank (CDB), and Export-Import Bank-were established to free the four "specialized" state-owned commercial banks (SCBs) from directed lending. Exchange rate unified from January 1.
1995	The CIB reduced the number of its branches from 32 to 16.
1995	Commercial bank law was promulgated. This created conditions for commercial bank system formation and structure and provided the legal basis for changing specialized state banks to SCBs.
March 1995	The Central Bank Law was passed, legally confirming the PBC as the central bank.
1996	Other banks joined the BOC in offering deposits and loans denominated in foreign currencies and settlement for foreign trade transactions.
January 1996	The first nonstate-owned commercial bank, Minsheng bank, was established.
December 1996	China established full convertibility of the renminbi on the current account of the balance of payments.
1997–1998	China cut interest rates to promote spending and allowed greater flexibility to vary lending rates around the administered level.
1998	The PBC began to allocate credit based on asset-liability management rather than quotas under the credit plan.
1998	China injected Y 270 billion in capital to ameliorate the nonperforming loan (NPL) problems in state banks.
1998–2002	China's four major SCBs cut approximately 250,000 employees and 45,000 branches.
March 1998	The ninth National People's Congress designated financial reform as one of three policy reform goals (for national corporations and government) for the next three years.
October 1998	The Guangdong International Trust and Investment Corporation failed.
1999	The PBC replaced provincial and municipal branches with nine regional branches. The PBC relaxed controls on foreign banks' renminbi business.
1999–2000	China transferred more than Y 1.4 trillion in bad debts of the SCBs and CDB to four asset management companies (AMCs). They and their partner banks are Cinda-CCB and CDB; Great Wall-ABC; HuarongICBC; and Orient-BOC.
November 2001	Huarong signed agreement to sell Y 10.8 billion of NPL assets to a consortium led by Morgan Stanley. The consortium agreed to pay Huarong in cash about 9 percent of the face value of the loans.
December 2001	China became a member of World Trade Organization (WTO). As part of its accession commitments, China agreed to open substantially the financial and financial services markets to foreign interests over five years.

**Selective Chronology of Chinese Financial Reform with Focus on Banking,
1978–2007** *(continued)*

Date	Measures
December 2001	Huarong sold Y 1.97 billion of NPL assets to Goldman Sachs. They established a joint venture, Rongsheng Asset Management Co., to resolve the loans. Soon thereafter, Huarong and the Morgan Stanley Consortium followed by setting up the joint venture First United Asset Management Corporation.
December 2001	China Orient arranged sale of a US$217 million NPL portfolio to the U.S.-based Chenery Associates.
February 2002	The proposal was made to separate bank regulation and supervision from the PBC (at the Central Financial Work Conference, Beijing).
2002	Banking scandals occurred. Wang Xuebing, the former head of the BOC and the CCB was investigated for alleged corruption and subsequently jailed.
January 2003	Citigroup was approved to take a 5 percent stake in Shanghai's Pudong Development Bank for US$72 million.
January 22–24, 2003	The Chinese Communist Party met to complete the separation of the bank regulatory function from the PBC, with a view to curbing the mounting NPLs of the banks.
January 30, 2003	The PBC promulgated requirements to standardize the work of commercial banks in collecting and reporting statistical information on intermediary services.
February 2003	The PBC approved Wenzhou City, Zhejiang Province, to conduct broad financial and banking reforms. The reform included lifting the ban on private investment in commercial banks in urban areas and freeing interest rates for loans to small enterprises.
March 2003	The National People's Congress amended the Central Bank Law and launched a new banking regulator, the China Banking Regulatory Commission (CBRC), as a part of the comprehensive restructuring of the State Council.
April 25, 2003	The CBRC assumed the functions of banking regulation and supervision from the PBC.
August 2003	Eight provinces and municipalities initiated a pilot reform of their rural credit cooperatives (RCCs).
August 25, 2003	Liu Mingkang, chairman of the CBRC, encouraged foreign banks to participate in the country's banking reform by buying stakes in domestic banks. He promised that his commission would improve its capacity to supervise foreign banks by referring to the Core Principles for Effective Banking Supervision.
August 2003	Foreign invested banks in Jinan, Fuzhou, Chengdu, and Chongqing (in addition to Shanghai, Shenzhen, Tianjin, and Dalian) were allowed to initiate renminbi-based business before the end of 2003.
September 2003	The PBC increased the reserve requirement by 1 to 7 percent for all commercial lenders, thereby removing an estimated Y 150 billion ($18 billion) of liquidity from the banks.
December 1, 2003	China raised the maximum equity share for a single foreign investor in a joint venture bank from 15 to 20 percent. Foreign banks are also allowed to provide renminbi services to Chinese businesses (but not individuals) in the 13 major cities.

Selective Chronology of Chinese Financial Reform with Focus on Banking, 1978–2007 *(continued)*

Date	Measures
December 2003	The government launched the latest round of banking reform, with a $45 billion capital injection from PBC's foreign exchange reserves into the BOC and the CCB (US$22.5 billion each) through an intermediary company, Central Huijin Investment Ltd. The reforms were to include transforming the banks into joint-stock companies, introducing foreign and domestic strategic investors, and (subsequently) listing them on the stock market.
2003-2004	Huarong auctioned Y 22.5 billion of NPL assets. Winning bidders included Citigroup, J.P. Morgan, Goldman Sachs, Union Bank of Switzerland, Morgan Stanley, and Lehman Brothers.
December 27, 2003	Sixth Session of the Standing Committee of the 10th National People's Congress adopted Law of the People's Republic of China on Banking Regulation and Supervision.
February 10, 2004	The CBRC said China encourages domestic private funds and foreign investors to become shareholders in Chinese commercial banks.
February 11, 2004	Premier Wen Jiabao called for financial reform to accelerate and promised steady reform of the interest rate system.
February 11, 2004	The CBRC and the PBC articulated 10 measures to guide the reform of the four big SCBs.
March 2, 2004	Premier Wen Jiabao ordered BOC and CCB to complete reforms within three years to transform themselves into true commercial banks.
March 11, 2004	The CBRC issued a guideline for BOC's and CCB's public offering.
March 18, 2004	The Chinese government required the BOC and the CCB to set up joint-stock units by the end of September 2004.
March 2004	China Securities Regulatory Commission (CSRC) reprimanded Shenzhen Development Bank for failing in its fiduciary duties during its negotiations with Newbridge. China Minsheng also disclosed that it faked a shareholder meeting in 2000 prior to an IPO in Shanghai.
April 12, 2004	The PBC increased further the mandatory reserve requirements of the major commercial banks to 7.5 percent from 7 percent. The ratio for more poorly performing banks rose to 8 percent from 7.5 percent.
April 16, 2004	Central bank governor Zhou Xiaochuan warned that reform of the four SCBs is likely to be delayed owing to bureaucratic delays.
April 20, 2004	The CBRC announced its intention to expand the scope of pilot reforms for RCCs in the second half of the year.
April 2004	Yangtze Special Situations Fund emerged in Hong Kong, the first in the country to invest in nonperforming assets of Chinese banks. The ADB approved an equity investment of up to $45 million in the fund.
May 2004	The PBC announced plans to issue bonds to remove Y 200 billion ($24 billion) in NPLs from the portfolios of the BOC and the CCB.
May 19, 2004	The CBRC urged the ABC and the ICBC to intensify their restructuring efforts before the industry fully opens to foreign competition in 2007.
June 2004	The CCB split into two: a company group and a shareholding company, the China Construction Bank Corporation, which will receive the CCB's best assets and become the listed unit.

Selective Chronology of Chinese Financial Reform with Focus on Banking, 1978–2007 *(continued)*

Date	Measures
June 2004	Cinda purchased Y 280 billion ($34 billion) in distressed assets from CCB and BOC, combined.
June 2004	Guizhou Huaxi Rural Cooperative Bank was set up in Guizhou Province as a new model for reforming RCCs.
June 30, 2004	Bank of Communications (BoCom) finished financial restructuring.
June 17, 2004	The CBRC set rules on the issuance of subordinated bonds by commercial banks.
July 21, 2004	The CBRC laid out a six-phase plan to dispose of the NPLs of the BOC and CCB and to restructure the institutions as self-financing joint-stock banks.
August 17, 2004	The CBRC issued administrative rules for automotive loans.
August 18, 2004	BoCom completed equity transfer to HSBC.
August 26, 2004	BOC transformed into a joint-stock company; Huijin Company exercised the rights of shareholder on behalf of the state.
September 1, 2004	The CBRC established rules for implementing the regulation of the People's Republic of China governing foreign-funded financial institutions.
September 21, 2004	CCB transformed into a joint-stock company; Huijin Company exercised shareholder rights on behalf of the state.
November 1, 2004	The PBC (with the CSRC and CBRC) set administrative rules for short-term financing bills of securities firms "to promote the development of money market and expand the financing channels of securities firms."
November 2004	Regulatory changes were introduced to speed up the transfer of NPLs to foreign investors. The AMCs were to report proposed sales to the National Development Reform Commission within 30 days of agreement, and the commission was to respond within 20 working days.
December 2004	Details of NPL transactions (to foreign investors) must be submitted to SAFE within 15 working days of completion.
December 2004	China Orient agreed to purchase Y 130 billion ($15.6 billion) of the CCB portion of Cinda's portfolio.
December 2004	Great Wall invited bids for assets valued at $18.1 billion.
December 11, 2004	Foreign banks were allowed to initiate renminbi business, as agreed to for China's membership in the WTO.
January 2005	Foreign investors were permitted to remit out of China funds related to NPL disposals if they reported transaction details to SAFE.
February 18, 2005	The PBC, the MOF, the State Development and Reform Commission, and the CSRC issued joint public notice ("Provisional Administrative Rules on International Development Institutions' Issuance of Renminbi [RMB] Bonds") "to standardize activities of international development institutions' issuance of RMB bonds and promote development of China's bond market."
April 2005	ICBC received $15 billion in recapitalization from the government.
April 20, 2005	The PBC and CBRC set administrative rules for pilot securitization of credit assets.

Selective Chronology of Chinese Financial Reform with Focus on Banking, 1978–2007 *(continued)*

Date	Measures
May 11, 2005	The PBC set administrative rules on forward bond transactions in the national inter-bank bond market.
June 2005	State Council allowed Huijin to inject about $1.5 billion into China Galaxy Securities, one of China's biggest state-owned brokers.
June 1, 2005	PBC announced the administrative rules for the issuance of financial bonds in the national interbank bond market "to promote the development of the bond market, regulate the issuance of financial bonds, and safeguard the lawful rights of the investors."
June 13, 2005	The PBC set rules for the information disclosure of asset-backed securities "to regulate information disclosure of asset-backed securities, safeguard the legal rights of investors, ensure a smooth progress of the pilot asset-backed securities, and promote the healthy development of the inter-bank bond market."
June 17, 2005	Bank of America announced plan to spend $3 billion to buy a 9 percent stake in the CCB, China's third-biggest state bank, with an option to increase its holding to 19.9 percent. Temasek of Singapore planned to purchase the remaining 5.1 percent of CCB shares that are available to foreign shareholders under current regulations.
August 2005	BoCom offered shares at 1.6 times book value in a $1.9 billion initial public offering (IPO).
August 2005	Central Huijin Investment Company made plans to inject Y 2.5 billion ($308 million) into the country's third-largest broker, Shenyin & Wanguo Securities Co.; Huijin was to receive 33 percent stake in Shenyin & Wanguo.
August 2005	ICBC issued multibillion-yuan subordinated debt. The bank planned to issue Y 35 billion, but subscription reached Y 85.5 billion.
August 2005	A fifth AMC, Huida Asset Custody Co. Ltd., was established to help in disposal of nonperforming assets of the PBC.
October 27, 2005	CCB shares were scheduled to begin trading in Hong Kong SAR as part of China's biggest IPO to date. The IPO was expected to raise $6.1-$7.7 billion.
December 2006	This is the deadline for China to open its financial markets as agreed to under WTO protocols; China will lift all geographic restrictions relating to foreign-bank-offered services in domestic currency (to foreign and domestic companies and individuals). During 2006, both BOC and CCB are expected to have completed IPOs.
2007	The ABC and ICBC are scheduled to complete reforms sufficient to permit both to make IPOs.

Sources:
Anne Hyland Hong Kong. "China Bid To Fast-Track Banking Reform" *Australian Financial Review.* January 21, 2003 Tuesday; "BANK REFORM GOES BEYOND IPO." *Business Daily Update.* April 6, 2004; Benjamin Morgan.
"China Pumps 45 Billion Dollars Into Two State Banks". *Agence France Presse.* January 6, 2004 Tuesday.
"BIG FOUR BANKS TO CARRY OUT INTERNAL REFORMS." *Sinocast China Business Daily News* February 11, 2004; "Big Four Listings On Course Despite Cool Moves." *The Standard*, May 18, 2004 Tuesday; CBRC, "Rules and Regulations," http://www.cbrc.gov.cn.

Selective Chronology of Chinese Financial Reform with Focus on Banking, 1978–2007 *(concluded)*

"CBRC TO EXPAND REFORM SCOPE OF RURAL CREDIT COOPERATIVES." *Sinocast China Business Daily News*. April 19, 2004.

"CCB, BOC Ordered To Set Up Joint-Stock Units By Q3, Pave Way For Stake Sale." AFX.COM. March 18, 2004 Thursday; "Central Bank to bail out broker." China Economic Net. August 4, 2005 http://en.ce. cn/Markets/Equities/200508/04/t20050804_4341851.shtml;. "CCB to launch world's biggest IPO." *China Daily*, October 10, 2005 http://www.chinadaily.com.cn/english/doc/2005–10/10/content_483788.htm; "Central theme." *China Daily*, August 27, 2005.

"China Bank Regulator Urges Last Two State-Owned Banks To Speed Up Reform." *AFX European Focus*, May 19, 2004 Wednesday; "China Encourages Foreign Banks To Buy Stakes In Domestic Banks." AFX.COM. August 26, 2003 Tuesday; "CHINA ENCOURAGES PRIVATE, FOREIGN FUNDS TO JOIN IN COMM'L BANKS." Xinhua. February 9, 2004; *China Financial Watch*, July 12, 2004;.

"China's biggest bank issues multi-billion-yuan subordinated debt." *People's Daily*, August 20, 2005; *China Securities*, May 14, 2004. "China Launches Sweeping Banking Reform In E. China City." *Xinhua*. Feb. 20, 2004; "China Outlines Reform Steps For Bank China, Construction Bank." *Agence France Presse*, July 21,2004 Tuesday.

"China Promotes "Triple-Win" Opening Scheme For Its Banking Sector." *Xinhua*. December 1, 2003, Monday; "China's Central Bank Plans Bonds To Finance Purchase Of Bad Debt: Official." *Agence France Presse*, May 19, 2004 Wednesday; "China to Set up 5th AMC." CRI Online, August 2, 2005.

"Chinese Central Bank Hikes Reserve Ratio Again." *Agence France Presse*. April 12, 2004 Monday; "Chinese Say Bank Insolvent." *Washington Post* page A14, January 12, 1999.

"Citigroup 'Cautiously Optimistic' On China Bank Reform." AFX.COM. January 8, 2004 Thursday; *Economic Information Daily*, May 14, 2004; Elliot Wilson, "CCB REVAMP A MILESTONE IN REFORMS" *The Standard*, June 11, 2004.

"Finance and Insurance." *People's Daily Online* http://english.people.com.cn/data/China_in_brief/ Economy/Finance%20and%20Insurance.html.

García-Herrero 2004; George Zhibin Gu, "A clearer path ahead for China's banks?" *Asia Times Online* http://www.atimes.com/atimes/China/GG02Ad05.html; GUIYANG, "China Reshuffles Rural Financial Service System", *Xinhua Economic News Service*, June 24, 2004, Thursday.

"ICBC Applies to Issue Bonds." *China Daily*. June 28, 2005 http://www.china.org.cn/english/ BAT/133341.htm; *Lardy* 1998.

People's Bank of China, "China Monetary Policy Report Quarter 4, 2004"; "People's Bank of China", "Regulations" http://www.pbc.gov.cn/english/; *People's Bank of China Yearbook 2003*.

People's Daily, May 14, 2004; Philip B. Gilligan, "China's NPLs: Trends and Future Issues" Technical Briefing, http://www.deacons.com.hk/eng/knowledge/knowledge_225.htm May 2005; *South China Morning Post*, Hong Kong SAR, December 30, 2002; "Reform Of China's Ailing State Banking Sector Likely To Be Delayed." Agence France Presse. April 16, 2004 Friday.

"Rules On Foreign Debts Of Foreign Banks -1," *Xinhua Economic News Service*, June 24, 2004. *The Capital Guided To China's Securities Markets*. An ISI Publication. 1994.

The Ministry/Commission Profile at 'www.Chinaonline.Com' http://www.Chinaonline.Com/Refer/ Ministry_Profiles/PBCL3.Asp; Tian Sulei."Chinese Banks Cut Payroll To Enhance Competitiveness." *Xinhua*. Nov. 12, 2003.

"WORLD AWAITS CHINA'S BANKING REFORMS." *China Post*. December 23, 2003.

Xinhua New Agency, Feb.11, 2004; Xinhua News Agency, March 3, 2004; Youngsuk, Oh. 1991. Chinese Special Economic Zones And Its Implication To Korean Businesses, Policy Analysis 91–05, Korea Institute For International Economic Policy.

Appendix II. Selected Financial Statistics*

Table 2.A2.1. Assets Distribution of Financial Institutions

	End of 2002 Q3		End of 2003 Q3		End of 2004 Q3		End of 2005 Q3	
	Assets (Y trillion)	Share (%)	Assets (Y trillion)	Share (%)	Assets (Y trillion)	Share (%)	Assets (Y trillion)	Share (%)
State-owned commercial banks	13.24	59.7	15.31	56.1	16.67	54.1	19.53	53.3
Other commercial banks	2.75	12.4	3.67	13.5	4.47	14.6	5.57	15.3
City commercial banks	1.00	4.5	1.36	5.0	1.59	5.2	1.91	5.2
Foreign-funded banks	0.29	1.3	0.33	1.4	0.50	1.9	0.59	1.8
Urban credit cooperatives	0.11	0.5	0.13	0.5	0.16	0.5	0.18	0.5
Rural credit cooperatives	2.14	9.6	2.57	9.5	2.96	9.7	3.13	8.6
Other financial institutions	2.66	12.0	3.82	14.0	4.31	14.0	5.61	15.3
Totals	22.19	100.0	27.19	100.0	30.66	100.0	36.52	100.0
China's GDP (Y trillion)	**2002** 12.03		**2003** 13.58		**2004** 15.99		**2005** 18.23	

Sources: The People's Bank of China, *Quarterly Statistical Bulletins*, 2005–4, 2004–4, 2003–4, 2002–4, Annual Reports and authors' calculations. In December 2005, the National Bureau of Statistics amended the former GDP figures as a result of China's inaugural economic census. The GDP figures reported here reflect this. The preliminary GDP figure for 2005 was released in January 2006.

Table 2.A2.2. Distribution of Select Deposits to Financial Sector, 2004: Q4 End Balance

	Demand Deposits (in trillions of yuan)	Quasi-Money (includes time deposits, household deposits, and other deposits)	Foreign Currency Deposits	Deposits of Other Financial Institutions Included in Broad Money
SCBs	4.33	9.07	0.88	0.09
Other commercial banks	1.52	1.96	0.23	0.07
UCCs	0.06	0.10	---	---
RCCs	0.50	2.23	0.01	0.00
Finance companies	0.20	0.28	0.01	0.00
Specific depository institutions	---	0.10	0.00	0.00
Postal savings deposits	---	1.08	NA	NA
Total	7.45	15.81	NA	NA

Source: *PBC Annual Report 2004.*

Notes: Total represents total for the entire financial sector and therefore does not represent the sum of the above categories. Also, fiscal deposits are not included here. Foreign currency deposits for specific depository institutions were approximately Y 4 billion. Deposits of RCCs included in broad money were approximately Y 2 million, of finance companies approximately Y 40 million, and of specific depository institutions approximately Y 200 million.

Table 2.A2.3. Branch and Employment Statistics for the Banking Sector (end-2000, and end-2003)

	2000		2003	
	Number of offices	Number of staff, workers	Number of offices	Number of staff, workers
PBC	2,222	169,302	2,199	160,020
SCBs	120,907	1,600,514	88,489	1,415,214
Industrial and Commercial Bank of China	31,673	471,097	24,129	389,045
Agricultural Bank of China	50,546	509,572	36,138	511,425
Bank of China	12,925	192,279	11,609	171,777
Construction Bank of China	25,763	427,566	16,613	342,967
Policy banks	2,272	62,297	2,328	64,762
Joint-stock commercial banks	4,769	105,023	4,786	136,780
Total	130,170	1,937,136	97,802	1,776,776

Source: China Statistical Yearbook 2004

Table 2.A2.4a. Nonperforming Loans (NPLs) of Major Commercial Banks (SCBs) and Joint-Stock Commercial Banks (JSCBs)

	2004:Q1	2004:Q2	2004:Q3	2004:Q4	2005:Q1	2005:Q2	2005:Q3
Outstanding balance (in trillions of yuan)	2.08	1.66	1.70	1.72	1.71	1.16	1.17
Share in total loans (%)	16.61	13.32	13.37	13.21	12.70	8.79	8.70

Source: China Banking Regulatory Commission (CBRC).

Table 2.A2.4b. NPLs of SCBs Only

	2004:Q1	2004:Q2	2004:Q3	2004:Q4	2005:Q1	2005:Q2	2005:Q3
Outstanding balance (in trillions of yuan)	1.89	1.52	1.56	1.58	1.57	1.01	1.02
Share in total loans (%)	19.15	15.59	15.71	15.57	15.00	10.12	10.11

Source: China Banking Regulatory Commission (CBRC).

Table 2.A2.4c. NPLs of JSCBs Only

	2004:Q1	2004:Q2	2004:Q3	2004:Q4	2005:Q1	2005:Q2	2005:Q3
Outstanding balance (in trillions of yuan)	0.188	0.140	0.140	0.143	0.146	0.150	0.153
Share in total loans (%)	7.12	5.16	5.03	4.94	4.9	4.66	4.51

Source: China Banking Regulatory Commission (CBRC).

Table 2.A2.5: Accumulated Disposal of Nonperforming Assets by the Four Asset Management Companies

(In trillions of yuan)

	2004:Q1	2004:Q2	2004:Q3	2004:Q4	2005:Q1	2005:Q2
Overall	0.529	0.567	0.588	0.675	0.689	0.717
Huarong	0.146	0.170	0.175	0.210	0.214	0.220
Great Wall	0.170	0.176	0.183	0.210	0.214	0.229
Orient	0.089	0.092	0.097	0.105	0.107	0.110
Cinda	0.124	0.129	0.133	0.151	0.154	0.158

Source: CBRC.

Appendix III.

Regulators in the Chinese Financial System

National Development and Reform Commission	Lead regulator of the primary corporate bond market. Controls master issuance quota. Authorizes new issue applications. No responsibility for the secondary market or post-issue disclosure.
People's Bank of China (PBC)	Sets interest rates on new issues. Regulates the interbank bond market and trading platform (China Foreign Exchange Trade System).
China Securities Regulation Commission (CSRC)	Securities market regulator. Supervises listed companies, securities companies and other intermediaries, securities investment funds, stock exchanges, new listings, and continuing disclosure for listed securities.
China Insurance Regulatory Commission	Insurance industry regulator. Determines permitted investments for insurance companies.
China Banking Regulatory Commission (CBRC)	Banking regulator. Determines permitted activities (corporate bond guarantees, intermediary business, permitted investments).
Ministry of Finance (MOF)	Supervises National Social Security Fund (NSSF) and its investment activities.
Ministry of Labor and Social Security	Supervises NSSF, corporate pension funds, and their investment activities.
Shanghai and Shenzhen stock exchanges	Stock exchange operators. Supervises new listings and continuing disclosure (regulated by CSRC).
China Foreign Exchange Trade System	Trading platform for interbank foreign exchange and money market transactions. Also trading platform for government and financial bonds among members of the interbank bond market. Supervised by PBC.
China Government Securities Depository Trust and Clearing Co. Ltd. (CDC)	Central depository for government, financial, and corporate bonds, as well as central bank bills. Regulated by MOF and PBC.
China Securities Depository and Clearing Company (CSDCC)	Subdepository of CDC for the portion of corporate bonds that have been granted a listing and have been transferred to the CSDCC, and for bonds issued by securities companies. Also, the central depository for the Shanghai and Shenzhen stock exchanges. Regulated by CSRC.

Source: Scott and Ho (2004).

Appendix IV. Case Study: Hongkong and Shanghai Banking Corporation's (HSBC's) US$1.75 Billion Investment in the Bank of Communications (BoCom)

Transaction Background	Win-Win Partnership

Transaction Background

- On August 6, 2004, HSBC announced its acquisition of a 19.9 percent stake in BoCom, China's fifth largest bank, for US$1.75 billion in cash, which represents 1.76 times more than the year-end 2003 book value and 1.4 times more than the post-money book value.
- The transaction was signed immediately after the completion of a massive recapitalization, which entails a US$6.4 billion nonperforming loan carve-out and a US$2.2 billion capital injection from the Chinese government and the National Social Security Fund
- The transaction is a landmark in the following aspects:
  - It was by far the largest foreign investment to that date in China's financial service sector.
  - It was one of the largest foreign equity investments in China.
  - It was one of the largest minority investments in financial institutions world-wide.
  - BoCom became the first major bank in China to complete a comprehensive restructuring and a massive recapitalization, setting an example for the country's financial reform.
  - The transaction provided a highly structured joint venture arrangement for cooperation in credit cards, including distribution of co-branded cards on a nationwide basis.
- Established in 1908, BoCom is one of the earliest commercial banks in China. It was re-established as the first joint-stock commercial bank with a nationwide license in 1987.
  - It serves more than 30 million customers through more than 2,700 branches throughout the nation, with a business focus in wealthy regions.
  - It has about 3.5 and 3 percent market share of domestic deposits and loans market, respectively. It is ranked third and sixth in funds custody business and overall card issuance in China, respectively.
- HSBC Group is one of the largest banking and financial services organizations in the world:
  - It provides a comprehensive range of financial services with more than 9,500 offices world-wide and more than 110 million customers.
  - It is a market leader in Hong Kong, with the largest operation of foreign banks in China. It has 10 branches on the mainland, and it has carried out several stake acquisitions in the Chinese financial industry, including the acquisition of an 8 percent stake in Bank of Shanghai and a 10 percent stake in Ping An insurance.

Win-Win Partnership

- Through the transaction, BoCom will
  - Leverage HSBC to further implement internal restructuring in line with international practices and further strengthen capital base on top of recapitalization.
  - Strengthen market position through cooperation in credit cards and other businesses and through technical support from HSBC.
  - Pave the way for overseas initial public offering, likely the first of any major Chinese bank.
- Through the transaction, HSBC will
  - Gain immediate access to a nationwide distribution network in China and complement HSBC's existing operations in China, already the strongest of any foreign player.
  - Pave the way for further increase in ownership.
  - Establish unique credit card platform to overtake Citibank-Shanghai Pudong venture.
  - Cooperate in other businesses to provide broad-based growth platform in China.
- Positive Media/Research Reponses
  - "The deal gives HSBC the biggest footprint of any foreign bank on the Chinese mainland and offers BoCom international management expertise." (Financial Times)
  - "Organic growth will be slow and costly, so teaming up with a local bank is the best strategy to tackle the retail market and Bank of Communications is the best fit amongst all the banks." (Barclays Capital)

Bibliography

Barnett, Stephen, 2004, "Banking Sector Developments," in *China's Growth and Integration into the World Economy: Prospects and Challenges*, ed. by E. Prasad, IMF Occasional Paper No. 232 (Washington: International Monetary Fund).

Bottelier, Pieter, 2004, "China's Emerging Domestic Debt Markets," Working Paper No. 202 (Stanford, California: Stanford Center for International Development), January.

Bottelier, Pieter, 2005a, "Managing China's Transition Debt: Challenges for Sustained Development," in *Financial Sector Reform in China*, ed. by Yasheng Huang, Tony Saich, and Edward Steinfeld (Cambridge, Massachusetts: Harvard University Asia Center).

————, 2005b, Testimony to the 8/11/05 hearing of the U.S.-China Economic and Security Review Commission on *The General Health of China's Banking System*, Washington.

"China's Foreign Debt Surges to 233.4 Billion U.S. Dollars," 2005, *People's Daily Online*, June 8. Available via the Internet: http://english.people.com.cn/200506/08/eng20050608_189073.html

"China's Trust Investment Companies Report Growing Business," 2005, *People's Daily Online*, January 19.

Federal Reserve Bank of San Francisco, 2005, "Foreign Banks' New China Strategy," *Asia Focus*, Country Analysis Unit (San Francisco, July).

Fu, Xiaoqing (Maggie), and Shelagh Heffernan, 2005, "China: The Effects of Bank Reform on Structure and Performance," Faculty of Finance Working Paper No. WP-FF–19–2005 (London: Cass Business School, City University).

García-Herrero, Alicia, and Daniel Santabárbara, 2004, "Where Is the Chinese Banking System Going with the Ongoing Reform?" Documentos Ocasionales No. 0406 (Madrid: Banco de España).

Gilligan, Philip B., 2005, "China NPLs: Trends and Future Issues" Technical Briefing. Available via the Internet: http://www.deacons.com.hk/eng/knowledge/knowledge_225.htm. (The briefing is an amended version of "Banking Regulation in China," by Philip B. Gilligan, in "Regulation of Foreign Banks," by M. Gruson and R. Reisner (LexisNexis).)

Hope, Nicholas C., and Lawrence J. Lau, 2004, "China's Transition to the Market: Status and Challenges," Working Paper No. 210 (Stanford, California: Stanford Center for International Development), March.

Hope, Nicholas C., Dennis Tao Yang, and Mu Yang Li, eds., 2003, *How Far Across the River? Chinese Policy Reform at the Millennium* (Stanford, California: Stanford University Press).

Hu, Fred, 2004, "China's Credit Boom: Causes and Implications," paper presented at the Stanford Center for International Development conference, "China's Policy Reforms: Progress and Challenges," Beijing, May 24–25.

Karacadag, Cem, 2003, "Financial System Soundness and Reform," in *China: Competing in the Global Economy*, ed. by W. Tseng and M. Rodlauer (Washington: International Monetary Fund).

Kuijs, Louis, 2005, "Investment and Saving in China," Policy Research Working Paper No. 3633 (Washington: World Bank), May.

Lardy, Nicholas R., 1998, *China's Unfinished Economic Revolution* (Washington: Brookings Institution Press).

———, 2003, "When Will China's Financial System Meet China's Needs?" in *How Far Across the River? Chinese Policy Reform at the Millennium*, ed. by N. Hope, D. Tao Yang, and M. Yang Li (Stanford, California: Stanford University Press).

McKinnon, Ronald, and Gunther Schnabl, 2002, "Synchronized Business Cycles in East Asia: Fluctuations in the Yen/Dollar Exchange Rate and China's Stabilizing Role," SCID Working Paper No. 156 (Stanford, California: Stanford Center for International Development).

People's Bank of China (PBC), 2004a, *Annual Report 2003* (Beijing), April.

———, 2004b, "Banking Survey." Available via the Internet: http://www.pbc.gov.cn/english/diaochatongji/tongjishuju/gofile.asp?file=2004S4.htm

———, 2005, "Financial Industry Performance Remained Stable." Available via the Internet: http://www.pbc.gov.cn/english/detail.asp?col=6400&id=546.

———, various years, *Quarterly Statistical Bulletin* (Beijing).

Prasad, Eswar, ed., 2004, *China's Growth and Integration into the World Economy: Prospects and Challenges*, IMF Occasional Paper No. 232 (Washington: International Monetary Fund).

Qian, Yingyi, and Jinglian Wu, 2003, "China's Transition to a Market Economy: How Far Across the River?" in *How Far Across the River? Chinese Policy Reform at the Millennium*, ed. by N. Hope, D. Tao Yang, and M. Yang Li (Stanford, California, Stanford University Press).

Scott, David H., and Irene S.M. Ho, 2004, "China's Corporate Bond Market: Creating New Options for Infrastructure Finance" (Washington: World Bank), June.

Sheng, Andrew, Xiao Geng, and Wang Yuan, 2004, "Property Rights and 'Original Sin' in China: Transaction Costs, Wealth Creation, and Property Rights Infrastructure," paper presented at Stanford Center for International Development's third annual conference on Chinese policy reform, Stanford, California, October 14–16.

Shih, Victor, Qi Zhang, and Mingxing Liu, 2004, "Comparing the Performance of Chinese Banks: A Principal Component Approach," Working Paper 8/2004 (unpublished; Chicago: Northwestern University).

Tay, Sue Anne, 2005, "China's Asset Management Companies a Liability," *Asia Times*, July 7.

Tseng, Wanda, and Markus Rodlauer, eds., 2003, *China: Competing in the Global Economy* (Washington: International Monetary Fund).

World Bank, 1996, *The Chinese Economy: Fighting Inflation, Deepening Reforms* (Washington), May.

————, 2005, "China Quarterly Update" (Washington), February.

Yang, Ya-Hwei, 2004, "Development and Problems in China's Financial System" Discussion Paper No. 04-E–06 (Taiwan Study Center).

Youngsuk, Oh, 1991, "Chinese Special Economic Zones and Its Implication to Korean Businesses," Policy Analysis 91–05 (Korea Institute for International Economic Policy).

3

The Banking System Structure in China and India

Luo Ping*

A comparison of China and India is both exciting and challenging, and should ideally lead to a serious consideration of various policy implications. In this context, our conference today marks the beginning of a long journey. In my remarks, I will try to compare the banking sectors in China and India, largely focusing on structure and robustness as well as the effectiveness of the banking supervisory systems.

General Comment

Both China and India are large, developing economies with huge populations, which help to contribute to their economic weight in the world. The transformation of both countries has strong implications for the rest of the world. No wonder some people believe that the emergence of China and India as economic giants should serve as a wake-up call for the developed world. It is true that China and India possess cheap skilled labor, reform-minded governments in favor of a more market-oriented economy, and huge domestic markets. Both countries have proven to be capable of managing their economies. And fortunately, both countries have maintained high growth rates, roughly 9 percent for China and 8 percent for India over the past couple of years.

---

*Luo Ping is a senior supervisor in the China Banking Regulatory Commission.

However, it is important to note that high growth for the two economies is critical, because they depend on a high growth rate to generate enough job opportunities for millions of people joining the labor force each year. Given their inherent constraints, it will take ages for both economies to catch up with the developed world, particularly as measured by per capita income. Even if China can continue its high growth rate for another 10 years, and assuming the United States stopped growing, it would reach only one-tenth of the per capita income of the United States by then. Therefore, I would have thought, of course, that on the part of the developed countries, in full recognition of the need to boost domestic consumption (particularly for the large economies), it would be better to engage and integrate these two developing countries into the global economy rather than treat them as potential threats by enacting arbitrary trade barriers.

The Role of the Banking Sector in the Economy

As far as the banking sector is concerned, it may well be true that the two countries share many attributes, particularly in terms of industry structure. First of all, the two countries heavily depend on bank finance to support economic growth, and capital markets are less developed. In China, the total assets in the banking sector represent more than 90 percent of the assets in the financial sector. And in India, the commercial banking sector represents about 74 percent of total financial system assets. Nonbank financial institutions make up the balance in India, of which 8.6 percent are term-lending institutions and 15.4 percent are investment institutions. Some of these institutions could be considered as banking institutions according to the broader definition in China. Moreover, the proportion of commercial banking sector financial assets in both countries is likely to rise further.

Another strikingly common attribute of the banking system in the two economies is dominant state ownership. This stands in stark contrast to other developing economies and has strong implications for the conduct and performance of the banking sector in general. In China, until very recently, all major commercial banks except one or two were controlled by the central and local governments, as are virtually all small commercial banks. China's banking sector is relatively concentrated. The four large banks, known as state-owned commercial banks until the recent diversification of ownership, plus the Bank of Communications (BoCom), also largely owned by the central government, account for nearly two-thirds of commercial bank assets.

It is true that following the equity participation of foreign institutional investors and public listing overseas, as is the case with the Construction Bank of China (CCB) and BoCom, the ownership structure of China's state-owned banks has changed quite significantly. However, there is a general perception that the government will keep majority holdings in these large banks up to at least 51 percent going forward.

The High Degree of State Ownership in the Banking Sector

The high degree of state ownership of commercial banks has traditionally been accompanied by a strong emphasis on lending to state-owned enterprises (SOEs) in China. The large state-controlled banks are heavily concentrated in lending to SOEs whereas the second- and third-tier, joint stock, and city commercial banks are somewhat more oriented toward nonstate enterprises.

The Indian banking system can be characterized by a large number of banks with mixed ownership. However, 27 public sector banks—namely, banks owned and controlled by the state—continue to dominate the Indian commercial banking landscape. Together, these banks account for three-quarters of the market share. Even though these public sector banks have access to capital markets, government policy is to ensure that its equity interest does not, as a result of public issues by banks, go below 51 percent.

As is the case with many developed and developing countries, the efficiency of the state-owned banks has been a concern for both the Chinese and Indian governments. And the Indian government also openly admitted that public sector banks have been consistently outperformed by private sector banks. The effort to restructure the state-owned banks is still a work in progress in the two countries. Both governments have continued to launch many new initiatives to further promote progress in this area.

The Chinese government has expressed often that the purpose of reforming the state-owned banks is to transform them into genuinely commercial entities. Against this background, the government has injected a massive amount of money to recapitalize CCB, Bank of China (BOC), Industrial and Commercial Bank of China, and BoCom, to restore their solvency and pave the way for ensuing corporate restructuring. Other elements of the reform package include further disposal of nonperforming loans (NPLs), restructuring into joint stock limited companies (that is, corporatization), offering shares to strategic foreign investors, public listing on international and/or domestic stock markets, recovery of the government's investment, and retreat of the government holding.

Furthermore, the China Banking Regulatory Commission (CBRC), which has the mandate to monitor the progress of reforming the state-owned banks, set out a number of performance criteria for assessment purposes in March 2004 when the central Huijin Investments Company—the government investment arm for capital injection into the state-owned banks—was not yet fully functional. These include 0.6 percent of return on assets and 11 percent of return on equity. At present, the central Huijin SAFE Investment Company, now the largest shareholder for the former state-owned banks, has not released any performance indicators, at least not publicly. It is true that both CCB and BOC meet almost all the performance indicators.

As their owner, the Indian government has recently enlarged autonomy to the public sector banks and will monitor their performance through the Statements of Intent, which have been drawn up by the managements of the public sector banks. The Statements of Intent relate to growth parameters, profitability parameters, performance with respect to national priorities, and credit management.

Clearly, in the review of the Statements of Intent for 2005 and 2006, the Indian government is not happy with the projections on the efficiency parameters of public sector banks. The government admitted that the Indian banking sector is known not to have offered very good returns on capital. The gap is significant in India as compared with other emerging markets. The return on assets of Indian banks stood at 0.7 percent, against 1.2 percent for Singapore, 1.36 percent for Malaysia, 1.42 percent for Korea, and 1.6 percent for Brazil.

It is true that the Indian government does not intend to prod public sector banks to set overambitious and unrealistic targets. However, they have made clear that they cannot accept targets which do not strategically mobilize the inherent advantages of Public Sector Banks in terms of their footprint, manpower, and, above all, sovereign ownership for achieving sustained improvement in efficiency, profitability, and growth.

The Robustness of the Banking Sector

According to Standard & Poor's, the Indian banking sector is fundamentally stronger than China's, at least for now. Indian banks' ratio of gross nonperforming assets—including NPLs, parts of restructured assets, and foreclosed properties—stood at 8–10 percent as of March 2005 compared with 31–35 percent for the Chinese banks as of December 31,

2004. According to the CBRC, the NPL ratio for major commercial banks in China stood at 10 percent by the end of August 2005.

The difference in asset quality can be explained by a number of factors, according to Standard & Poor's. For example, there are structural differences in the economic development models. Indian banks play an indirect role in the government fiscal operations, providing funds to the central government through their subscription to government bonds in line with statutory liquidity ratio requirements. In contrast, Chinese banks, the state-owned banks in particular, are directly used as fiscal instruments to fund state-owned enterprises. Further, Indian banks' credit risk management systems are comparatively more advanced than China's, mainly because Chinese banks spent decades under policy lending regulations that placed very low priority on developing a credit risk management platform.

In terms of capital adequacy, with relatively better interest margins (the benign interest rate regime continued to favor the Indian banking sector, with net interest margin for the public sector banks inching up from 2.98 percent in 2003–04 to 3.03 percent in 2004–05), low provisioning needs, and stronger net profitability, Indian banks have been able to build a stronger capital base than Chinese banks.

The Robustness of the Banking Supervisory System

Overall, a cursory review of public information would suggest that the Indian banking supervisory system is also, to some extent, stronger than that in China. Two indicators are quite meaningful. Basically, a large part of China's banking sector is insolvent and the priority is to restore the banking sector to normal. Therefore, China cannot afford to introduce a deposit insurance scheme quickly, because the fund would not be enough to absorb the stock problem. Similarly, China cannot adopt Basel II because it asks for not 8 percent of capital requirement but more likely 10–12 percent at a minimum. However, India has moved quite a long way in these two areas, which is a sign of a strong supervisory system and a strong banking system as well.

Neither the existence of deposit insurance nor preparations for Basel II are particularly meaningful indicators of the strength of the supervisory system; the issues are much more basic, including sound rules for asset classification, risk management, measuring capital adequacy at full provisioning, and rules enforcement. First, India has already set up a deposit insurance scheme to provide a degree of cover for both depositors and lenders. The Deposit Insurance and Credit Guarantee Corp. is wholly owned by the Reserve Bank of India, operating separate insurance funds to protect bank depositors and banks with exposures to priority sectors identified and supported by the government. The Deposit Insurance Scheme covers all classes of banks in India, including cooperative banks. Deposit insurance is compulsory and the cover per depositor per bank account is Rs. 100,000 and covers about 75 percent of total banking system deposits. The premium payable under the scheme by insured banks is equal to five basis points of total deposits and will increase to 10 basis points from 2005 onward.

In clear contrast, despite the government-orchestrated financial restructuring of banks in general, 30 percent of China's banking sector, measured in terms of assets, is still undercapitalized. These include many small city commercial banks, not to mention credit cooperatives, where efforts to restore their solvency are still under way.

In full recognition of the benefits of a deposit insurance system, the central bank in China has started to formulate the detailed arrangements for such a system. However, a number of risks inherent in the deposit insurance system need to be addressed, such as moral hazard (particularly following the full liberalization of interest rates), potential cross subsidy to the disadvantage of large and well-capitalized banks, and practical difficulty in assigning a risk-adjusted premium. Therefore, a deposit insurance system for China can only be expected to become a reality after a few more years. And this is most likely to happen when the entire banking sector has been made sounder.

Further evidence for the argument is India's readiness to adopt Basel II, a set of more demanding capital standards, designed originally for internationally active banks in G-10 countries only. As complex as Basel II is, India is determined to implement it effective March 31, 2007. They will initially adopt the standardized approach for credit risk and the basic indicator approach for operational risk. After adequate skills are developed, both by the banks and also by the supervisor, some banks may be allowed to migrate to the internal ratings-based approach (IRB). Despite the benefit of a favorable perception overseas that India is conforming to best international standards, it is estimated that the banking sector may see a net depletion of 200 basis points in capital adequacy following the adoption of Basel II, as it asks for more capital for emerging markets. For one thing, operational risk is just an add-on. Of course, this may entail raising fresh capital. And in the case of public sector banks, the room for raising further capital would be constrained by the policy requirement to keep the government's shareholding at 51 percent or more. It is important to note that in March 2001, the Reserve Bank of India required all banks to meet a higher minimum capital requirement of 9 percent, up from the previous 8 percent.

China, on the other hand, does not have the luxury to shift to Basel II so soon, because many banks are now trying hard to come to grips with Basel I. In light of market conditions, the Chinese supervisor intends to mandate the IRB approach only for large Chinese banks in perhaps five years' time, while continuing to adopt Basel I for the rest of the banking industry.

To conclude, China and India both have accomplished a great deal in reforming and improving their banking industries in recent years. Because state ownership will continue to dominate the banking sector in each country, the major challenge for the governments in China and India will be to ensure that banks can operate as genuinely commercial businesses by striking a proper balance between their roles as owners and as supervisors of banks. Following foreign equity participation and the public listing of China's state-owned banks, corporate governance of these banks is changing dramatically. Public sector banks in India should presumably move more quickly in improving their governance, because they have been listed for quite some time already, although domestically. Despite supportive government policies toward the banking sector and an extensive branch network, both China's reforming state-owned banks and India's public sector banks still need to demonstrate that they are the right mechanisms to deliver and maximize shareholders' value, which in turn fosters the development of the national economies going forward.

PART II

FINANCIAL SECTOR REFORMS: SECURITIES MARKETS

4

Development of the Securities Market in India

G.N. Bajpai[*]

Exchanges in religion, culture, education, and medicine between China and India began thousands of years ago. India, for example, hosted distinguished Chinese scholars like Fa Hien in the fourth century CE and Hieun Tsang in the seventh century CE, while China welcomed the great Indian physician Sushrutha, who is considered to be the father of surgery, some 2,500 years ago.

The two societies, Chinese and Indian, have approached social and economic development from diverse angles. Whereas the Chinese system functions in a political framework of Maoist ideology with a steadily rising role of nonstate organizations and individual citizens, India has followed the Westminster Parliamentary democratic system, where social and political factors strongly influence economic decisions.

China embarked on modern economic development as a "cooperative venture" on the principle of equality via deep state intervention. On the other hand, post independence India's command and control economy was built on collaboration between the public and private sectors. In the late 1970s, China chose to experiment with liberalization to facilitate private ownership and global participation and began moving from a sluggish, inefficient, and centrally planned model to a more market-oriented economy. It expanded the authority of local agriculture officials in place

---

*G.N. Bajpai is the former Chairman of the Securities and Exchange Board of India (SEBI) and also former Chairman of the Life Insurance Corporation of India.

of the old collectivization model and plant managers in industry. China permitted a wide variety of small-scale private enterprises in services and light manufacturing, and opened the economy to increased foreign trade and investment.

In the early 1990s, India began to liberalize and integrate globally and launched a program of reforms in response to a fiscal and balance of payments crisis. The program, consisting of stabilization-cum-structural adjustment measures, was put in place with a view to attain macroeconomic stability and higher rates of economic growth. The reforms in the industrial, trade, and financial sectors were much wider and deeper.

Undoubtedly, China has raced ahead of India. Particularly in manufacturing, it has become a global outsourcing center. India has emerged as an information technology powerhouse, with services contributing a major part of growth of the back office of the whole world. It is not the intention of this presentation to either compare the magnitudes of development in the two economies or delineate the reasons for them. What I seek to communicate is that the two emerging (great) economies have pursued different models and distinct paths but have gained enviable success.

Financial Infrastructure

The financial system of the country, including policies, institutions, and judicial system is the engine of economic growth. It is increasingly believed that sustainable economic growth takes place where there is a spirit of enterprise. India's record in managing risks is enviable. That the cascading effect of the East Asian crisis did not cause even ripples in the Indian financial system speaks volumes about the strength and resilience of its financial infrastructure.

Development of the Securities Market

A securities market is a place where the suppliers and users of capital meet to share one another's views, and where a balance is sought among diverse market participants. The securities separate individual acts of saving and investment over time, space, and entities, and thus allow savings to occur without concomitant investment. Moreover, yield-bearing securities make present consumption more expensive relative to future consumption, inducing people to save more. The composition of savings changes, with less of it being held in the form of idle money or unproductive assets, simply because more divisible and liquid assets are available.

The securities market acts as a brake on channeling savings to low-yielding enterprises and impels enterprises to focus on performance. It continuously monitors performance through movements of share prices in the market and threats of takeover. These characteristics improve the efficiency of resource utilization and thereby significantly increase returns on investment. As a result, savers and investors are not constrained by their individual abilities, but enabled by the economy's capability to invest and save, which inevitably enhances savings and investment in the economy. Thus, the securities market converts a given stock of investable resources into a larger flow of goods and services and augments economic growth. In fact, the literature is full of theoretical and empirical studies that have established a causal robust (statistically significant) two-way relation between developments in the securities market and economic growth.

The Indian securities market dates to the eighteenth century, when the securities of the East India Company were traded in Mumbai and Kolkata. However, the orderly growth of the capital market began with the setting up of the Bombay Stock Exchange in July 1875 and Ahmedabad Stock Exchange in 1894. Eventually, 22 other exchanges in various cities were set up.

Given the significance of the securities market and the need for the economy to grow at a projected 8 percent a year, the managers of the Indian economy have been assiduously promoting the securities market as an engine of growth to provide an alternative yet efficient means of resource mobilization and allocation. Further, the global financial environment is undergoing unremitting transformation. Geographical boundaries have disappeared. The days of insulated and isolated financial markets are history. The success of any capital market largely depends on its ability to align itself with the global order.

To realize national aspirations and keep pace with the changing times, the securities market in India has gone through various stages of liberalization, bringing about fundamental and structural changes in the market's design and operation. These changes have resulted in broader investment choices and a drastic reduction in transaction costs. Efficiency, transparency, and safety have also increased integration with the global markets. The opening up of the economy for investment and trade, the dismantling of administered interest and exchange rates regimes, and setting up of sound regulatory institutions have facilitated these changes.

Regulatory Efficacy

The securities market in India was underdeveloped, opaque, dominated by a handful of players, and concentrated in a few cities. Manipulation and unfair practices were perceived to be rampant, prompting an overseas researcher to describe the market as a "snake pit." The transformation of the Indian securities market started with the establishment of the Securities and Exchange Board of India (SEBI) in 1989, initially as an informal body and in 1992 as a statutory autonomous regulator with the twin objectives of protecting the interests of investors and developing and regulating the securities market over a period of time. SEBI has been empowered to investigate, examine, visit company premises, summon records and persons, and inquire and impose penalties commensurate with misconduct. The first and foremost challenge for the fledgling regulator was to create a regulatory and supervisory framework for the market, a job that proved formidable, because vested interests resisted every new step. However, with the designing and notification of 32 regulations and guidelines, during its decade and a half of existence, the apparatus steadily evolved and has adapted to the situation.

SEBI has instituted a consultative process of framing regulations. All reports, concept papers, and policy proposals are posted on SEBI's website (www.sebi.gov.in) for comments from market participants and the public. The comments are compiled and taken into account before regulations are finalized. Even draft regulations are put on the website, so legal experts can comment on the law's correspondence with the spirit of the initiatives. This openness has a profound impact not only in terms of valuable input and gauging public opinion before framing regulations and guidelines but also in terms of improving quality, acceptability, and ease of implementation. SEBI has formed a number of committees of eminent experts and market practitioners to support it in the design of reforms for different aspects of securities markets. The regulator posts all its orders, including those delivered on appeals against its orders, on its website. On request, it provides informal guidance on payments of nominal fees and issues an action letter so that the participants can seek clarification on any aspect and adopt an appropriate business strategy that conforms to the applicable regulations.

SEBI has put timelines for performance of its various functions, such as registration and renewal, on the website. These measures work as a self-disciplining mechanism within SEBI and provide full transparency to its functioning.

Primary Market

The primary market, which at one time was flooded with a number of issues floated by dubious promoters, depriving gullible investors of their lifetime savings, has since been transformed. The changes in this area have been epic and include detailing of complete profiles of promoters, comprehensive disclosures, the existence of tangible assets, and a track record of profit as also reporting end uses of funds to the Board as a part of corporate governance. Recently, when the story of Google's initial public offering (IPO) was being touted in the media worldwide as one of the greatest innovations of recent times for raising risk capital, the *Financial Times*, London, carried the following observation:

> The World's Biggest Democracy can show Google how to conduct an online IPO. . . .[I]n India you cannot apply on the web but investors can access one of the world's largest financial networks with 7000 terminals scattered around 350 cities. And every step of the book building process is public. . . .[T]he Indian system is a refreshing example of a transparent IPO market but it is also a rare one, especially in the insider-friendly Asian markets.

All the IPOs since the reforms started have been a success and, barring a few exceptions, are trading at a premium over the issue price. The regulatory framework has been modified to provide options to Indian firms for raising resources either domestically, globally, or both. These options help discover prices and reduce the cost of funds. A number of Indian firms have raised money through American depository receipts, global depository receipts, and external commercial borrowings. Two-way fungibility is permitted to enhance liquidity.

During 2004–05, a sum of Rs. 282.56 billion, as opposed to Rs. 232.71 billion in 2003–04 (which was larger than the amount raised in the 10 years of the earlier primary market boom), was raised through the primary market. In fact, the corporate sector and central and state governments together raised a total of Rs. 3.75 trillion from the securities market during 2004–05. Thankfully, so far, no major mishap has occurred recently.

If a Rip van Winkle woke up from a prolonged, deep slumber of a couple of years, he would be amazed to see the quality of the secondary market of India. The deafening noise of an outcry trading system has been replaced with the silence of the electronic consolidated anonymous limit order book, with price-time priority matching accessible through more than 10,000 terminals spread over 400 cities and towns across the Indian subcontinent, something perhaps without a parallel in the world. Transaction costs are low, compared with those of the most developed markets.

The Indian settlement system conforms to the Committee on Payment and Settlement–International Organization of Securities Commissions principles and G–30 committee (January 2003, under the chairmanship of Sir Andrew Large) recommendations, which even the most developed markets of the world are proposing to implement by the end of 2006. The institution of central counterparty (CCP), which provides full novation and guarantees settlement, has eliminated counterparty risk entirely. More than 99 percent of the dematerialization of market capitalization and straight-through processing, mandatory for all institutional trades, have enabled the Indian settlement system to function seamlessly, notwithstanding size and spread.

On a T+2 cycle, all securities are fully cleared electronically through a CCP on a rolling settlement. The CCP of the exchanges, which operates a tight risk management system and maintains a short (T+2) and consistent settlement cycle, is now financially able to meet the obligations for four to five consecutive settlements even if all the trading members default in their obligations. The dynamic risk management system comprises capital adequacy norms, trading and exposure limits, index-based market-wide circuit breakers, and margin (mark to market) requirements. The encashability of the underlying liquidity of the margins, comprising cash, bank guarantees, and securities, is evaluated periodically. The real-time monitoring of broker positions and margins and automatic disablement of terminals with value-added risk margining, built on much higher sigma deviation than the best of the markets in the world, have reduced the operational risk to the lowest ebb. In a recent unfortunate, very sharp (more than 25 percent in two days) fall of the market in May 2004, the strength of the system's risk management was tested. There was not a single broker failure or default, and on the third day (after the two consecutive days of decline) the market functioned as if nothing unusual had happened. Even the CCP was not required to fund any broker-dealer's obligations.

The three-legged corporate compliance stool—disclosure, accounting standards, and boardroom practices—has lifted India to a global pedestal in corporate governance. In a study titled *What Works in Securities Laws?* Professors Rafael La Porta, Florencio Lopez de Silanes, and Andrei Shleifer comment, "India scores 100% as far as disclosure standards are concerned." The Indian accounting standards are aligned with international accounting standards and are "principle based." One of the most sophisticated pension fund managers, CalPERS, gave a score of three (the maximum that could be awarded) via permissible equity market analysis when voting for India as an investment destination. Its September

2004 report, CLSA–CG Watch says, "In terms of consolidation, segmental reporting, deferred tax accounting and related party transactions, the gap between Indian and U.S. Generally Accepted Accounting Principles (GAAP) is minimal."

Regarding corporate governance it might be worthwhile to recall what an Economist Intelligence Unit 2003 study said: "Top of the Country class, as might be expected, is Singapore followed by Hong Kong SAR and somewhat surprisingly, India where overall disclosure standards have improved dramatically, accounting differences between local and U.S. standards have been minimized and the number of companies with a majority of independent directors has risen significantly." The CLSA–Emerging Markets Study on Corporate Governance gives India a score of 6.2, which is next only to 7.5 for Singapore and 6.7 for Hong Kong SAR, and this happened before the implementation of the Narayana Murthy Committee recommendations, said to be effective from January 1, 2006. None of the Indian companies listed on the New York Stock Exchange (NYSE) or on the NASDAQ, to public knowledge, has sought the benefit of transition time for the implementation of SOX requirements. What could possibly be more comforting to any regulator or investor than the CLSA–Emerging Markets Study comment "The Securities and Exchange Board of India (SEBI) continues to raise the bar for good corporate governance."

It is not appropriate to compare the Indian securities market with those of Singapore and Hong Kong SAR. Singapore and Hong Kong SAR are city-states and have a much smaller spectrum to watch: listed companies, broker-dealers, investors, and even number of transactions. The Indian securities market is next only to the U.S. market in terms of size. Even though by all criteria of economic research, market capitalization and trades in U.S. dollar terms determine market size, in actual operations, the market participants and the regulators have to grapple with the number of listed securities, market participants, and the volume of transactions—areas where India stands out. The National Stock Exchange (NSE) is the third-largest exchange in the world, next only to the NYSE and NASDAQ, in the number of transactions, followed by the Bombay Stock Exchange, the fifth largest in the world. India has the largest electronic order book; NYSE and NASDAQ books are quote driven. In the matter of single-stock futures, India leads the world, followed by EURONEXT, which is not even 25 percent its size. Even in index futures, NSE volumes are next only to the Chicago Mercantile Exchange and Eurex. No other market in the world, including that of Japan, compares with the volume of transactions of Indian markets.

The focus of development and the quality of regulation have not centered only on primary and secondary markets, they have also been directed at quality of intermediation and enforcement. The mutual fund industry of India, which has gone through a host of reforms via regulatory interventions, today has some outstanding features such as benchmarking mutual fund schemes, valuation norms, uniform cutoff time, and comprehensive risk management. An independent study organized by the Asian Development Bank, the Cadgon report testifies to this.

Investors and issuers can take comfort and make transactions with confidence if intermediaries and their employees (1) follow a code of conduct and deal with probity and (2) are capable of providing professional services. All intermediaries in the securities market are now registered and regulated by SEBI. A code of conduct has been prescribed for each intermediary as well as for their employees, in addition to applicability of fit and proper person regulatory standards. Further, capital adequacy and other norms have been specified and a system of monitoring and inspecting their operations has been instituted to enforce compliance. Disciplinary action is taken against them for violating any ground rules. All the intermediaries in the market are mandated to have a compliance officer, who reports noncompliance observations directly and independently to SEBI.

The state of the market today bears testimony to the role SEBI plays. It is no wonder that a study by the Society for Capital Market Research and Development (October 2004) revealed that there has been great improvement in the general public's perception of capital market regulation in India since 2001.

The Economic Survey 2003–04 by the government of India had the following to say: "The securities markets have made enormous progress in recent years. India's equity market is now being increasingly recognized as a success story on the world scale." These reforms have boosted the confidence of investors (domestic and international) in the Indian securities market. There are four parameters to ascertain the level of investor confidence: (1) investments by foreign institutional investors (FIIs), (2) growth of the mutual funds industry, (3) subscriptions to IPOs, and (4) an increase in the number of accounts with the depositories. According to figures from the 2003–04 financial year, mutual funds mobilized net resources of about Rs. 480 billion, equivalent to about one-fourth of incremental bank deposits. Mutual funds' assets increased from Rs. 1.1 billion at the end of March 2003 to Rs. 2.0 billion at the end of October 2005. Indian companies raised about Rs. 33 billion through euro issues. The year 2004 witnessed a net FII (portfolio money) inflow of US$10 billion. The volume of issuance in the primary market increased from Rs. 41 billion in 2002–03 to Rs. 282.56 billion in 2004–05.

The two benchmark stock market indices, namely the SENSEX and S&P CNX NIFTY, generated astounding returns of 83 percent and 81 percent, respectively, during 2002–03 and 2003–04. Market capitalization grew from Rs. 7 trillion at the end of March 2003 to Rs. 14 trillion at the end of March 2004, and to Rs. 23 trillion as of August 2005, indicating that the equity market is bigger than the banking system. The primary issues in the last year added at least Rs. 2 trillion in market capitalization. The trading in cash segment of exchanges increased from Rs. 932,062 in 2002–03 to Rs. 1,658,787 in 2004–05. Trading in derivatives increased from Rs. 442,341 to Rs. 2,563,165 during the same period. The turnover in government securities increased from Rs. 1,941,621 to Rs. 2,639,897. The impact cost went down to 0.1 percent in 2003–04, reflecting substantial improvement in liquidity. The number of demand accounts with depository participants has increased considerably during the past three years, from 3.8 million to 8 million, and is increasing on average at the rate of more than 100,000 per month. The number of investor complaints received by SEBI has been sharply decreasing over the years.

The efficacy of the market, where entry and exit are possible at will and the liquidity has spread from being skewed to just about 100 to more than 500 securities, is a matter of substantial comfort. More than 2,500 securities (equities) are traded for more than 100 days in a year. Overseas investors are no longer glued to research and assessments of index stocks and have been observing keenly and investing in the mid-cap segment.

The changes in the market have been very fast-paced; they have been possible with the cooperation of all the market participants, other regulators, and the government of India.

However, I would not like to give the impression that in the Indian securities market everything is fine and needs no improvement, polishing, or refurbishing. In fact, the dynamics of the global environment dictate that those charged with the responsibility of bringing about changes must always seek out learning by experience, criticism, and judgments. The market depth needs to be supplemented with further product diversification—mortgage- and asset-backed securities, warrants, and disinvestment in the public sector. The debt market of India, though large and next in size only to Japan in Asia, lacks vibrancy and does not provide adequate options for meeting medium- to long-term funds required for greenfield projects, in particular. Infrastructure funding (essential for continued high economic growth) has become an issue in the absence of a vibrant debt market. There is no market for below-investment-grade paper, or junk bonds.

SEBI's agenda should include making the corporate debt market vibrant: cash and futures, operationalization of Indian deposit receipts, and corporatization and demutualization of stock exchanges (which has already begun with Stock Exchange, Mumbai) where the ownership, management, and trading rights reside with three different sets of entities in order to avoid conflict of interest. The Central Listing Authority and ombudsman should become fully functional. The settlement cycle should migrate to T+1. New products should be introduced to meet the needs of all kinds of market participants. MAPIN (unique identification) should be extended to cover all market participants. Regulations should be revised and amended on a continuing basis to keep them in tune with market developments. National training and skill delivery institutes should be organized to build a cadre of professionals to fulfill specialized functions in the securities market. There is a need to spread an equity culture and build institutions, such as pension funds, to enlarge the market and reduce volatility.

The regulation of listed companies, a job performed in a fragmented manner by SEBI and the Ministry of Company Affairs, needs to be consolidated to eliminate regulatory arbitrage, by unscrupulous operators and blurring of regulatory accountability.

Further, regulation is an evolutionary process and has to be refined on an ongoing basis. Thus, SEBI would and should continue to travel on the learning curve to reorient and reconfigure ground rules (regulations), investigating abilities, and investor protection measures. India will do well because it is fully convinced that securities markets allow people to do more with their savings, ideas, and talents than would otherwise be possible. Development of securities markets will also allow increasingly larger numbers of citizens to participate in some form and to share an opportunity to profit from economic gains. Let me conclude with an opinion expressed recently by Steve Vickers, President of International Risk, published on Finance Asia.com on September 29, 2005: "The stock market has been transformed from a proverbial den of thieves to one of the most transparent automated and well regulated in the world—with record foreign institutional investment inflows a testimony to this."

Appendix I

Fact Sheet on the Indian Capital Market

Number	Market Participants	March 31, 2004	March 31, 2005	September 30, 2005
1	Securities Appellate Tribunal (SAT)	1	1	1
2	Regulators (DEA, MCA, RBI, SEBI)	4	4	4
3	Depositories	2	2	2
4	Depository participants	431	477	499
5	Clearing corporations (NSCCL, BOISL)	2	2	2
6	Stock exchanges (Cash segment)	23	22	22
7	Stock exchanges (Derivatives segment)	2	2	2
8	Negotiated Dealing System (for government securities)	1	1	1
9	Brokers (Cash segment)	9,368	9,129	9,163
10	Corporate brokers (Cash segment)	3,746	3,733	3,786
11	Sub-brokers (Cash segment)	12,815	13,684	16,419
12	Derivative brokers	829	994	1,048
13	Foreign Institutional Investors (FIIs)	540	685	793
14	Portfolio managers	60	84	102
15	Custodians	11	11	11
16	Registrars to an issue/Share transfer agents	78	83	88
17	Merchant bankers	123	128	126
18	Bankers to an issue	55	59	60
19	Debenture trustees	34	35	34
20	Underwriters	47	59	58
21	Venture capital funds—domestic	45	50	62
22	Venture capital investors—foreign	9	14	30
23	Mutual funds	37	39	38
24	Credit rating agencies	4	4	4
25	Approved intermediaries (Stock lending schemes)	3	3	3

Source: *SEBI Bulletin*, November 2005.

Notes: DEA (Department of Economic Affairs, Ministry of Finance, Government of India), MAC (Ministry of Company Affairs, Government of India), RBI (Reserve Bank of India), and SEBI (Securities Exchange Board of India).

Appendix II

Securities Regulations and Guidelines in Effect

Regulations

1. SEBI (Stockbrokers and Sub-Brokers) Regulations, 1992
2. SEBI (Prohibition of Insider Trading) Regulations, 1992
3. SEBI (Merchant Bankers) Regulations, 1992
4. SEBI (Portfolio Managers) Regulations, 1993
5. SEBI (Registrars to an Issue and Share Transfer Agents) Regulations, 1993
6. SEBI (Underwriters) Regulations, 1993
7. SEBI (Debenture Trustees) Regulations, 1993
8. SEBI (Bankers to an Issue) Regulations, 1994
9. SEBI (Foreign Institutional Investors) Regulations, 1995
10. SEBI (Custodian of Securities) Regulations, 1996
11. SEBI (Depositories and Participants) Regulations, 1996
12. SEBI (Venture Capital Funds) Regulations, 1996
13. SEBI (Mutual Funds) Regulations, 1996
14. SEBI (Substantial Acquisition of Shares and Takeovers) Regulations, 1997
15. SEBI (Buyback of Securities) Regulations, 1998
16. SEBI (Credit Rating Agencies) Regulations, 1999
17. SEBI (Collective Investment Schemes) Regulations, 1999
18. SEBI (Foreign Venture Capital Investors) Regulations, 2000
19. SEBI (Procedure for Board Meeting) Regulations, 2001
20. SEBI (Issue of Sweat Equity) Regulations, 2002
21. SEBI (Procedure for Holding Inquiry by Inquiry Officer and Imposing Penalty) Regulations, 2002
22. SEBI (Prohibition of Fraudulent and Unfair Trade Practices Relating to Securities Markets) Regulations, 2003
23. SEBI (Central Listing Authority) Regulations, 2003
24. SEBI (Ombudsman) Regulations, 2003
25. SEBI (Central Database of Market Participants) Regulations, 2003
26. SEBI (Self-Regulatory Organizations) Regulations, 2004
27. SEBI (Criteria for Fit and Proper Person) Regulations, 2004

Guidelines

1. SEBI (Employee Stock Option Scheme and Employee Stock Purchase Scheme) Guidelines, 1999
2. Guidelines for Opening of Trading Terminals Abroad (Issued in 1999)
3. SEBI (Disclosure and Investor Protection) Guidelines, 2000
4. SEBI (Delisting of Securities) Guidelines, 2003
5. SEBI (STP Centralized Hub and STP Service Providers) Guidelines, 2004
6. Comprehensive Guidelines for Investor Protection Fund/Customer Protection Fund at Stock Exchanges (Issued in 2004)

Schemes

1. Securities Lending Scheme, 1997
2. SEBI (Informal Guidance) Scheme, 2003

Source: Securities and Exchange Board of India.

Appendix III

Major Reforms in the Primary Market

- Merit-based regime to disclosure-based regime. Disclosure and Investor Protection Guidelines issued.
- Pricing of public issues determined by the market.
- System of proportional allotment of shares introduced.
- Banks and public sector undertakings allowed to raise funds from the primary market.
- Accounting standards close to international standards.
- Corporate Governance Guidelines issued.
- Discretionary allotment system to QIBs has been withdrawn.
- Foreign Institutional Investors (FIIs) allowed to invest in primary issues within the sectoral limits (including GSec).
- Mutual funds are encouraged in both the public and private sectors and have been given permission to invest overseas.
- Guidelines were issued for private placement of debt.
- Securities and Exchange Board of India promotes Self-Regulatory Organizations.
- Allocation to retail investors increased from 25 percent to 35 percent.
- Separate allocation of 5 percent to domestic mutual funds within the QIB category.
- Freedom to fix face value of shares below Rs. 10 per share only in cases where the issue price is Rs. 50 or more.
- Shares allotted on a preferential basis as well as the pre-allotment holding are subjected to lock-in period of six months to prevent sale of shares.

Source: Securities and Exchange Board of India (SEBI).

Appendix IV

Major Reforms in the Secondary Market

- Registration of market intermediaries made mandatory.
- Capital adequacy norms specified for brokers and sub-brokers of stock exchanges.
- Guidelines issued on Listing Agreement between stock exchanges and corporates.
- Settlement cycle shortened to T+2.
- Stock exchanges and other intermediaries, including mutual funds, inspected.
- Regulation of Substantial Acquisition of Shares and Takeovers, 1997.
- Foreign institutional investors (FIIs) allowed to invest in Indian Capital Market, 1992.
- Order-driven, fully automatic, anonymous screen-based trading introduced.
- Depositories Act, 1996, enacted.
- Guidelines issued on corporate governance.
- Fraudulent and unfair trade practices, including insider trading, prohibited by Securities and Exchange Board of India.
- Straight-through processing introduced and made mandatory for institutional trades.
- Margin trading and securities lending and borrowing schemes introduced.
- Separate trading platform, Indonext, for small and medium-sized enterprises (SME) sector launched.
- Notification of corporatization and demutualization of stock exchanges.
- Settlement and trade guarantee fund and investor protection fund set up.
- Comprehensive risk management system (capital adequacy, trading and exposure limit, margin requirement, index-based market-wide circuit breaker, online position monitoring, automatic disablement of terminals) put in place.
- Comprehensive surveillance system put in place.
- Securities Appellate Tribunal set up July 28, 1997.
- Mutual funds and FIIs to began entering the unique client code (UCC) pertaining to the parent entity at the order-entry level and entered UCCs for individual schemes and subaccounts for the post-closing session.
- Introduction of exchange traded derivatives in India in June 2000.

Source: Securities and Exchange Board of India (SEBI).

Appendix V

Volume: Cash Segment of National Stock Exchange (NSE)

Month/Year	No. of Companies Listed[1]	No. of Companies Permitted[1]	No. of Companies Available for Trading[1,2]	Number of Trading Days	Number of Companies Traded	Number of Trades (Lakh)	Traded Quantity (Lakh)	Turnover (Rs.)	Average Daily Turnover (Rs.)	Average Trade Size (Rs.)	Demat Securities Traded (Lakh)	Demat Turnover (Rs.)	Market Capitalization (Rs.)[1]	S&P CNX Nifty Index[3] High	Low	Close	CNX Nifty Junior Index[4] High	Low	Close
1999-00	720	479	1,152	254	NA	984	242,704	839,052	3,303	85,244	153,772	711,706	1,020,426	1,818.15	916.00	1,528.45	5,365.90	1,631.90	3,695.75
2000-01	785	320	1,029	251	1,201	1,676	329,536	1,339,510	5,337	86,980	307,222	1,264,337	657,847	1,636.95	1,098.75	1,148.20	3,771.80	1,570.20	1,601.80
2001-02	793	197	890	247	1,019	1,753	278,408	513,167	2,078	29,270	277,717	512,866	636,861	1,207.00	849.95	1,129.55	1,676.25	1,038.75	1,566.95
2002-03	818	107	788	251	899	2,398	364,065	617,989	2,462	25,776	364,049	617,984	537,133	1,153.30	920.10	978.20	1,690.35	1,231.95	1,259.55
2003-04	909	18	787	254	804	3780	713,301	1,099,534	4,329	29,090	713,301	1,099,534	1,120,976	2,014.65	920.00	1,771.90	3,702.60	1,259.75	3,392.05
2004-05	970	1	839	255	856	4,508	797,685	1,140,072	4,471	25,283	797,685	1,140,072	1,585,585	2,183.45	1,292.20	2,035.65	4,705.25	2,493.70	4,275.15
Apr-04	918	18	795	20	771	319	53,686	100,951	5,048	31,600	53,686	100,951	1,171,828	1,912.35	1,771.45	1,796.10	3,875.55	3,398.00	3,639.80
May-04	928	16	804	21	776	357	54,651	98,920	4,710	27,697	54,651	98,920	950,494	1,837.95	1,292.20	1,483.60	3,756.65	2,493.70	2,846.90
Jun-04	940	12	813	22	787	336	41,987	84,898	3,859	25,298	41,987	84,898	979,700	1,566.50	1,437.90	1,505.60	3,018.40	2,723.50	2,903.35
Jul-04	929	12	815	22	793	377	63,058	93,836	4,265	24,918	63,058	93,836	1,066,087	1,638.70	1,472.55	1,632.30	3,162.85	2,804.75	3,082.10
Aug-04	936	9	820	22	799	358	57,543	86,856	3,948	24,260	57,543	86,856	1,143,075	1,658.90	1,573.70	1,631.75	3,206.15	3,006.70	3,199.00
Sep-04	945	7	824	22	809	367	62,666	88,508	4,023	24,124	62,666	88,508	1,227,550	1,760.80	1,619.90	1,745.50	3,543.60	3,204.55	3,504.25
Oct-04	950	6	828	22	814	299	47,274	75,698	3,785	25,233	47,274	75,698	1,253,825	1,829.45	1,737.85	1,786.90	3,653.40	3,403.70	3,481.55
Nov-04	954	6	829	20	816	327	62,548	82,035	4,102	24,859	62,548	82,035	1,446,292	1,963.80	1,776.70	1,958.80	3,913.60	3,466.65	3,884.55
Dec-04	957	6	832	23	821	475	99,326	115,593	5,026	24,339	99,326	115,593	1,579,161	2,088.45	1,944.50	2,080.50	4,468.35	3,849.05	4,453.30
Jan-05	958	5	833	19	820	410	81,575	99,732	5,249	24,343	81,575	99,732	1,557,444	2,120.15	1,894.40	2,057.60	4,549.85	3,999.75	4,247.80
Feb-05	964	4	837	20	825	425	89,665	99,989	4,999	23,551	89,665	99,989	1,614,597	2,110.15	2,036.60	2,103.25	4,427.45	4,213.95	4,388.20
Mar-05	970	1	839	22	831	459	83,705	113,055	5,139	24,626	83,705	113,055	1,585,585	2,183.45	1,971.15	2,035.65	4,705.25	4,113.40	4,275.15
2005-06 (so far)																			
Apr-05	973	1	836	20	829	367	51,265	82,718	4,136	22,527	51,265	82,718	1,517,908	2,084.90	1,896.30	1,902.50	4,413.40	4,016.85	4,024.40
May-05	977	1	842	22	830	413	56,516	86,802	3,946	21,020	56,516	86,802	1,654,995	2,099.35	1,898.15	2,087.55	4,369.05	3,998.80	4,364.55
Jun-05	987	1	855	23	843	477	70,485	111,397	4,843	23,374	70,485	111,397	1,727,502	2,226.15	2,061.35	2,220.60	4,573.05	4,351.25	4,393.25
Jul-05	999	1	868	20	856	503	84,134	123,008	6,150	24,449	84,134	123,008	1,848,740	2,332.55	2,171.25	2,312.30	4,991.50	4,396.15	4,919.10
Aug-05	1,006	1	875	22	864	570	100,717	145,731	6,624	25,548	100,717	145,731	1,957,491	2,426.65	2,294.25	2,384.65	5,173.05	4,786.45	5,053.00
Sep-05	1,016	1	883	21	872	576	91,996	145,393	6,923	25,229	91,996	145,393	2,098,263	2,633.90	2,382.90	2,601.40	5,419.90	4,955.75	5,303.50
Oct-05	1,019	1	881	20	876	463	57,670	120,810	6,040	26,077	57,670	120,810	1,927,645	2,669.20	2,307.45	2,370.95	5,443.40	4,609.15	4,714.45

Source: NSE.

Note: A lakh is a unit corresponding to 100,000.

[1] At the end of the period.

[2] Excludes suspended companies.

[3] S&P CNX NIFTY Index commenced November 3, 1995.

[4] CNX NIFTY Junior Index commenced November 4, 1996.

Appendix VI

Volume: Cash Segment of Bombay Stock Exchange (BSE)

Month/ Year	Number of Companies Listed[1]	Number of Companies Permitted[1]	Number of Companies Available for Trading[1]	Number of Trading Days	Number of Scrips	Number of Trades (Lakh)	Traded Quantity (Lakh)	Turnover (Rs.)	Average Daily Turnover (Rs.)	Average Trade Size (Rs.)	Demat Securities Traded (Lakh)	Demat Turnover (Rs.)	Market Capitalization (Rs.)[1]	BSE Sensex[2]			BSE=100[3]		
														High	Low	Close	High	Low	Close
1999–00	5,815	0	8,028	251	4,330	740	208,635	686,428	2,735	9,270	NA	NA	912,842	6,150.69	3,183.47	5,001.28	3,906.41	1,379.71	2,902.20
2000–01	5,869	0	9,826	251	3,927	1,428	258,511	1,000,032	3,984	7,002	NA	NA	571,553	5,542.81	3,436.75	3,604.38	3,055.14	1,633.90	1,691.71
2001–02	5,782	0	7,321	247	5,347	1,277	182,196	307,292	1,244	24,060	NA	NA	612,224	3,759.96	2,594.87	3,469.35	1,830.98	1,209.93	1,716.28
2002–03	5,650	12	7,363	251	2,679	1,413	221,401	314,073	1,251	2,223	NA	NA	572,197	3,538.49	2,828.48	3,048.72	1,763.49	1,411.32	1,500.72
2003–04	5,528	12	7,264	254	2,610	2,028	390,441	503,053	1,981	24,806	376,304	4,79,472	1,201,206	6,249.60	2,904.44	5,590.60	3,373.24	1,446.53	2,966.31
2004–05	4,731	36	6,897	253	2,382	2,374	477,171	518,715	2,050	21,849	431,307	451,080	1,698,428	6,954.86	4,227.50	6,492.82	3,756.07	2,226.36	3,481.86
Apr-04	5,292	15	7,098	20	1,907	156	25,669	44,864	2,243	28,702	20,587	38,033	1,255,347	5,979.25	5,599.12	5655.09	3,210.50	2,958.54	3,025.14
May-04	5,296	15	7,223	21	1,768	170	25,907	45,938	2,188	27,014	22,688	39,732	1,023,128	5,772.64	4,227.50	4,759.62	3,090.17	2,226.36	2,525.35
Jun-04	5,271	15	7,560	22	1,780	149	19,122	36,990	1,681	24,894	17,385	32,588	1,047,258	5,012.52	4,613.94	4,795.46	2,658.05	2,446.87	2,561.16
Jul-04	4,730	15	7,087	22	1,991	175	28,624	39,449	1,793	22,583	26,938	35,664	1,135,588	5,200.85	4,723.04	5,170.32	2,771.06	2,518.01	2,755.22
Aug-04	4,735	15	7,133	22	2,093	178	30,446	38,195	1,736	21,501	28,391	33,232	1,216,566	5,269.22	5,022.29	5,192.08	2,813.28	2,682.78	2,789.07
Sep-04	4,733	15	7,148	22	2,314	205	36,955	39,603	1,800	19,301	33,537	33,518	1,309,317	5,638.79	5,155.96	5,583.61	3,020.29	2770.29	2,997.97
Oct-04	4,721	27	6,903	20	2,213	174	29,309	34,608	1,730	19,946	26,860	30,296	1,337,191	5,803.82	5,558.14	5,672.27	3,115.52	2,965.77	3,027.96
Nov-04	4,725	27	6,908	20	2,459	201	42,343	35,742	1,787	17,808	37,139	30,449	1,539,595	6,248.43	5,649.03	6,234.29	3,347.10	3,016.74	3,339.75
Dec-04	4,730	27	6,942	23	2,425	274	62,644	50,226	2,184	18,327	56,775	43,963	1,685,988	6,617.15	6,176.09	6,602.69	3,589.26	3,311.21	3,580.34
Jan-05	4,730	36	6,916	19	2,432	220	53,521	43,888	2,310	19,952	48,571	37,839	1,661,532	6,696.31	6069.33	6555.94	3,641.25	3,269.37	3,521.71
Feb-05	4,732	36	6,946	20	2,455	251	61,626	49,686	2,484	19,787	56,299	43,353	1,730,940	6,721.08	6508.33	6,713.86	3,626.76	3,497.96	3,611.90
Mar-05	4,731	36	6,897	22	2,382	222	61,005	59,528	2,706	26,779	56,137	52,412	1,698,428	6,954.86	6,321.31	6,492.82	3,756.07	3,387.31	3,481.86
2005-06 (so far)																			
Apr-05	4,736	35	7,204	20	2,446	136	33,370	37,809	1,890	27,809	29,506	31,187	1,635,766	6,954.86	6,321.31	6,154.44	3,756.07	3,387.31	3,313.45
May-05	4,734	35	7,040	22	2,531	170	43,369	43,359	1,971	25,501	38,716	36,941	1,783,221	6,772.74	6,140.97	6,715.11	3,628.00	3,302.80	3,601.73
Jun-05	4,738	36	7,097	IT,	2,568	204	63,309	58,479	2,543	28,661	57,017	51,109	1,850,377	7,228.21	6,647.36	7,193.85	3,829.03	3,575.16	3,800.24
Jul-05	4,743	36	7,129	20	2,577	219	67,719	61,899	3,095	28,281	67,623	61,840	1,987,170	7,708.59	7,123.11	7,635.42	4,112.89	3,786.08	4,072.15
Aug-05	4,752	38	7,166	22	2,669	272	101,503	75,933	3,451	27,954	101,290	75,824	2,123,900	7,921.39	7,537.50	7,805.43	4,248.89	4,027.09	4,184.83
Sep-05	4,746	38	7,134	21	2,552	284	87,055	81,291	3,871	28,589	86,846	81,159	2,254,376	8,722.17	7,818.90	8,634.48	4,606.07	4,191.65	4,566.63
Oct-05	4,748	38	7,167	20	2,421	183	36,496	59,102	2,955	32,213	36,420	59,049	2,065,611	8,799.96	7,685.64	7,892.32	4,666.82	4,057.46	4,159.59

Source: BSE.

Note: A lakh is a unit corresponding to 100,000.

[1]At the end of the period.

[2]BSE Sensex commenced January 2, 1986.

[3]BSE-100 Index commenced April 3, 1984.

Appendix VII

Volume: Derivatives Segment at National Stock Exchange (NSE)

Month/ Year	Number of Trading Firms	Index Futures Number of contracts	Index Futures Turnover (Rs.)	Stock Futures Number of contracts	Stock Futures Turnover (Rs.)	Interest Rate Futures Number of contracts	Interest Rate Futures Turnover (Rs.)	Index Options Call Number of contracts	Index Options Call Notional Turnover (Rs.)	Index Options Put Number of contracts	Index Options Put Notional Turnover (Rs.)	Stock Options Call Number of contracts	Stock Options Call Notional Turnover (Rs.)	Stock Options Put Number of contracts	Stock Options Put Notional Turnover (Rs.)	Total Number of contracts	Total Turnover (Rs.)	Open Interest Number of contracts	Open Interest Turnover (Rs.)
Jun-00 to Mar-01	211	90,580	2,365	NA	NA	NA	NA	NA	NA	NA	NA	NA	NA	NA	NA	90,580	2,365	NA	NA
2001-02	247	1,025,588	21,482	1,957,856	51,516	NA	NA	113,974	2,466	61,926	1,300	768,159	18,780	269,370	6,383	4,196,873	101,925	93,917	2,150
2002-03	251	2126763	43,951	10675786.4	286,532	NA	NA	269,721	5,671	172520	3,577	2456501	69,644	1,066,561	30,490	16,768,909	439,854	97,025	2,194
2003-04*	254	17,192,274	5,54,462	32,485,160	1,305,949	1,013	20	1,043,894	31,801	688,520	21,022	4,258,595	168,174	1,338,654	49,038	56,886,776	2,130,649	235,792	7,188
2004-05	253	21,635,449	772,174	47,043,066	1,484,067	0	0.0	1,870,647	69,373	1,422,911	52,581	3,946,979	132,066	1,098,133	36,792	77,017,185	2,547,053	592,646	21,052
Apr-04	20	2,164,528	79,560	3,829,403	121,048	0	0.0	115,378	4,347	80,733	2,968	292,628	9,640	85,998	2,736	6,568,668	220,299	249,845	7,668
May-04	21	2,551,985	82,149	3,322,799	92,628	0	0.0	196,198	6,824	100,430	3,469	246,630	7,717	63,156	1,976	6,481,198	194,763	179,487	4,696
June-04	22	2,152,644	64,017	3,125,283	78,392	0	0.0	158,784	4,914	117,041	3,559	193,687	5,339	75,380	2,084	5,822,819	158,306	201,871	5,367
July 04	22	1,971,231	61,125	3,492,774	94,009	0	0.0	189,179	6,059	124,352	3,856	262,755	7,614	94,222	2,682	6,134,513	175,345	206,709	5,964
Aug-04	22	1,803,263	57,926	3,577,911	99,591	0	0.0	127,779	4,192	98,618	3,193	284,013	8,499	86,919	2,604	5,978,503	176,006	261,185	7,332
Sep-04	22	1,463,682	49,500	3,768,178	107,123	0	0.0	124,547	4,282	93,808	3,164	365,187	10,763	116,304	3,547	5,931,706	178,380	446,299	13,353
Oct-04	20	1,320,173	47,191	3,660,047	111,695	0	0.0	138,099	5,030	97,628	3,500	357,625	11,684	93,342	3,124	5,666,914	182,224	321,545	9,845
Nov-04	20	1,023,111	38,277	3,600,135	113,525	0	0.0	131,218	4,979	102,223	3,814	363,158	11,971	94,810	3,239	5,314,655	175,805	371,842	12,239
Dec-04	23	1,447,464	58,333	5,238,498	179,387	0	0.0	130,557	5,355	108,650	4,356	481,349	16,952	108,951	3,845	7,515,469	268,227	426,606	15,221
Jan-05	19	1,931,290	76,151	4,551,564	159,564	0	0.0	176,682	7,188	143,416	5,786	362,345	13,502	81,618	3,100	7,246,915	265,290	388,354	13,604
Feb-05	20	1,729,103	71,546	4,167,787	151,743	0	0.0	168,594	7,128	144,627	5,998	367,707	13,890	83,843	3,247	6,661,661	253,551	404,809	14,900
Mar-05	20	2,076,975	86,398	4,708,687	175,363	0	0.0	213,632	9,074	211,385	8,918	369,895	14,496	113,590	4,608	7,694,164	298,857	592,646	21,052
2005-06 (so far)																			
Apr-05	20	3,332,361	65,598	4,225,623	106,129	0	0.0	361,544	7,295	295,020	5,981	307,994	8,203	105,955	2,764	8,628,497	195,969	576,056	12,243
May-05	22	3,545,971	70,465	4,466,404	112,882	0	0.0	382,530	7,720	353,975	7,056	288,137	7,642	100,602	2,609	9,137,619	208,380	670,705	15,863
Jun-05	23	3,626,288	77,218	5,783,428	163,096	0	0.0	421,480	9,092	331,753	7,041	385,640	11,677	104,478	3,122	10,653,067	271,246	997,984	24,545
Jul-05	20	3,451,684	77,399	6,537,794	199,638	0	0.0	358,867	8,130	389,154	8,642	376,129	11,735	84,989	2,623	11,198,617	308,166	1,024,749	27,198
Aug-05	22	4,278,829	100,813	7,124,266	234,817	0	0.0	444,294	10,620	485,001	11,372	350,370	11,935	81,453	2,750	12,764,213	372,307	892,678	24,788
Sep-05	21	4,701,774	118,905	6,995,169	236,945	0	0.0	523,948	13,370	583,081	14,550	363,872	12,917	85,897	3,069	13,253,741	399,756	783,718	23,063
Oct-05	20	6,849,732	170,100	6,526,919	214,398	0	0.0	695,311	17,632	715,208	17,954	309,120	10,753	80,134	2,822	15,176,424	433,660	803,773	21,083

Source: NSE.

Notes: Notional Value of Outstanding Contracts for FUTIDX—Open Interest * Closing price of index future Notional Value of Outstanding Contracts for FUTSTK—Open Interest * Closing price of stock future Notional Value of Outstanding Contracts for OPTIDX - Open Interest * Closing price S&P CNX Nifty Notional Value of Outstanding Contracts for OPTSTK—Open Interest * Closing price of Underlying security Notional Turnover (Strike Price 4 − Premium) * Quantity, Index futures, index options, stock options, stock futures, and interest rate futures were introduced in June 2000, June 2001, July 2001, November 2001, and June 2003, respectively. Volume of derivatives in BSE is negligible. Revised figures.

Appendix VIII

Volume: Trends in Foreign Institutional Investors (FIIs) Investment

Period	Gross Purchases (Rs.)	Gross Sales (Rs.)	Net Investment (Rs.)	Net Investment[1] (millions of US$)	Cumulative Net Investment[1] (millions of US$)
1999–00	56,856	46,734	10,122	2,339	11,237
2000–01	74,051	64,116	9,934	2,160	13,396
2001–02	49,920	41,165	8,755	1,846	15,242
2002–03	47,060	44,371	2,689	562	15,804
2003–04	144,858	99,094	45,765	9,949	25,754
2004–05	216,953	171,072	45,881	10,172	35,926
Apr–04	19,692	12,972	6,720	1,483	27,237
May–04	15,655	19,201	–3,546	–806	26,431
Jun–04	10,894	11,168	–274	–57	26,374
Jul–04	11,247	10,534	713	157	26,531
Aug–04	12,856	10,335	2,521	550	27,080
Sep–04	13,097	10,522	2,575	556	27,637
Oct–04	16,063	14,035	2,028	439	28,075
Nov–04	21,302	13,117	8,185	1,783	29,858
Dec–04	25,841	15,702	10,140	2,229	32,087
Jan–05	17,502	17,819	–317	–75	32,012
Feb–05	24,360	15,151	9,209	2,101	34,113
Mar–05	28,444	20,517	7,927	1,813	35,926
2005–06 *(so far)*					
Apr–05	16,210	17,686	–1,475	–338	35,588
May–05	15,619	17,005	–1,386	–318	35,271
Jun–05	25,960	20,702	5,259	1,210	36,481
Jul–05	25,717	17,956	7,760	1,784	38,264
Aug–05	28,359	23,737	4,621	1,062	39,327
Sep–05	26,651	22,194	4,457	1,023	40,349
Oct–05	27,166	31,794	–4,627	–1,054	39,295

Source: Securities and Exchange Board of India (SEBI).
[1]Net investment in millions of U.S. dollars at monthly exchange rate.

Appendix IX

Trends in Mobilization of Funds by the Mutual Fund Industry

(In rupees)

Period	Gross Mobilization				Redemption[1]				Net Inflow				Assets at the End of the Period
	Private sector	Public sector	UTI	Total	Private sector	Public sector	UTI	Total	Private sector	Public sector	UTI	Total	
1999–00	43,726	3,817	13,698	61,241	28,559	4,562	9,150	42,271	15,166	–745	4,548	18,970	107,946
2000–01	75,009	5,535	12,413	92,957	65,160	6,580	12,090	83,829	9,850	–1,045	323	9,128	90,587
2001–02	147,798	12,082	4,643	164,523	134,748	10,673	11,927	157,348	13,050	1,409	–7,284	7,175	100,594
2002–03	284,095	23,515	7,096	314,706	272,026	21,954	16,530	310,510	12,069	1,561	–9,434	4,196	109,299
2003–04	534,649	31,548	23,992	590,190	492,105	28,951	22,326	543,381	42,545	2,597	1,667	46,808	139,616
2004–05	736,463	56,589	46,656	839,708	728,864	59,266	49,378	837,508	7,600	–2,677	–2,722	2,200	149,600
Apr–05	63,753	11,193	4,206	79,152	50,403	10,194	4,586	65,183	13,350	999	–380	13,969	153,214
May–04	55,356	–3,227	3,341	55,469	50,793	–3,178	2,476	50,091	4,562	–49	865	5,378	154,018
Jun–04	62,776	3,973	4,090	70,840	60,327	3,922	4,792	69,041	2,450	51	–702	1,799	155,875
Jul–04	57,961	5,005	6,669	69,635	58,783	4,657	6,458	69,898	–822	348	211	–263	157,747
Aug–04	64,060	30,240	3,090	97,390	65,527	36,481	4,629	106,638	–1,468	–6,241	–1,540	–9,249	155,686
Sep–04	68,359	–19,949	2,923	51,334	72,353	–25,448	3,526	50,430	–3,993	5,500	–603	904	153,108
Oct–04	52,074	3,441	2,769	58,284	54,949	4,280	2,772	62,000	–2,875	–839	–3	–3,716	147,995
Nov–04	47,229	3,786	2,376	53,391	48,473	4,118	2,882	55,472	–1,244	–332	–506	–2,082	149,581
Dec–04	75,048	4,762	3,450	83,260	76,320	5,637	3,759	85,717	–1,272	–875	–309	–2,456	150,537
Jan–05	51,801	5,308	3,099	60,207	50,041	4,398	3,205	57,644	1,760	910	–106	2,563	150,378
Feb–05	53,512	5,712	3,993	63,217	54,767	4,968	3,821	63,556	–1,255	745	171	–339	153,253
Mar–05	84,535	6,345	6,650	97,529	86,127	9,237	6,473	101,837	–1,593	–2,892	177	–4,308	149,600
2005–06 *(to date)*													
Apr–05	63,049	5,015	3,849	71,913	52,693	4,099	3,847	60,638	10,357	917	2	11,275	158,422
May–05	54,135	3,264	5,107	62,506	48,962	3,836	4,178	56,976	5,173	–572	928	5,529	167,978
Jun–05	63,887	6,584	4,106	74,577	66,128	6,447	4,532	77,108	–2,241	136	–426	–2,531	164,546
Jul–05	70,145	5,855	5,282	81,283	64,130	6,087	5,014	75,231	6,015	–231	268	6,052	175,916
Aug–05	91,833	8,608	7,515	107,956	80,277	6,679	6,239	93,195	11,555	1,929	1,277	14,761	195,784
Sep–05	78,791	11,736	7,156	97,683	78,625	9,414	7,828	95,868	165	2,322	–672	1,815	201,669
Oct–05	**81,429**	**8,868**	**8,068**	**98,366**	**79,696**	**7,528**	**7,024**	**94,249**	**1,733**	**1,340**	**1,044**	**4,117**	**200,209**

Source: Securities and Exchange Board of India (SEBI).

Notes: (i) The former UTI has been divided into the UTI mutual fund (registered with the Securities and Exchange Board of India (SEBI)) and the specified undertaking of UTI (not registered with SEBI). The above data contain information only for the UTI mutual fund.

(ii) Net assets pertaining to funds of funds schemes are not included in the above data.

(iii) Data for UTI-I are included up to January 2003.

[1] Includes repurchases as well as redemption.

IDBI— MF (earlier a public sector mutual fund) has now become Principal MF (a private sector mutual fund).

Appendix X

Daily Return and Volatility: Select World Stock Indices

(In percent)

Year/Month	United States		United Kingdom		France		Australia		Hong Kong SAR		Singapore		Malaysia	
	Return	Volatility	Return	Volatility	Return	Volatility	Return	Volatility	Return	Volatility	Return	Volatility	Return	Volatility
2000	-0.04	1.40	-0.04	1.20	0.00	1.48	0.00	0.85	-0.05	1.98	-0.10	1.47	0.07	1.40
2001	-0.06	1.36	-0.07	1.37	-0.10	1.64	0.02	0.80	-0.12	1.76	-0.06	1.45	0.01	1.33
2002	0.11	1.64	-0.11	1.73	-0.16	2.22	-0.05	0.70	-0.08	1.22	-0.08	1.03	-0.03	0.75
2003	0.08	1.06	0.09	1.16	0.11	1.37	0.15	0.93	0.12	1.07	0.12	1.17	0.09	0.72
2004	0.04	0.70	0.03	0.65	1.58	0.00	1.58	0.00	0.04	1.03	0.06	0.78	0.06	0.72
Nov. 04– Oct. 05	0.03	0.67	0.05	0.55	0.07	0.70	0.06	0.58	0.04	0.73	0.05	0.62	0.02	0.53

(In percent)

Year/Month	Brazil		Mexico		South Africa		Japan		SENSEX		S&P CNX Nifty	
	Return	Volatility	Return	Volatility	Return	Volatility	Return	Volatility	Return	Volatility	Return	Volatility
2000	-0.04	2.00	-0.09	2.20	-0.01	1.31	-0.11	1.4	-0.12	2.20	-0.06	1.96
2001	-0.05	2.14	0.05	1.48	0.10	1.39	-0.09	1.55	-0.09	1.72	-0.07	1.59
2002	-0.07	1.89	-0.02	1.40	-0.05	1.19	-0.09	1.44	-0.01	1.10	0.01	1.06
2003	0.34	2.06	0.11	1.07	0.14	1.2	0.12	1.44	0.23	1.19	0.23	1.26
2004	0.06	1.80	0.15	0.94	0.07	0.91	0.03	1.04	0.04	1.61	0.03	1.76
Nov. 04– Oct. 05	0.10	1.58	0.12	1.03	0.13	0.78	0.11	0.79	0.13	1.04	0.11	1.07

Source: Basic data are taken from Bloomberg L.P.

References

La Porta, Rafael, Florencio Lopez de Silanes, and Andrei Shleifer. "What Works in Securities Laws?" Available via the Internet: www.nber.org/papers/w9882

CLSA-CG Watch, CLSA Asia Pacific Markets (Subsidiary of Calyon Credit Lyonnais) Headquartered in Hong Kong SAR, September 2004.

CLSA Emerging Markets Study, CLSA Asia Pacific Markets (Subsidiary of Calyon Credit Lyonnais) Headquartered in Hong Kong SAR, September 2004.

Cadgon report, Study by Asian Development Bank with the help of Government of India under expert, Mr. Cadgon.

Society for Capital Markets, Research and Development Society. Delhi, India.

Steve Vickers, President International Risk, Published in FinanceAsia.Com, September 29, 2005.

5

Development of Securities Markets: The Indian Experience

Narendra Jadhav[*]

A satisfactory pace of economic growth in any economy is contingent upon availability of adequate capital. A well-developed securities market, while acting as a provider of funding for economic activity at the macro level, plays specific roles in an economy: it diffuses stress on the banking sector by diversifying credit risk across the economy, supplies funds for long-term investment needs of the corporate sector, provides market-based sources of funds for meeting the government's financing requirements, provides products with the flexibility to meet the specific needs of investors and borrowers, and allocates capital more efficiently.

The main impulse for developing securities markets, including both the equity and debt segments, depends on country-specific histories and, more specifically in the context of the financial system, it relates to creating more complete financial markets, preventing banks from taking on excessive credit, risk diversification in the financial system, financing government debt, conducting monetary policy, sterilizing capital inflows, and providing a range of long-term assets. Prior to the early 1990s, most financial markets in India faced pricing controls, entry barriers, transaction restrictions, high transaction costs, and low liquidity. A series of reforms since the early 1990s have aimed to develop the various segments of financial markets by phasing out the

---

[*]Naredra Jadhav is Principal Adviser and Chief Economist, Department of Economic Analysis and Policy, Reserve Bank of India.

administered pricing system; removing barrier restrictions; introducing new instruments; establishing an institutional framework; upgrading the technological infrastructure; and evolving efficient, safe, and more transparent market practices.

Corporate Securities: The Equity Segment

Capital markets have historically played an important role in channeling long-term resources for commerce and industry in many countries, such as the United States and the United Kingdom, whereas in some other countries, including Japan and Germany, corporate investments are largely financed through intermediary-based sources. The Indian capital markets are some of the oldest in Asia. Traditionally, however, the Indian financial system since independence has been based on financial intermediaries rather than capital markets. Given the developmental needs of the country in the past and the inability of the markets to generate and allocate funds effectively for long-term development projects, the bank-based financial system best suited the country's needs.

During the 1990s, however, the growing needs of the economy and the forces of liberalization changed the face of the Indian financial system drastically, and the capital markets assumed a prominent place in the resource allocation process of the economy. In recent years, the Indian financial system seems to be gradually maturing to a point at which both the intermediary- and market-based systems coexist, thus drawing the benefits of both systems.

The policy environment governing the capital markets evolved rapidly in the 1990s to pave the way for vibrant, liquid, and transparent markets. The major reforms in the Indian capital market since the 1990s are presented below:

- In 1992, the Capital Issues (Control) Act (1947) was phased out, enabling the corporate sector to raise capital from markets without the permission of regulators, subject to sufficient disclosures in the offer documents. A book-building mechanism for the pricing of new capital issues was introduced in 1995, whereby the offer price of an initial public offering is based on the demand for the issue. The book-building mechanism has proved to be both cost and time effective in India.
- Buyback of shares helps improve liquidity in shares of companies and helps the corporate sector enhance investors' wealth. Securities and Exchange Board of India (SEBI) issued the SEBI (buyback of

securities) regulations in 1998, under which a company is permitted to buy back its shares from shareholders.

- The market microstructure for the Indian capital markets evolved to become free and fair during the 1990s. The stringent disclosure norms have improved the information flow to small investors, and the stricter corporate governance practices prescribed for listed companies have helped curb insider trading and price-rigging practices.

- To control excess volatility in the markets, circuit breakers have been introduced on the stock exchanges. Effective June 2, 2001, index-based marketwide circuit breakers applicable on the Bombay Stock Exchange (BSE) Sensex and the S&P CNX NIFTY (the two major indexes of stock prices) are operational at 10 percent, 15 percent, and 20 percent on movement on either side of any of the indices.

- Management of various risks, such as counterparty risks and credit risks, is important in promoting the safety and efficiency of the capital market. To provide necessary funds and ensure timely completion of settlement in cases of member brokers' failure to fulfill their settlement obligations, major stock exchanges have set up settlement guarantee funds (SGFs). These funds are like self-insurance schemes, with the members contributing to the fund. SGFs have played a key role in ensuring timely settlement, especially during periods of market turbulence. Furthermore, the clearinghouses set up by each of the stock exchanges have substantially reduced counterparty risk in the settlement system. Various risk management mechanisms, such as capital adequacy requirements, trading and exposure limits, and daily margins composed of mark-to-market margins and value at risk margins, are now in place.

- Technology has played an important role in changing market practices in India. The Indian stock markets have moved away from open outcry system to an online electronic trading system, in line with best international practices. The electronic system has improved efficiency in the price discovery mechanism, lowered transaction costs, promoted transparency in transactions, and helped improve integration across stock exchanges throughout the country.

- Until recently, the majority of scrips on Indian securities markets was traded in physical form. Trading securities in physical form slows down transactions, adversely affecting the liquidity of the markets, increasing trading costs, and also contributing to problems relating to bad deliveries, theft, and forgery. Compulsory dematerialization has resulted in the overwhelming majority of securities being traded in electronic form.

- Technology has also enabled faster movement of funds across the country. Electronic funds transfer, combined with dematerialization of securities, has created an environment conducive to the reduction of settlement cycles on the stock markets. Shorter settlement cycles reduce the risk involved in transactions and speculative activity, and infuse more liquidity into the markets. The Indian stock markets, which previously followed a Monday-to-Friday settlement cycle, gradually switched to a rolling settlement cycle. The rolling settlement cycle was reduced to T+3 effective April 2002 and further to T+2 effective April 2003 in line with best international practices. In addition to their effect on trading, the technological developments have made their mark in the clearing and settlement process, paving the way for efficient and sophisticated systems.
- The Indian capital markets in the 1990s deepened and widened, with a larger investor base and emergence of a wide range of innovative and hybrid instruments. On the investor-base side, foreign institutional investors (FIIs), which have been allowed to invest in Indian equities since 1992, have now emerged as the biggest institutional investors on Indian capital markets. Mutual funds, especially private sector mutual funds, have also emerged as active institutional investors.
- On the instrument side, derivative instruments, such as index futures, stock futures, index options, and stock options, have become important instruments of price discovery, portfolio diversification, and risk hedging. Various risk-containment measures, including margins, positions, and exposure limits, are in place to ensure smooth functioning of the derivatives market.
- Indian companies can now raise funds freely in the international capital markets through the use of various instruments, such as American Depository Receipts (ADRs) and Global Depository Receipts (GDRs), foreign currency convertible bonds, and External Commercial Borrowings. ADRs and GDRs have two-way fungibility, meaning that investors (foreign institutional or domestic) in any company that has issued ADRs and GDRs can freely convert the ADRs and GDRs into underlying domestic shares, and vice versa. This is expected to improve liquidity in the markets and eliminate arbitrage between domestic and international markets.

The Indian equity market has developed tremendously since the 1990s. The market has grown exponentially in terms of resource mobilization, number of listed stocks, market capitalization, trading volume, and investor base. Along with this growth, the profiles of the investors, issuers, and intermediaries have changed significantly. The market has witnessed a fundamental institutional change, resulting in drastic reduction in transaction costs and significant improvement in efficiency, transparency, and safety. In the 1990s, reform measures initiated by the SEBI, such as market-determined allocation of resources, rolling settlement, sophisticated risk management, and derivatives trading, greatly improved the framework and efficiency of trading and settlement. Almost all equity settlements take place at two depositories. As a result, the Indian capital market has become qualitatively comparable to many developed markets.

As a result of the reforms undertaken in the liberalization period, the capital market in India has deepened. The prevalent conditions in the primary and secondary markets seem to have affected corporate decisions to finance project costs either through the equity markets or through loans. A large amount of funds to finance project costs has traditionally been raised through loans from financial intermediaries. Industrial liberalization, however, led to an increasing number of companies tapping the primary capital market to mobilize resources in the early 1990s. In the second half of the 1990s, following deceleration in the industrial sector and subdued conditions in the stock market, the corporate sector again shifted to the loans route, and the amount raised through new capital issues declined. More recently, there has been a revival of the primary market owing to a recovery in the stock markets as well as improvement in the investment climate and macroeconomic outlook (Figure 5.1).

There has been a change in the pattern of financing of the Indian corporate sector. The share of capital market–related instruments in the total funds, which picked up in the first half of 1990s, has declined in the current decade so far. The trend might change with an upturn in the capital market. The share of financial intermediaries in total funds also has declined. There has been a greater reliance on internal sources. During the 1980s and 1990s, internal sources of funds as a percentage of total sources ranged around 30–40 percent, whereas during recent years it has increased to more than 50 percent and even came close to 70 percent in 2002–03. Correspondingly, there has been a reduction in reliance on external financing. As a result of corporate reliance on internal generation of funds, there has been a noticeable decline in the debt-equity ratio (Table 5.1).

A notable feature of the 1990s was the substantial growth of the private placement market. The private placement market emerged as the preferred source of financing for corporations, including public sector enterprises, state-level undertakings, and development financial institutions (DFIs). The resources raised through the private placement market, which

Figure 5.1. Resource Mobilization by the Private Corporate Sector through Equity

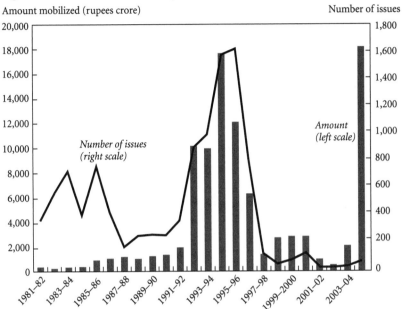

stood at Rs. 13,361 crore (1 crore = 10 million) in 1995–96 increased to Rs. 85,102 crore in 2004–05. Currently, the size of the private placement market is estimated to be four times that of the public issues market.

The euro issues market became operational and developed in the 1990s. The amount raised through euro issues was as high as Rs. 7,898 crore in 1993–94 but declined afterward to Rs. 3,353 crore in 2004–05. Even though the amounts raised by new euro issues show a declining trend, the scrips listed on international markets are being actively traded.

The stock markets witnessed a long and sustained rally starting in May 2003, which continued throughout 2004 and 2005 despite intermittent disturbances. Notably, unlike in the past, this rally has been broad-based, encompassing almost all sectors. The BSE Sensex closed at the historical high of 8,500.26 on September 20, 2005, mainly because of strong buying support from domestic and foreign institutional investors, strong industrial growth, and satisfactory progress of the monsoon.

Turnover, which is an indicator of market liquidity, has shown a sustained increase, both on the BSE and the National Stock Exchange (NSE), in the stock market rally. Substantial liquidity has also shifted to the derivatives market, which started trading in June 2000. Turnover in

Table 5.1. Pattern of Sources of Funds for Indian Corporates

Item	1985–86 to 1989–90	1990–91 to 1994–95	1995–96 to 1999–2000	2000–01 to 2003–04
Internal Sources	31.9	29.9	37.1	61.4
External Sources	68.1	70.1	62.9	38.6
Of which:				
Equity capital	7.2	18.8	13.0	9.7
Borrowings	37.9	32.7	35.9	10.4
Of which:				
Debentures	11.0	7.1	5.6	−1.2
From banks	13.6	8.2	12.3	19.0
From financial institutions	8.7	10.3	9.0	−1.4
Trade dues and other current liabilities	22.8	18.4	13.7	17.7
Total	100.0	100.0	100.0	100.0
Memorandum items:				
Share of capital market–related instruments (debentures and equity capital)	18.2	26.0	18.6	8.4
Share of financial intermediaries (borrowings from banks and financial institutions)	22.2	18.3	21.3	17.5
Debt-equity ratio	88.4	85.5	65.2	62.8

Source: Articles on "Finances of Public Limited Companies," *RBI Bulletin* (various issues).
Note: Data pertain to nongovernment nonfinancial public limited companies.

the derivatives market remains much higher than in the cash markets (Figure 5.2).

Market capitalization, which is a barometer of the size of the stock market and the market value of investors' wealth, has similarly shown a steady increase. The market capitalization of the BSE and the NSE as of end-March 2005, at Rs. 1,698,428 crore and Rs. 1,585,585 crore, respectively, represents all-time-high levels mainly because of a surge in stock prices and listing of new securities (Figure 5.3). The market capitalization of the BSE as a percentage of GDP, which roughly accounts for 95 percent of market capitalization countrywide, increased from 16.2 percent in 1990–91 to 54.7 percent in 2004–05.

The price/earnings (P/E) ratio, which reflects the valuations of scrips vis-à-vis their earnings, was much higher in the 1992–94 period as compared with the present ratio (Figure 5.4). Despite unprecedented price levels, the P/E ratio for Indian equities has remained attractive thanks to strong growth in corporate earnings. A high P/E ratio indicates overvalued scrips as compared with corporate earnings; thus the current low P/E ratio points toward the potential of the Indian stock markets, notwithstanding the current high prices.

Figure 5.2. Turnover in Cash and Derivatives Segment of the NSE Stock Exchange
(In rupees crore)

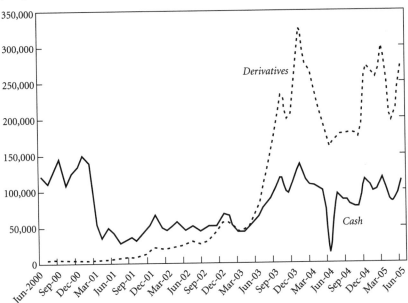

The Indian stock markets have become more stable thanks to the strengthening of the market design and risk containment measures. This is reflected in a sharp decline in the volatility of stock prices, measured by the coefficient of variation for the BSE Sensex (Figure 5.5).

Liberalization and consequent reform measures have drawn the attention of foreign investors, leading to a rise in portfolio investment in the Indian capital market. FIIs emerged as the largest institutional investors in the Indian equity market in the 1990s. Apart from providing institutional character to the capital markets, FIIs inject global liquidity into the markets and reduce the cost of capital. From the perspective of FIIs, investments in various countries provide an excellent measure of portfolio diversification and hedging, and also take advantage of arbitrage opportunities. Over recent years, India has emerged as a major recipient of portfolio investment among emerging market economies. Because of such large inflows, reflecting the confidence of cross-border investors in the prospects of the Indian securities market, India received positive portfolio inflows each year except one. The stability of portfolio flows toward India contrasts with the large volatility of portfolio flows in most emerging market economies. FII

Figure 5.3. Trends in Market Capitalization
(In rupees crore)

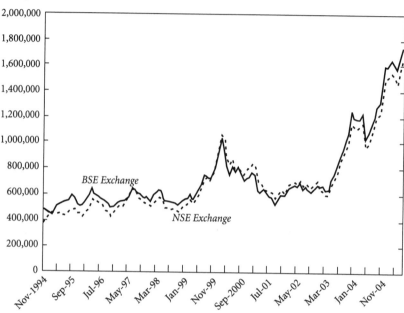

investment in equities in 2004–05 was Rs. 44,123 crore, which was one of the highest investments in equities in a single year by FIIs.

Corporate Securities: Debt Segment

From the perspective of developing countries, a liquid corporate bond market can play a critical role in supporting economic development. It supplements the banking system to meet the requirements of the corporate sector for long-term capital investment and asset creation. It provides a stable source of financing when the equity market is volatile. Further, with the decline in the role of DFIs, there is an increasing realization of the need for a well-developed corporate debt market as an alternative source of finance.

A number of policy initiatives were taken during the 1990s to activate the corporate debt market in India. The interest rate ceiling on corporate debentures was abolished in 1991, paving the way for market-based pricing of corporate debt issues. In order to improve the quality of debt issues, rating was made mandatory for all publicly issued debt instruments,

Figure 5.4. Price-Earnings Ratio of BSE Sensex Scrips and Average BSE Sensex

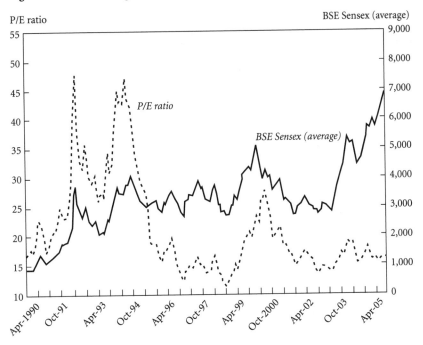

P/E ratio

BSE Sensex (average)

irrespective of their maturity. The role of trustees in bond and debenture issues has strengthened over the years. All privately placed debt issues are required to be listed on the stock exchanges and follow the disclosure requirements. However, despite the policy initiatives, corporate debt still constitutes a small segment of the debt market in India. Whereas the primary market for debt securities is dominated by the private placement market, the secondary market for corporate debt is characterized by poor liquidity, although this has improved in recent years.

The developed financial markets are characterized by a sound financial and legal infrastructure, which is necessary for the development of a corporate bond market, supported by a well-functioning regulatory system. The United States is, by far, the most suitable example of a country whose corporate bond market is deep, efficient, and liquid. The bond markets in the United Kingdom and euro-area countries are also reasonably developed. The markets for debt securities in Western European countries and Japan are much smaller than in the United States, not only in absolute terms but also as a percentage of GDP. Unlike the developed financial systems, the corporate bond market has a very short history of develop-

Figure 5.5. Quarterly Coefficient of Variation of BSE Sensex
(In percent)

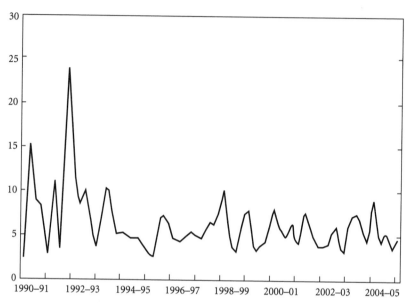

ment in the emerging market economies. A comparative position of the corporate debt market in developing countries and the United States is presented in Table 5.2.

Historically, India had a bank-dominated financial system, which was supplemented by DFIs to provide long-term project finance. However, the financial system has undergone a marked change in recent years. With the conversion of DFIs into banks, a gap has been created for long-term finance. Commercial banks, given the short-term nature of their liabilities, may not be able to fill the gap in long-term finance. In view of this, India's corporate sector requires long-term finance to supplement its resources. In this context, development of the corporate bond market will play a strategic role in the near future.

The corporate debt market in India has existed since independence. Public limited companies have been raising capital by issuing debt securities. In 1985–86, state-owned public sector undertakings began issuing bonds. However, in the absence of a well-functioning secondary market, such debt instruments remained illiquid. In recent years, because of falling interest rates and adequate availability of funds, corporate debt issuance has shown a noticeable rise, especially through private placements (Table 5.3).

Table 5.2. Comparative Position of the Indian Corporate Debt Market, 2002

	India	Malaysia	Hong Kong SAR	Singapore	United States	Korea	China
	(In billions of U.S. dollars)						
GDP	510	95	164	91	10,445	462	1,238
Government bonds	143	47	11	31	6,685	225	201
Corporate bonds	19	36	34	27	9,588	156	212
Bank loans to corporate sector	156	135	678	210	6,976	609	2,073
Equity	170	123	463	102	11,010	216	463
	(In percent)						
Corporate bonds to GDP	4	38	21	30	92	34	17
Corporate bonds to total bonds	12	43	76	47	59	41	51
Corporate bonds to bank loans	12	27	5	13	137	26	10
Corporate bonds to equity	11	29	7	26	87	72	46

Sources: Bank for International Settlements, Deutsche Bank, World Bank, and World Federation of Stock Markets.

Corporations continue to prefer private placement of debt issues rather than floating public issues. Resource mobilization through private placement picked up from Rs. 13,361 crore in 1995–96 to Rs. 85,102 crore in 2004–05. The dominance of private placement has been attributed to several factors, such as ease of issuance, cost efficiency, primarily institutional demand, and so forth. About 90 percent of outstanding corporate debt has been privately placed. In the private placement market, 57 percent of issuances are by financial institutions and banks, in both the public and private sectors. Public sector companies account for 58 percent of privately placed issues. About 26 percent represent issues by public sector undertakings and central and state government guaranteed bonds.

The secondary market activity in the debt segment, in general, remains subdued at both the BSE and the Wholesale Debt Market Segment (WDM) of the NSE, partly because of a lack of a sufficient number of securities and partly because of a lack of interest by retail investors. In order to improve secondary market activity in this segment, the Union Budget for 1999–2000 abolished the stamp duty on the transfer of dematerialized debt instruments. This enabled a pickup in the turnover in corporate debt at the NSE from Rs. 5,816 crore in 2002–03 to Rs. 17,521 crore in 2004–05. The share of turnover in corporate debt securities in total turnover in the WDM segment of the NSE, however, remains small at about 2 percent.

Table 5.3. Resource Mobilization by the Corporate Sector
(In rupees crore)

Year	Public Equity Issue	Debt Issues Public issues	Debt Issues Private placements	Debt Issues Total (3+4)	Total Resource Mobilization (2+5)	Share of Private Placements in Debt Issues (4/5*100)	Share of Debt in Total Resource Mobilization (5/6*100)
1	2	3	4	5	6	7	8
1995–96	14,493	5,970	13,361	19,331	33,824	69.12	57.15
1996–97	7,928	7,483	15,066	22,549	30,478	66.81	73.99
1997–98	1,701	2,957	30,099	33,056	34,756	91.05	95.11
1998–99	2,622	6,743	49,679	56,422	59,044	88.05	95.56
1999–00	3,230	4,475	61,259	65,734	68,964	93.19	95.32
2000–01	3,111	3,251	67,836	71,087	74,198	95.43	95.81
2001–02	1,025	6,087	64,876	70,963	71,988	91.42	98.58
2002–03	1,233	3,634	66,948	70,582	71,815	94.85	98.28
2003–04	3,427	4,424	63,901	68,325	71,752	93.53	95.22
2004–05	18,024	3,868	85,102	88,970	106,994	95.65	83.15

India is fairly well placed as far as prerequisites for the development of the corporate bond market are concerned. There is a developed government securities market that provides a reasonably dependable yield curve. The major stock exchanges have trading platforms for transactions in debt securities. Infrastructure for clearing and settlement also exists. The Clearing Corporation of India Limited (CCIL) has been successfully settling trades in government securities, foreign exchange, and money market instruments. The existing depository system has been working well. The settlement system has improved significantly in recent years. The settlement in government securities has moved over to delivery versus payment (DVP III)[1] since March 29, 2004. Real Time Gross Settlement (RTGS) has become operational for commercial bank transactions in certain cities. The presence of multiple rating agencies provides an efficient rating mechanism in India.

The Indian corporate debt market has, however, remained confined to AAA or AA+/AA rated borrowers. Most investors are institutions, with very few retail investors; hence, the disintermediation process is not complete. Transparency is limited in both the primary and the secondary markets, liquidity is poor, and many bonds are held until redemption. The legal recourse in case of nonpayment of interest and principal is complicated, and bankruptcy laws provide little comfort. The legal and

---

[1]Under the DVP III mode of settlement, both the securities leg and the funds leg of transactions are settled on a net basis.

regulatory requirements, accounting and auditing standards for issuers, and the infrastructure for trading, clearing, and settlement need to be further developed.

Government Securities Market

A well-developed government securities market facilitates market-based conduct of monetary policy and provides a domestic credit risk–free rupee yield curve as a benchmark for prices of other securities. However, prior to 1991, the government securities market was not developed, because of inefficient market practices and lack of proper institutional infrastructure. Subscriptions to government securities emanated mainly from the reserve bank, as it monetized the budget deficits of the government and banks as part of fulfilling its statutory obligations. The main factor that inhibited the development of the sovereign yield curve in India in the pre-reform period was the prevalence of artificially low administrative coupon rates on these securities that were out of alignment with other interest rates in the economy. The coupon rates remained virtually unchanged up to 1979–80. Thereafter, although coupon rates were revised upward, especially for securities of longer tenor, the yield of a 30-year government bond remained lower than the maximum bank deposit rate. The reserve bank, despite being the debt manager for the government, did not have control over volume, maturity, and term structure of interest rates in the government securities market. This was mainly on account of the absence of any limit to the automatic monetization of central government budget deficits. Consequently, the market remained narrow, with captive participation from institutions as dictated by statutory requirements. Apart from the reserve bank holding securities on its own account, the major investors were banks, insurance companies, provident funds, and other trust funds. The reserve bank did not have special representatives in the market and had to make use of the services of stockbrokers. The non-remunerative yields and captive nature of the government securities market impeded secondary market activity. The maturity structure of government securities remained highly skewed in favor of longer terms of more than 15 years.

The reform process for the government securities market focused on the following major areas:

- It was necessary to phase out the administered interest rate system and bring in market discovery of prices of government securities to ensure broad-based participation. Accordingly, an auction-based system for issuances of government dated securities was initiated in June 1992. The auctioning system has been essentially of a multiple-price variety, whereby successful winning bids are filled at the bid price. Occasionally, however, for dated securities, with a view to eliminate the typical "winner's curse" problem of the multiple-price method and to broaden investor participation, a uniform price auction has been adopted, whereby successful bidders pay a flat price, called the cut-off price. Furthermore, to diversify participation, allotment is also made through noncompetitive bids outside the notified amount to state governments, nongovernment provident funds, other central banks, and individuals.

- An appropriate network of intermediaries (Discount and Finance House of India in 1988, Securities Trading Corporation of India in 1994, and primary dealers (PDs) in 1995) was created with the objective of strengthening the securities market infrastructure. A PD provides a minimum bidding commitment, maintains a minimum success ratio, and underwrites and offers two-way quotes in the government securities market. The PD system enables a lowering of the government's market borrowing cost as far as possible consistent with a prudent degree of rollover risk. There were 18 PDs in March 2004, which accounted for more than one-quarter of outright turnover in the government securities market. Efforts have also been made to make participation in this market wider and voluntary. The statutory liquidity ratio (SLR), the proportion of net demand and time liabilities that a bank had to keep as investments in government and other approved securities, was brought down from 38.5 percent to its minimum value of 25 percent during the first half of the 1990s. The reserve bank's monetization of government debt through subscriptions of government dated securities was also reduced; the reserve bank's primary subscriptions occur now with the objective of managing liquidity or to devolve the gilt on its own account when market conditions are not conducive to unloading the same through sales under open market operations once market conditions improve. Foreign institutional investors were permitted in the gilt market in July 1997. The retailing of government securities was promoted by allowing the trading of government securities on the stock exchanges on an anonymous screen-based, order-driven basis to provide countrywide access.
- The reserve bank shifted from passive to active management of public debt as the practice of automatic monetization of the central government deficit through ad hoc treasury bills was phased out and

replaced by a scheme of ways and means advances (WMAs). Because the ad hoc treasury bills bore a fixed coupon rate of 4.6 percent and WMAs are extended at interest rates linked to the bank rate, the abolition of ad hoc treasury bills has served as a major landmark for migrating to a system of market-related interest rates in the government securities market.

- Attempts were made to introduce new instruments to suit diverse investor requirements; for example, zero coupon bonds (January 1994), floating rate bonds (September 1995), capital indexed bonds (December 1997), and bonds with call and put options (July 2002). However, plain vanilla bonds have remained the mainstay. Since 1999–2000, a policy of reissuance of key securities through price-based auctions has enabled passive consolidation of public debt, helped emergence of benchmark securities, and promoted liquidity in the government securities market. Active consolidation of public debt was undertaken under a debt buyback scheme in July 2003 under which high-cost and illiquid securities issued in the past were bought back by the government in exchange for new securities at the prevailing market yield.

- A policy priority has been to improve the market practices in government securities in line with best international practices. Efforts have been made to calibrate technological upgrades of trading, payment, and settlement structure in the gilt market in a phased manner to make it safer, transparent, and efficient. Settlement risk was lowered with the introduction of the delivery versus payment (DvP) system in July 1995, which ensures settlement by synchronizing the transfer of securities with cash payment. The DvP graduated into the third stage in April 2004, with settlement of both securities and funds on a net basis. CCIL commenced operations on February 15, 2002, in clearing and settlement in government securities. Backed by an SGF, CCIL acts as central counterparty and provides guaranteed settlement. The Negotiated Dealing System, which was set up simultaneously, provides online electronic bidding at the auctions and permits paperless settlement of transactions in government securities with electronic connectivity to CCIL and the DvP system. Measures were introduced in May 2002 for holding government securities in a dematerialized instead of physical fashion, which had carried the potential risk of irregularities through nondelivery. Screen-based, order-driven trading of gilts was also allowed in stock exchanges as of January 2003. The operationalization of RTGS was undertaken in March 2004 for continuous processing and settlement

Figure 5.6. Market Loans and Interest Rate of Central Government Borrowing

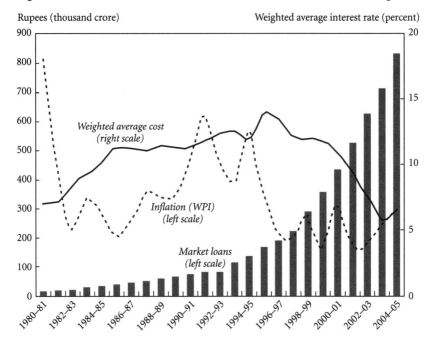

transfer of funds to minimize payment risk. Efforts have been made to widen the investor base in the government securities market. The Reserve Bank of India authorized banks and primary dealers to open Constituent Subsidiary General Ledger accounts for their constituents for wider participation in the government securities market. The cumulative debt investment for FIIs was raised from US$1 billion to $1.75 billion, with the ceiling on corporate debt at $0.5 billion being kept over and above the government securities ceiling of $1.75 billion.

The switchover to the system of market-related interest rates has allowed the government to increase market loans substantially since the early 1990s (Figure 5.6). Reforms brought flexibility on both the supply and demand sides of the government securities market. On the supply side, the reserve bank undertook active debt management by modulating the maturity structure of primary gilt issuances as required. It was shortened from 16 years in 1990–91 to 5.5 years in 1996–97 to reduce the costs of government borrowing. However, subsequently, with a view to avoiding bunching of repayments, the maturity structure of government securities was lengthened to 15 years in 2003–04. Availability of ample liquidity enabled the reserve bank to lengthen the maturity of gilt issuances, with substantial reduction in weighted average yield from 13.7 percent in 1996–97 to 5.7 percent in 2003–04. Strikingly, the auctioning system has facilitated a market-related softening of the interest cost of government borrowing as opposed to artificial lowering of the interest cost in the pre-reform-administered interest rate regime.

On the demand side, the investor base for government securities has widened from commercial banks, financial institutions, and provident and pension funds to co-operative banks, regional rural banks, mutual funds, and nonbank financial companies in recent years. The reserve bank's share of the total stock of government securities has steadily declined, reflecting its sterilization operations as well as its policy of keeping private placements and devolvements on its own account to a minimum. Strikingly, despite SLR reductions, banks have been voluntarily maintaining gilt investments much above the stipulated levels, especially during phases of slack in credit time, slowdown in the demand for credit and market expectations of interest rate softening. Mutual funds dedicated exclusively to investments in government securities or gilt funds have been set up to encourage retailing of gilts. Furthermore, a scheme of noncompetitive bidding reserving for individuals up to 5 percent of the auctions' notified amounts was introduced in January 2002.

These developments have enabled the evolution of a smooth yield curve in the government securities market. The maturity of the yield curve has gradually lengthened in recent years. Persistent rallies in government securities prices have progressively shifted the yield curve down. Furthermore, with the prevalence of liquidity overhang and the repurchase (repo) rate as an anchor of short-term rates, the yield curve has progressively flattened in the past few years (Figure 5.7). Transactions in the secondary market in the government securities market have expanded at a phenomenal pace, increasing from Rs. 1, 22,942 crore in 1996–97 to Rs. 2,723,621 crore in 2004–05. The sharp increase, especially in recent years, reflected a sustained rally in the prices of the government securities market as well as increased use of the repo market.

Assessment of Reforms and Future Challenges

The progress made by the Indian capital markets in the post-liberalization phase in terms of implementing international standard practices, widening and deepening capital markets, and technological progress has been

Figure 5.7. Yield Curves in Government Securities
(In percent)

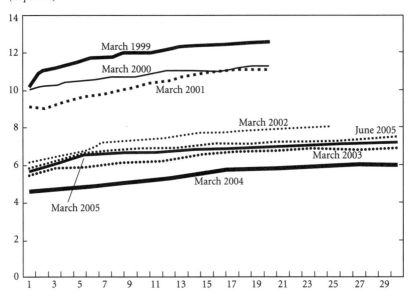

remarkable. It should, however, be noted that this period was also marked by the greatest turmoil the markets have ever witnessed. With timely and appropriate policy initiatives, systemic failures were avoided. Some of the fundamental problems relating to Indian capital markets include a huge number of illiquid stocks; lack of depth, with a few companies accounting for the majority of trading volume; a low delivery ratio; and concentration of trading with a few brokerage houses. Although some of these problems are chronic and difficult to solve for any regulatory authority, they underline the need to develop capital markets further.

With the initiation of financial sector reforms, the avenues for raising long-term finance for the Indian corporate sector are undergoing a shift. Whereas the corporate sector now has increased access to international capital markets, the channeling of funds from the traditional source of long-term finance to the corporate sector—DFIs—has been slowing down. With some of these DFIs converting into universal banks, one can expect a boost in the flow of medium- to long-term financing from the banking sector to the corporate sector, because these DFIs have an existing client base and expertise in the evaluation and monitoring of project financing. After the East Asian crisis, a unanimous view has emerged that a multiagency approach to meeting the demand for long-term funds would be both effective and efficient. Under such an approach, the equity market, the debt market, banks, and financial institutions should together meet the long-term financing needs of the corporate sector.

The development of the corporate debt market is, however, still relatively inadequate. Most investors are institutions, with very few retail investors. Transparency is limited in both the primary and secondary markets, liquidity is poor, and many bonds are held until redemption. The legal recourse in case of nonpayment of interest and principal is complicated, and bankruptcy laws afford little comfort. To develop the corporate bond market, conscious efforts have to be made to increase the supply of high-quality paper, creating an adequate institutional investor base, ensuring a variety of instruments of differing maturities, and mounting supporting infrastructure. Emphasis also needs to be placed on efficient legal systems as important infrastructure for deep and liquid bond markets. Among legal reforms, bankruptcy laws and capacity to seize collateral are particularly important. Experience also indicates that in many emerging economies, because the risk is transferred to the creditor in bond markets as compared to banks, there is a preponderant bias toward bank deposits among household savers in many countries. In other words, development of the domestic corporate debt market is bound to be a long process, and banks will have to continue to be dominant in the financial systems of most emerging market economies.

Some success has also been achieved in creating a deep and liquid government securities market as the investor base has widened with the participation of nonbank players, limited primary purchases of the reserve bank, and market-related movement of coupon rates. The elimination of automatic monetization by the reserve bank and reduction of the statutory preemption of banks have provided much-needed autonomy for the conduct of the monetary policy. Considerable progress has been made in establishing a state-of-the-art institutional framework, risk-management systems, clearing and settlement systems, and transparency in debt management operations in the government securities market. However, several challenges remain. First, the need for better coordination of the debt and monetary management functions continues, because the timing and amounts of issuance of government securities may not always coincide with the requirements of monetary management. Progress has already been made in this direction: a half-yearly calendar for issuance of government securities minimizes uncertainty on the part of both the debt manager and the investors. Second, there is a need to introduce new instruments, such as longer-term repos, rollover of repos, and separate trading of coupon instruments with the operationalization of Separate Trading for Registered Interest and

Principal of Securities. Capital Indexed Bonds with modified features will be introduced shortly to offer inflation-linked returns on both the coupons and the principal repayments. Third, the derivatives market is evolving in India and, therefore, its development has to be cautiously planned to avoid pitfalls. There is a need to harmonize the regulatory prescriptions for over-the-counter (OTC) and exchange-traded interest rate derivatives. Furthermore, in order to strengthen the OTC derivatives market and to mitigate the risks involved, a clearing arrangement through CCIL also needs to be worked out. The trading volume of government securities in the stock exchanges continues to suffer. Finally, market operation mechanisms need to be worked out for the phase commencing April 2006, when the Reserve Bank of India will not participate in the primary market of government securities. An appropriate role needs to be designed for the primary dealers for successful completion of primary auctions during this phase.

References

Allen, F., and D. Gale, 2000, *Comparing Financial Systems* (Cambridge, Massachusetts: MIT Press).

Bose, Suchismita, and Dipankar Coondoo, 2003, "A Study of the Indian Corporate Bond Market," *Money & Finance, ICRA Bulletin* (January–March).

Endo, Tadashi, 2004, "Debt Market Development in Emerging Economies: Major Issues and Challenges," paper presented at the World Bank Seminar, Colombo, Sri Lanka, June 9.

Mohan, Rakesh, 2004, "A Decade of Reforms in Government Securities Market in India and the Road Ahead," speech delivered at the FIMMDA-PDAI conference, Dubai, *RBI Bulletin* (November).

National Stock Exchange of India Ltd., 2004, *Indian Securities Market—A Review*, Volume VII.

Patil, R.H., 2004, "Corporate Debt Market: New Beginnings," *Economic and Political Weekly* (March 20) pp. 1237–46.

Reddy, Y.V., 2002, "Developing Bond Markets in Emerging Economies: Issues and Indian Experience," speech delivered at the FIMMDA-PDAI conference, Bangkok, *RBI Bulletin* (April).

Singh, A., 1995, "Corporate Financial Patterns in Industrializing Economies," International Finance Corporation Technical Paper No. 2 (Washington: World Bank and International Finance Corporation).

6

Accelerating the External and Internal Opening Up of China's Securities Industry

Xinghai Fang, Ti Liu, and Donghui Shi*

Now we have set the economic development objectives. But how are we going to achieve them? Well, we need to abide by the principles of social and economic development and pursue two 'opening-ups,' that is, opening up to the outside world and opening up within the country itself. Opening up to the outside is important, because no country could develop by isolation. International communication and transference of expertise, technology and capital from the outside is all necessary. Opening up within the country means reform.

—Deng Xiaoping (April 1985)

Inadequacies of the Current Policy on Opening Up the Securities Industry

The current arrangement for opening up the securities industry is part of China's World Trade Organization (WTO) commitment. It now seems that there are some major oversights in the arrangement:

---

*The authors are, respectively, Deputy Chief Executive, Lead Research Manager, and Assistant Director of Research of Shanghai Stock Exchange (SSE). We thank Kate Yang of SSE's International Department for her excellent assistance and translation.

A foreign securities firm can set up operations in China, but only in the form of a joint venture, of whose shares it can hold no more than 33 percent. This restriction has turned away many world-class securities firms. The key reason is that as a minority shareholder, a firm cannot control the joint venture and thus subject its highly valued business reputation to the risk of mismanagement by the joint venture (JV). Moreover, its status as a small shareholder limits its economic incentives in the joint venture, which in turn prevents it from adequate involvement in the institutional and long-term development of the JV company. Perhaps, by opening up, China seeks to attract management expertise rather than capital. However, without a certain percentage of equity investment, the foreign partner's concern about the management of the joint venture will be too limited to have any meaningful influence.

The business scope of a JV securities firm is extremely limited. Currently, a JV securities firm can obtain a license to become an underwriter and/or a financial advisor, but cannot operate as a broker or engage in proprietary investment or portfolio management. The extremely limited business scope for these joint ventures reduces foreign companies' willingness to come to China and hurts the competitiveness and long-term earning potential of an existing JV company, depriving it of the opportunity to provide a full spectrum of services.

Domestic partners for a JV securities firm are limited to existing Chinese securities firms. This restriction severely limits the choice of potential domestic partners for a joint venture, especially when we consider that many Chinese securities firms are not well run. Potential competition between the JV company and the parent domestic securities firm is another drawback. The current solution is to segregate business between the two, with the joint venture specialized in underwriting and the parent firm engaged in proprietary investment, brokerage, and portfolio management. However, this has to some extent given rise to two incomplete companies and has served only to postpone rather than to solve the potential conflict of interest.

Indeed, opening up the securities industry has been painfully slow. Foreign investment is limited. The firms that are attracted are not the most competitive. The performance of the few joint ventures that have formed is unsatisfactory. Goldman Sachs adopted an ultra-complex model to ensure management control over its joint venture, but we have to wait to see whether the arrangement works. By contrast, foreign investors in the Chinese insurance industry can hold up to 50 percent of the equity in a joint venture life insurer and controlling equity in a property insurer. As a result, many JV companies have partnered with first-class international insurance companies. In the banking industry, foreign commercial banks are allowed to have wholly owned operations in China. The banking industry will be entirely opened up at the end of the WTO grace period in December 2006. By that time, foreign commercial banks will be able to conduct any banking business anywhere within China. It is not hard to imagine that foreign investment in the banking sector will be all the more vigorous then.

Unfounded Concerns About Opening Up the Securities Industry Faster

The purpose of accelerating the opening up of the securities industry is to enhance its overall competitiveness and strength. A frequently mentioned concern about opening up is that major international players would squeeze the less competitive domestic counterparts out of business. An often-cited example is the British securities industry; its key domestic companies were almost all acquired by stronger foreign rivals (mostly American firms) following the opening up of the industry in the mid-1980s, though London's status as an international financial center was consolidated as a result. Surely, the British experience is an important precedent for China to consider. However, the opening up experiences in Japan, Korea, and Taiwan Province of China have been very different. Even after these markets were fully opened up, domestic companies maintained a considerable market share advantage over their international counterparts.

The question is then, what will happen to China after it opens its securities markets? The answer is almost certain. The British and U.S. business communities share the same language and a similar culture. Domestic firms have little advantage over their foreign counterparts. However, the Chinese business environment is distinctly different from that of Britain, and is close to those of Japan, Korea, and Taiwan Province of China. In addition, China is a big market. It is quite impossible for a handful of international players to monopolize this market.

We should have confidence that Chinese firms will do well in the Chinese market because financial services contain so many local elements. China's telecommunications equipment and household appliance industries survived and thrived following the opening up of their markets. The insurance industry offers a more applicable experience. When American International Assurance Company entered the Shanghai market in 1992, it grabbed considerable market share from local companies with its unique method of managing sales. However, domestic companies learned quickly and recovered their lost market share shortly.

Even for Britain, had it not opened its securities market in the 1980s and made itself home to major international players, British firms would not have been able to keep London a global financial center—Frankfurt or Amsterdam could have overtaken London to become the new financial center in Europe. India offers another positive lesson for opening up. The Indian securities market opened in 1992 with no restrictions on foreign shareholding or scope of business. Today, the Indian market is considered on a par with those of developed countries, though foreign companies account for no more than 40 percent of the market. Moreover, as time goes by domestic companies are likely to grow in relative strength.

A second concern about opening up is that China would be deprived of a chance to build its national brand names in the securities industry. A commonly cited example is the Chinese auto industry. However, the real reason that China has no leading brand names in cars is not because the industry was opened up too quickly, but because foreign auto builders were allowed to enter into partnerships with only Chinese state-owned enterprises. These state-owned firms have neither urgency nor long-term incentives for innovation. From the 1950s through the 1980s, the auto industry in China was totally closed. Had foreign car makers been allowed to team up with top private companies in China, Chinese brand names would have been established by now—only wholly private brands can bring in strong profits.

A third concern about opening up is that the Chinese securities industry may end up at a disadvantage if that opening up is unilateral while other markets fail to give Chinese firms equal access. We believe, however, that the primary issue in making the policy decision is whether opening up is beneficial to our own industry. If the answer is yes, we should pursue it. Whether or not we will receive equal treatment in a foreign market is a separate issue. In addition, we think that Chinese securities firms are not yet ready to test themselves in a market such as New York or London. When China National Offshore Oil Corporation failed in its bid for Unocal, some people suggested that we should slow down the opening up of China's financial industry.

Recommendations to Accelerate Opening Up the Securities Industry

The necessity of opening up is well argued by Deng Xiaoping as quoted in the beginning of this essay. The three restrictions listed in the first part are China's minimum WTO commitments, but we have never said that opening up our securities industry could not go beyond our commitments or proceed faster than we had promised. Considering the current conditions of our domestic securities companies, a preferred model for accelerating opening up would be to allow foreign companies to acquire for a fee domestic securities firms that are on the brink of bankruptcy. After acquisition, the foreign company would inherit the business licenses of the acquired domestic firm and obtain controlling shares within the new firm. This model is attractive to foreign companies because it allows them a full license, control over the new company, and access to the expanding Chinese market, at the limited cost of compensating for the historical losses (or even part of the losses) of the acquired domestic firm. At the same time, the model reduces the financial burden on the Chinese government to bail out failing securities firms. The new companies formed by such an acquisition will usually improve their management and competitiveness.

Acceleration of Opening Up Internally

Deng Xiaoping pointed out as early as 1985 that to open up within the country is to adopt reform. Almost all securities firms in China are still state-owned or state-controlled. It was not until a few years ago that some private companies became the controlling shareholders in a couple of securities firms. However, driven by majority shareholders' short-term interest in an environment of weak regulation, these privately controlled companies (such as Fuyou, Deheng, and Hengxin Securities) committed a series of violations. I believe, however, that these violations should not be a reason to slow down reform. In light of the shortage of regulatory capacity in the near future, effective reform can be achieved in the following manner:

Make senior and departmental managers shareholders of their own securities companies. One proposal is to start with management acquiring some company shares with their own cash. Later, they could increase their shares by converting part of the incremental net assets of the company into equity. This approach is probably the best way to heighten securities firms' risk awareness and increase their competitiveness against foreign rivals.

Allow securities professionals of Chinese citizenship from within or outside China to establish new firms. Licensing can start with brokerage-only firms for which limited capital investment and a few key sponsors are required. The success of a securities firm depends on quality professional leadership. Over the past few years, the Chinese securities market has seen a number of well-qualified professionals with extensive operational experience. If these people are allowed to set up their own firms, no doubt some high-quality companies will soon emerge.

We are looking forward to domestic securities firms (and asset management firms) holding a majority market share in a fully opened Chinese securities market. For this reason, we have to carefully plan for the pace of the opening up process so that domestic companies will be able to maintain their advantages. We believe that each year it is appropriate to admit three or four foreign-controlled securities firms to the Chinese market and to restructure or newly establish six or seven new firms controlled or managed by Chinese professionals.

Harms of Opening Up Slowly

The foremost harm of opening up slowly is entirely losing the market. Refusal to open up will save us some weak securities firms at the cost of losing the whole securities market. A Shanghai Stock Exchange survey shows that by the end of 2004, the aggregate floatable market capitalization of Chinese companies on overseas markets had exceeded the total market value of the two domestic stock exchanges in Shanghai and Shenzhen, and that the difference was expanding. Although Chinese issuance on overseas markets quickened during 2005 with the recent listing of China Construction Bank and Bank of Communications, new issuance on domestic markets has come to a full stop. Equity derivatives based on Chinese stocks are being developed in both Chinese and overseas markets. We cannot help but wonder which of these derivatives will be more representative of the Chinese economy or be better risk management instruments for investment into China—no doubt the foreign ones. Liquidity, which is the essence of a financial market, will be hard to recover once we lose it. It is highly urgent that we accelerate reform and opening up and improve the capabilities of securities firms and other financial intermediaries operating in the domestic market, to maintain the Chinese securities market. When the market is gone, how are Chinese securities firms going to survive?

It has become a consensus that the Chinese securities industry lacks innovation. Innovation in the Chinese market is, at best and mostly, a slight adjustment of products and ideas that have been well tested in overseas markets. However, if our market were filled with first-class investment banks from abroad, the innovation situation would be very different. Product innovation with regard to asset securitization is a good example. In spite of the restrictions in laws and regulations, China International Capital Corporation Limited (CICC) (a joint venture with Morgan Stanley) delivered the first Chinese asset securitization product

(Unicom Rental Scheme), now listed on the Shanghai Stock Exchange. But even after CICC made this breakthrough, other Chinese securities firms have exhibited neither efficiency nor momentum in following its example. Why? The innovative capacity of CICC lies in its incentive and risk control mechanisms and the talents it has attracted, which domestic firms lack. This example shows another harm of opening up slowly, namely, lagging behind the innovation frontier of international markets and the service demands of domestic companies and investors.

Conclusion

The Chinese experience of reform and opening up in the past 27 years has shown that diminished effort in these areas slows the development of an industry. In today's globalized world, an industry of a country that refuses to open up to competition will save a few weak players but lose the market as a whole. During his meeting with the president of ABN-AMRO Bank in April 2004, Vice Premier Huang Ju (who is in charge of the financial portfolio) pointed out that the opening up of China's capital market should be accelerated promptly and used as a spur to internal reform. It is time that we implement his advice.

PART III

FINANCIAL INTEGRATION

7

Domestic Financial Liberalization and International Financial Integration: An Indian Perspective

SUMAN BERY AND KANHAIYA SINGH*

India and China are both large, poor countries that have benefited from greater integration into the world economy; both are still at an early but crucial stage of their development path. In both countries, financial systems were relatively controlled for a long period: while they played an important role in resource mobilization, they were not accorded an important independent role in resource allocation. In both countries, the formal financial system remains dominated by publicly owned, deposit-money banks.

In both countries, increased international linkages of the wider economy have put a repressed financial system under strain. Domestic firms require financing at close to international terms in order to be competitive. Greater international trade and human links open up opportunities for de facto movement of capital, providing competition for domestic financial institutions. As planning gives way to the market, financial institutions have a potentially important role to play in investment project selection and monitoring. In brief, the whole machinery of rising productivity, which motivates market-led liberalization and of which glo-

*Suman Bery is Director-General, National Council of Applied Economic Research, and Kanhaiya Singh is a Fellow at the Indian National Council of Applied Economic Research.

balization is now an essential part, requires liberalization of the domestic financial system.

Contemporary systems of global production are driven increasingly by investment rather than just trade. Such foreign investment creates its own pressures for the financial system. Foreign capital needs to be able to enter and leave under predictable rules; pressures soon develop for domestic firms to enjoy similar privileges. Freedom for capital flows, in turn, has implications for the monetary and exchange systems.

Yet wholesale liberalization of capital flows also carries its own risks, both apparent and real. These include the risk of appreciation of the real exchange rate, the risk of sudden reversals of flows, and the risks of inflation. These risks of liberalization were noted early on (Diaz-Alejandro, 1985) even with respect to domestic liberalization. In the 1990s, financial crises in many emerging markets created a similar caution regarding the speed of external financial liberalization, although it continues to be considered a desirable final goal.

This chapter attempts to describe the links between domestic liberalization and financial integration for India, a journey which is still incomplete. The goal is to make accessible and transparent, particularly for an interested Chinese audience, the issues of sequencing that have arisen along the way. It may be mentioned that the Reserve Bank of India (RBI) has also provided considerable documentation on these issues; for example, Chapter VI of the *Report on Currency and Finance 2004–05* (RBI, 2005b).

In India's case there are two additional, linked, considerations that have begun to influence the debate on external financial integration. The first is the aspiration to develop Mumbai as a regional financial center; the second is for India to participate in broader initiatives for financial integration in Asia. These twin initiatives would both stimulate, and benefit from, greater integration between India's financial market and that of the region and of the rest of the world.

India's ambitions for Mumbai are, in turn, derived from two perceptions of India's underlying comparative advantage. The first is that finance is a skill-intensive service industry where India may be able to provide quality offshore services at a competitive price in software development and information-technology-enabled services. The second is that there is considerable talent of Indian origin in financial institutions worldwide. As China has successfully tapped the Chinese diaspora across Asia to strengthen its capabilities in manufacturing, India could succeed in doing the same in financial services. Indeed, it is perhaps not too fanciful to expect that, as China's own need for sophisticated financial services increases, Mumbai could offer an alternative to both Hong Kong SAR and Singapore for the provision of these services.

Domestic Financial Liberalization

The Origins of Financial Repression

Prior to its independence in 1947, India enjoyed a relatively liberal domestic financial system with capital account convertibility within the sterling area; indeed the Indian rupee was a medium of exchange throughout the Persian Gulf region. Exchange controls were introduced as a wartime measure (RBI, 2005b). The large sterling balances that India had accumulated during the war were blocked as Britain struggled to balance her external accounts with various creditors, notably the United States. Domestically, India's financial system was relatively sophisticated, with established stock and commodity exchanges, and domestic and foreign banks largely under private ownership.

A series of landmark events between the mid-1950s and the late-1960s transformed what had been a relatively liberal system into a highly repressed one. It may be mentioned that this evolution was in keeping with the larger world-wide intellectual trends of the time that were influenced by the work of John Maynard Keynes and the apparently successful modernization of the Soviet Union, which accorded the state an important role in manipulating the financial system to achieve the goals of planned development. This global consensus was reflected in the World Bank's active support of state-guaranteed development finance institutions (DFIs) in the 1950s and 1960s.

In 1955, the State Bank of India, India's largest bank, was nationalized; in 1956, independent India encountered its first foreign exchange crisis, leading to an intensification of both import and exchange controls. It was the beginning of a siege mentality with regard to foreign exchange availability that is only now slowly receding, 50 years later. The private banking system was criticized as the tool of the major industrial houses and for being insufficiently oriented to the needs of an agrarian country embarking on planned development. This perception led to the nationalization of 14 of the largest private domestic banks in 1969 as part of a populist move by then Prime Minister, Mrs. Indira Gandhi. (For a further account of the India's growth experience since independence, see Singh and Bery, 2005.) Foreign banks, though heavily controlled, were not nationalized. A further 6 smaller banks were nationalized in 1980.

Following nationalization, there was significant branch expansion. The number of bank branches rose from about 8,800 in 1969 to about 60,600 in 1991, and the share of rural branches increased from about 22 percent to 58 percent (Mohan and Prasad, 2005). This helped the government in mobilizing household savings. The ratio of broad money to GDP increased from 24 percent of GDP in 1970–71 to 46 percent in 1990–91, and 73 percent in 2004–05.

India became increasingly politically aligned with the Soviet bloc in the 1970s. This was largely in response to U.S. foreign policy in that era, both toward the subcontinent and in Southeast Asia. India's foreign policy stance manifested itself in domestic financial sector policies, which increasingly became populist, rigid, and directive. Although the implementation of such policies was facilitated by public ownership of the main banks, they were, in principle, applicable to all commercial banks. Interest rates ceased to have a significantly allocative role, and competition among banks was suppressed in favor of publicly managed consortia. Fiscal policy remained relatively prudent until the 1980s; nonetheless, public debt was administratively placed through compulsory portfolio requirements imposed on the banks and on other institutions such as insurance companies and provident funds. Capital markets remained privately owned and operated. Although the secondary market was relatively free, primary capital issues were subject to government control and scrutiny. Monetization of the fiscal deficit took place through the automatic acceptance by the RBI of what were known as ad hoc treasury bills; as these accumulated, they were packaged as dated securities. Finally, the exchange regime essentially remained the Bretton Woods system of adjustable pegs, with periodic, brusque adjustments usually associated with exchange crises (RBI, 2005b).

Before leaving this era of financial repression (whose heyday lasted from 1970 until the late 1980s, but whose influence can be felt even in 2006), a few observations are perhaps in order. First, throughout, important sectors of the financial markets (and institutions) remained in private hands. Thus the skill base was by and large retained, although the pressures for financial innovation were slight. Second, the Indian allergy to inflation ensured that the damage done by these policies was more at the microeconomic than the macroeconomic level. Third, as the Indian nonfinancial private sector continued to survive, if not thrive, the assets of the public sector banks remained free from dominance of public-sector corporations, in contrast to the experience of China and the COMECON countries.

Liberalization, 1985–91

Moves toward liberalization initially came out of concerns for monetary management, signaled by the so-called Chakravarty Committee report of 1985 (RBI, 1985). The committee recommended a gradual deregulation of banking system interest rates so that monetary policy could be conducted using more modern, market-oriented instruments rather than the blunt portfolio controls of that time. In addition, a working group was set up to analyze money market issues. Both committees continued to regard social goals and priority sectors as appropriate guiding principles for their recommendations, rather than issues of competition, innovation, stability, and soundness. They accordingly recommended a continuation of the overall administered rate structure with calibrated cross-subsidization.

Despite these new instruments, the repression of the financial system continued to be enforced through quantitative controls, specifically the cash reserve ratio (CRR) meant for containing liquidity growth and the statutory liquidity ratio (SLR) a tool of captive financing for the government.[1,2] At the end of 1990–91, the CRR and SLR stood at 15.5 and 38.25 percent, respectively; the two requirements together preempted more than half of the net demand and time liabilities. The actual ratio exceeded 60 percent because public sector banks preferred to hold excess SLR in preference to commercial loans. Owing to the absence of transparent, international standards for income recognition, the true quality of bank assets was not known widely outside the RBI—then, as now, the sole banking regulator for the scheduled commercial banks (RBI, 2005b, Chapter V).[3]

---

[1]Since 1962, the RBI has been empowered to vary the CRR between 3 and 15 percent of the total demand and time liabilities. CRR in excess of 3 percent is currently remunerated at 4 percent per annum (Reddy, 1999).

[2]Over and above the CRR, banks are required to maintain a minimum amount of liquid assets in cash, gold, and government securities, amounting to a specified share of their demand and time liabilities.

[3]The RBI is vested with regulatory and supervisory authority over commercial banks and urban cooperative banks (UCBs), DFIs, and nonbanking financial companies (NBFCs). On March 31, 2005, there were 289 commercial banks (89 Scheduled Commercial Banks), 196 Rural Regional Banks (RRBs), and 4 Local Area Banks, 1,872 UCBs, 8 DFIs, and 13,187 NBFCs. The Board for Financial Supervision has been constituted as a Committee of the Central Board of the RBI since November 1994 and is headed by the Governor with a Deputy Governor as Vice Chairperson and other Deputy Governors and four Directors of the Central Board as members. In respect of state and district central cooperative banks, while the RBI is the regulator, supervision is vested with the National Bank for Agriculture and Rural Development. The Insurance Regulatory and Development Authority regulates

Domestic Liberalization (1991–2005)

The process of reform

India's financial sector liberalization since 1991 has been a comprehensive program involving issues related to banking, capital markets, fiscal policy, and international financial integration. Issues of linkage and sequencing between these areas have been central. India makes heavy use of expert commissions to float and develop ideas and agendas. In apparent contrast to China, there is little formal use made of foreign advisors. The two key regulators, the RBI and the Securities and Exchange Board of India (SEBI) have increasingly taken to inviting comments and discussion on major regulatory and market development issues through the Internet, press debate, and conferences/meetings with stakeholders. The finance ministry initiates and drafts needed legislation for parliamentary review. An important stimulus for reform has been provided by a series of market frauds (or scams) that resulted in improvements in market institutions and infrastructure.

Responding to the balance of payments crisis in 1990, wide-ranging economic reforms were introduced in 1991. Two important committees were constituted in the financial sector: the Committee on Financial Systems (CFS), and the Committee on Banking Sector Reforms (CBSR)[4]. The CFS took note of excessive administrative and political interference in internal management and credit decision making in public sector banks and observed that the economic reforms in the real sectors of the economy could not realize their full potential without reform of the financial sector.

The CFS and CBSR (henceforth the first and the second Narasimham Committees) provided the blueprint for reforming the financial system. Based on the committees' recommendations, a series of measures were undertaken beginning in 1992. The suggested reforms included decontrol of interest rates, development of securities markets, building a credible risk-free yield curve, greater reliance on open market operations, auctions of government securities, phased decontrol of the capital account, and

---

the insurance sector while the Securities and Exchange Board of India (SEBI) regulates securities and mutual funds (RBI, 2005b).

[4] The report of the CFS was submitted in 1991. Mr. M. Narasimham, a former RBI governor was the chairman of the committee. Subsequent to this report, the government appointed another committee, the CBSR, again with Mr. Narasimham as committee chairman, to review the progress made in reforming the banking sector and to chart the actions needed to strengthen the foundation of the banking system. The CBSR report was submitted in April 1998. For a summary see RBI (1998).

establishing prudential norms and mechanisms for supervision of the banking sector in line with international standards and practices, specifically those proposed by the Basel Committee for banks with significant international operations (the so-called Basel I norms). Significantly, neither committee forcefully championed denationalization.

In its external payments regime, India made the transition to a managed float of the rupee in 1993 (RBI, 2005b). Concurrently, most restrictions on current transactions were removed, and India accepted the disciplines of Article VIII status (current account convertibility) at the IMF as of March 1993. The exchange rate regime is officially described as market-determined, with no target rate, but the RBI reserves (and exercises) the right to intervene in the market to resist speculative attacks and to guide the exchange rate in the directions of "appropriate" competitiveness. One measure of this intervention has been the accumulation of foreign exchange reserves, which reached US$150 billion by March 2006. By way of comparison, the equivalent figure at the end of March 2001 was US$54.1 billion. While part of this intervention has been designed to strengthen India's defense against a speculative attack, part has been designed to insulate the nominal exchange rate from what are perceived as temporary capital inflows (Lal, Bery, and Pant 2003; Patnaik, 2004; Joshi and Sanyal, 2004).

Interest rate regime liberalization and the lowering of statutory requirements

The framework of administered interest rates has been almost dismantled since 1997. In the case of deposit rates, only the rate on savings bank deposits remains under RBI control. At present, this is prescribed at 3.5 percent. The effective yield on deposits is lower, however, because interest is payable only on the minimum balance between the tenth day and the last day of each month. As for lending rates, the RBI now directly controls only the interest rate charged on export credit, which accounts for about 10 percent of commercial advances and indirectly controls the interest rate on small loans of up to Rs. 200,000, which accounts for about 20 percent of total advances[5]. Commercial banks are not allowed to exceed their Prime Lending Rate (PLR) in the case of loans up to Rs. 200,000.[6]

---

[5]For export credit, the RBI provides refinancing at concessional rates that mitigate the burden of this particular control on the banking system.

[6]Each commercial bank is statutorily required to declare its PLR in advance.

The RBI specifies an interest rate ceiling for nonresident Indians' foreign currency deposits and nonresident Indians' rupee deposits. Since July 2003, these are linked to the London Interbank Offered Rate (LIBOR) for selected international currencies, less 25 basis points for nonresident Indians' foreign currency deposits and plus 250 basis points for nonresident Indians' rupee deposits.

With these reforms and given larger trends in financial markets, as influenced by the RBI's monetary policy actions, the nominal deposit rate for 1–3 year maturities has dropped from 12.0 percent in 1991–92 to 4–5.25 percent in 2004–05, and the nominal lending rate has over the same period dropped from 16.0 to 10.25 percent.

The minimum cash reserve ratio has been lowered to 4.75 percent from 15.5 percent (prior to the reforms), and banks are paid interest on deposits in excess of the 3 percent statutory minimum at the rate of 6 percent, which is equal to the RBI policy-determined Bank Rate. The statutory liquidity ratio was gradually brought down from an average effective rate of 37.5 percent in 1992 to the statutory minimum of 25 percent in 1997, and it continues to be at that level, although actual holdings still remain in excess of the minimum.

Increasing role of private sector domestic and foreign banks

Since the start of reforms in 1991, private sector banks, both domestic and foreign, have been allowed more liberal entry, albeit with different degrees of freedom. By end-March 2004, the domestic private sector banks held 18.6 percent of assets, 17 percent of deposits, and 19.8 percent of advances. The corresponding numbers for foreign banks were 6.9 percent, 5.1 percent, and 7.0 percent. While there is thus a substantial presence of private banking in India, the public sector banks (the State Bank of India group and the nationalized banks) continue even now to dominate the Indian banking sector. Indian banks, led by the public sector banks, have also continued to expand their presence overseas.

Expansion of foreign banks in India and their acquisition powers over domestic private banks have been the subject of considerable attention and debate, as well as being governed by India's commitments under the General Agreement on Trade in Services. As India's economy has improved, foreign banks have sought to expand their presence, both by branch expansion and by acquisition of private banks. (Unlike China, there has been no interest in providing a minority "strategic stake" in public sector banks even though this is not prohibited by law.)

Following an announcement in the 2002–03 budget, foreign banks in India have been given more flexibility in their Indian operations wherein they are allowed to operate as branches of their overseas parent or as subsidiaries in India. Under a three-phase road map set out by the RBI on February 28, 2005, between March 2005 and March 2009 foreign banks satisfying the RBI's eligibility criteria will be permitted to establish a wholly owned banking subsidiary (WOS) or to convert their existing branches into a WOS. The WOS is required to have minimum capital of Rs. 3.0 billion with sound corporate governance. The WOS will be treated on par with the existing branches of foreign banks for branch expansion with flexibility to go beyond the existing World Trade Organization (WTO) commitments of 12 branches in a year and preference for branch expansion in under-banked areas. The RBI would also prescribe market access and national treatment consistent with WTO commitments and also other appropriate limitations consistent with international practices and the country's requirements. Permission for acquisition of shareholding in Indian private sector banks by eligible foreign banks will be limited to banks identified by the RBI for restructuring. Where such acquisition is by a foreign bank already present in India, a maximum period of six months will be given for conforming to the "one form of presence" concept. The second phase will commence in April 2009 after a review of the experience gained. Extension of national treatment to WOS, dilution of stake, and permitting mergers and acquisitions of any private sector banks in India by a foreign bank would be considered, subject to an overall investment limit of 74 percent (RBI, 2005a).

Strengthening prudential norms

In order to strengthen the banking system, the RBI has already introduced capital adequacy norms to ensure uniform measurement of regulatory capital consistent with the recommendations of the Basel Committee and income recognition (Basel I). The initial target was to obtain a capital-to-risk weighted assets ratio (CRAR) of 8 percent as required by Basel I. The government contributed about Rs. 40 billion (0.6 percent of the 1990–91 GDP) to the paid-up capital of public sector banks between 1985–86 and 1992–93 and again about Rs. 177 billion (about 1.9 percent of the 1995–96 GDP) between 1992–93 and 2001–02 (Mohan and Prasad, 2005). Constrained by competing fiscal demands, the government permitted banks to raise fresh equity to meet a shortfall in capital requirements. Public sector banks were also encouraged to raise Tier-II (i.e., debt) capital without a government guarantee, subject to certain limits linked to their capital. Several public sector banks also accessed capital in India and abroad through global depository receipts (GDR), while other banks raised subordinated debt through private placement for inclusion under Tier-II capital. Unlike the big Chinese banks, however, there is no appetite in India for the sale of strategic stakes to foreign banks. Where the domestic private sector banks are concerned, foreign equity holdings are currently restricted to a total of 74 percent, with no individual shareholder able to exercise more than 10 percent of voting rights, other than with the RBI's approval with sublimits for the three categories of foreign direct investment (FDI), foreign institutional investors (FIIs), and nonresident Indians (NRIs) (RBI, 2005a).[7] With these efforts, the Indian banking sector has achieved more than required capital adequacy in almost all the groups except two banks in the old private sector (Table 7.1).

After substantially complying with the Basel I requirements, Indian banks are now moving towards the New Capital Adequacy Framework on International Convergence of Capital Measurement and Capital Standards (Basel II) regime (November 2005), which entails three pillars for establishing minimum capital requirements (incorporating credit risk, operational risk, and market risk), supervisory review, and market discipline. The RBI has, in principle, accepted to adopt Basel II. Accordingly, all commercial banks in India except RRBs are required to adopt the Standardized Approach for credit risk and the Basic Indicator Approach for operational risk by March 31, 2007. Banks are encouraged to formalize their capital adequacy assessment process in alignment with their business plan and performance budgeting system.

In order to ensure a smooth transition to Basel II, the RBI has appointed a steering committee comprising senior officials from 14 banks. On the basis of the recommendations of the steering group, draft guidelines on implementation of the New Capital Adequacy Framework were formu-

---

[7]The guidelines require that: (1) important shareholders (i.e., with shareholding of 5 percent and above) are "fit and proper" as per the RBI's guidelines on acknowledgement for allotment and transfer of shares, (2) the directors and the Chief Executive Officer who manage the affairs of the bank are "fit and proper" and observe sound corporate governance principles, (3) banks have minimum capital/net worth for optimal operations and systematic stability, and (4) policies and processes are transparent and fair.

On the issue of aggregate foreign investment in private banks from all sources (FDI, FII, NRI), the guidelines stipulate that it cannot exceed 74 percent of the paid-up capital of a bank. If FDI (other than by foreign banks or foreign bank groups) in private banks exceeds 5 percent, the entity acquiring such stake would have to meet the "fit and proper" criteria indicated in the share transfer guidelines and get the RBI's acknowledgement for transfer of the shares. The aggregate limit for all FII investments is restricted to 24 percent, which can be raised to 49 percent with the approval of the board/shareholders. The current limit for all NRI investments is 24 percent, with the individual NRI limit being 5 percent, subject to the approval of the board/shareholders.

Table 7.1. Scheduled Commercial Banks: Frequency Distribution of CRAR (end-March 2005)

Bank Group	Negative	0–9 Percent	9–10 Percent	10–15 Percent	15 Percent and Above	Total
Public sector banks	0	0	2	22	4	28
SBI group	0	0	0	8	0	8
Nationalized banks	0	0	2	14	4	20
Private sector banks	0	2	4	16	7	29
Old private sector banks	0	2	2	11	5	20
New private sector banks	0	0	2	5	2	9
Foreign banks	0	0	1	10	19	30
All banks	0	2	7	48	30	87

Sources: RBI (2005a); off-site supervisory returns submitted by the banks.
Notes: Data for March 2005 are unaudited and provisional. SBI: State Bank of India. CRAR: capital-to-risk weighted assets ratio.

lated and issued to banks on February 15, 2005. An internal working group was also constituted for identifying eligible domestic credit rating agencies whose ratings may be used by the banks for computing capital for credit risk under Basel II (RBI, 2005a). It is the responsibility of bank management, however, to develop an internal capital adequacy assessment process and accounting standard.

In addition, the enactment of the Securitization and Reconstruction of Financial Assets and Enforcement of Security Interest (SARFAESI) Act, 2002 (with amendments in 2004), has offered great opportunities to step up loan recoveries and tighten credit administration procedures, which could further enhance the scope for greater profitability. The banks' readiness is reflected in significant improvements in CRAR and nonperforming assets (NPA) across the banking sector (Table 7.2) while maintaining reasonable profitability.

Strengthening regulatory and supervisory institutions

In order to strengthen the regulation and supervision of the banking system, a Board for Financial Supervision has been constituted as a Committee of the Central Board of the Reserve Bank since November 1994 and is headed by the Governor with a Deputy Governor as Vice Chairperson and other Deputy Governors and four Directors of the Central Board as members. The Board has focused on restructuring the inspection system, setting up off-site surveillance, enhancing the role of external auditors, and strengthening corporate governance, internal controls, and audit procedures, disclosures, and transparency.

Table 7.2. Select Financial Indicators

Item	Period	Scheduled Commercial Banks	DFIs	PDs	NBFCs	SUCBs
CRAR	March 2004	12.9	22.0	42.7	26.8	11.0
	March 2005	12.8	22.8	54.3	22.9	12.7
Gross NPAs to gross advances	March 2004	7.4	16.4	n.a.	8.2	30.4
	March 2005	5.2	11.5	n.a.	8.1	24.9
Net NPAs to net advances	March 2004	2.9	10.5	n.a.	2.4	20.8
	March 2005	2.0	3.7	n.a.	3.4	8.9
Return on total assets	2003–04	1.1	−0.2	5.9	2.5	0.4
	2004–05	0.9	1.1	−1.8	n.a.	0.3
Return on equity	2003–04	19.3	−1.2	19.9	13.6	n.a
	2004–05	14.0	4.8	−5.1	n.a.	n.a
Cost/income ratio	2003–04	45.6	0.2	16.9	14.1	24.9
	2004–05	49.3	0.2	297.0	n.a.	25.5

Source: RBI (2005a)

Notes: n.a.: not available. Data for March 2005 are provisional. Data for nonbank financial companies (NBFCs) pertain to deposit-taking NBFCs having an asset size of Rs. 10 crore and above. Data for 2005 in respect of NBFCs pertain to the period ended September 2004. Data for scheduled commercial banks pertain to domestic operations only and may not tally with the balance sheet data. Data in respect of Development Financial Institution (DFIs) as on March 2005 do not include IDBI due to its conversion into a banking company. In regard to UCBs, data for CRAR relate to 52 scheduled Urban Cooperative Banks (UCBs) while other data relate to 53 scheduled UCBs (out of 55). Data for scheduled UCBs are based on offsite surveillance statements.

Since March 1998, mandatory disclosures have also included profitability indicators such as the ratio of interest and noninterest income to working funds and the financial position of subsidiaries. And, since March 2000, banks have to disclose the maturity profile of loans and advances, investments, movements in nonperforming assets, and lending to sensitive sectors.

Greater stress is also given to timely identification and monitoring of the behavior of troubled banks. The role of external auditors has been extended to verifying and certifying almost all aspects of balance sheets including financial ratios. Concurrent audits have also been introduced.

With the increasing use of credit cards and electronic banking, supervision has taken on another dimension: integrity of e-money. As of October 2004, different banks had already issued about 37.85 million plastic cards covering a range of credit cards, debit cards, and smart cards (RBI, 2004). The RBI has constituted several working groups on electronic money, and the recommendations are being implemented.

Capital market reforms

The Capital Issues (Continuance of Control) Act, 1947,[8] was used to control the issue of capital in the Indian market up to 1992. Under this Act, any firm wishing to raise funds from the market had to obtain approval from the government, which also determined the amount, type, and price of the issue. In order to pave the way for market-determined allocation of resources, the 1947 Act was repealed in 1992 and the Securities and Exchange Board of India Act, 1992 was enacted with statutory power granted to SEBI to (a) protect the interest of investors in securities, (b) promote and develop the securities market, and (c) regulate the securities market. In addition to the SEBI Act, 1992, three other acts are applicable to the capital market. These are: the Securities Contract (Regulation) Act, 1956 (SC(R)A); the Companies Act, 1956; and the Depositories Act, 1996. The government has framed rules under all these three acts, and SEBI issues notifications and guidelines that must be complied with by market participants. The Department of Economic Affairs, Department of Company Affairs, the RBI, and the SEBI with clear areas of jurisdiction under different applicable Acts share the responsibility of regulating the securities market.

SC(R)A was amended in 1995 to lift a ban on the writing of options in securities, and was again amended in December 1999 to expand the definition of securities to include derivatives in order to bring these into the general frame of regulations applicable to any other security. In addition, a 30 year old ban on forward trading was withdrawn in order to make trading in derivatives a reality.

Historically, brokers owned, controlled, and managed stock exchanges in India, which often led to extreme volatility in the securities market. In March 2001, in order to corporatize the stock exchanges, the government proposed de-mutualization, whereby ownership, management, and trading membership would be segregated from one another. The government has offered tax incentives to facilitate this transformation.

---

[8]Control of Capital Issues was introduced through the Defense of India Rules in 1943 under the Defense of India Act, 1939, to channel resources to support the war effort. The control was retained after the war with some modifications as a means of controlling the raising of capital by companies and to ensure that national resources were channeled to serve the goals and priorities of the government, and to protect the interests of investors. The relevant provisions in the Defense of India Rules were replaced by the Capital Issues (Continuance of Control) Act in April 1947. (See *http://www.sebi.gov.in/chairmanspeech/histspeech.html* for more information.)

SEBI (Central Listing Authority) Regulations, 2003, were issued to provide for the constitution of a Central Listing Authority (CLA) by SEBI. In addition, the regulations provided for mandatory recommendation from CLA before listing in any stock exchange and appeal to SEBI and the Securities Appellate Tribunal in case of refusal of issuance of letter of recommendations from CLA. The CLA was constituted on April 9, 2003.

The National Stock Exchange of India Limited (NSE) was established during the early 1990s as a competing exchange under public ownership with state of the art technology to supplement the business at the Bombay Stock Exchange (BSE), both of which have traded in derivatives of securities since June 2000. The market presently offers index futures and index options on two indices and stock options and stock futures on 31 stocks. NSE quickly introduced a nationwide, on-line, and fully automated screen based trading system (SBTS). The SBTS electronically matches orders on a strict price/time priority, cutting costs and reducing risk of error.

Rolling settlement on a T+5 basis was introduced for all scripts in December 2001 to reduce the trading cycle (to as little as 1 day, in the case of specified scripts), which earlier used to take 14 days for specified scripts and 30 days in the case of other scripts. T+5 gave way to T+3 in December 2002, T+2 in April 2003, and now it is moving toward T+1. With a view to make the trading system more efficient and less time consuming, effective April 2004, Straight Through Processing became compulsory for all institutional trades.

The Companies (Second Amendment) Act, 2002, was enacted to provide for a new, modern, efficient, and time-bound Insolvency Law to provide for both rehabilitation and winding up of sick companies within a maximum time frame of two years. It envisaged the setting up of a National Company Law Tribunal with several Benches to be notified by the government all over the country.

Public debt

The RBI is the regulator of the market for government securities and it also services and manages the public debt for both the central and state governments. Following the scam of 1992, where lack of transparency in the pricing and settlement of government securities created a funding channel for stock market speculation, significant reforms have been made to markets for both bills and dated securities.

Until 1991, the government securities market consisted mainly of pre-determined, low-coupon, long-maturity loans. There was no benchmark rate for the market. In 1992, however, the government began borrowing at market interest rates through an auction system, and, by April 1997, it abolished the system of automatic monetization via ad-hoc treasury bills. These actions paved the way for rapid reforms. New instruments such as zero coupon bonds, floating rate bonds, bonds with call-put options, and capital-indexed bonds were introduced across the maturity spectrum. A system of primary dealers (PDs) was introduced with liquidity support and incentives for underwriting. This, along with permission for FIIs to invest in dated securities and treasury bills in the primary and secondary market segments, added depth and liquidity to the market. The transparency was increased by announcements of an auction calendar for treasury bills, online dissemination of information, creation of the Negotiated Dealing System for delivery, and settlement through the Clearing Corporation of India Limited (CCIL). Market participants can now hedge their risks through interest rate swaps and forward rate agreements on the over-the-counter market and through rate futures on exchanges (RBI, 2005b, Chapter VII). While market infrastructure has clearly become much more robust, and has facilitated the move from direct to indirect instruments, provision of adequate liquidity remains a challenge, perhaps aggravated by the RBI's habitual ambivalence to the role of brokers in the public debt markets. Liquidity is an even larger issue in the fragmented market for corporate debt, even though other elements of market infrastructure, such as independent and well-staffed rating agencies, have existed for a number of years.

With the legislative framework in place and responsive to market changes, the securities market is also becoming increasingly integrated with the international markets. Indian companies have been permitted to raise resources from abroad through issues of American Depository Receipts, GDRs, Foreign Currency Convertible Bonds, and External Commercial Borrowings (ECBs) and are also allowed listing on foreign stock exchanges under certain conditions. The FIIs enjoy full capital account convertibility. They can invest in a company under portfolio investment up to 24 percent of the paid-up capital of the company, which can be increased up to the sectoral cap/statutory ceiling if it is approved by the Indian company's board of directors and also its general body.

Money market development and innovations

In order to bring financial stability and facilitate the movement of the short-term money market rate within a corridor, a full-fledged liquidity adjustment facility (LAF) was established on June 5, 2000, to be operated through repo and reverse repo instruments. The LAF is now fully supported by a real time gross settlement system and a computerized public debt office. Liquidity is injected by the RBI through the Collateralized

Lending Facility to banks, export credit refinance to banks, and liquidity support to PDs in government securities. The absorption of liquidity takes place through fixed-rate reverse repos (rates being announced daily) and open market operations in government-dated securities by the RBI. However, it is important to note that these operations occur within the given framework of the CRR (that directly affects liquidity) and the Bank Rate which signals the central bank's medium-term view on short-term rates. The CCIL now handles most overnight transactions in the repo/reverse repo market.

Introduction of the LAF has been one of the most important recent changes in the money market. It gives the RBI the flexibility to affect liquidity and signal interest rates in the short-term money market. In order to provide the RBI with additional tools to cope with the recent surge in capital flows, however, the Government of India signed a memorandum of understanding with the RBI on March 25, 2004, detailing the rationale and operational modalities of a Market Stabilization Scheme (MSS) to be effective from April 2004. Under the MSS, the government would issue treasury bills and/or dated securities in addition to its normal borrowing requirements, so as to facilitate the RBI's efforts in absorbing liquidity from the system. The treasury bills and dated securities issued for MSS purposes are matched by an equivalent cash balance, which is held by the government in the RBI. The interest payments on treasury bills and/or dated securities outstanding under the MSS will be the only impact on government revenue and fiscal balances.

Thus, effective April 2004, the MSS became an important instrument of liquidity absorption and sterilization. Initially, an annual provision was made of Rs. 600 billion, which was increased to Rs. 800 billion for 2005–06.

In his budget speech in February 2000, the Indian Finance Minister mooted the idea of amending the RBI Act to accord greater operational flexibility to the Reserve Bank in conducting monetary policy and regulation of the financial system. Accordingly, the Reserve Bank of India (Amendment) Bill, 2005, was introduced in India's lower house of Parliament (the Lok Sabha), which aims at bestowing enabling powers on the RBI to use a larger variety of financial instruments than hitherto, including derivatives, and more flexibility to set the cash reserve ratio. Apart from these legislative changes, there remains a rich agenda of additional reform to improve the liquidity and efficiency of the money market further, both to serve commercial needs and to improve its sensitivity and responsiveness to the RBI's monetary policy actions. A few examples follow.

The repo market is still at an early stage of development. Reforms on the rollover of repos and on documentation are expected to pave the way for a deeper and more liquid repo market. With appropriate regulatory safeguards, guaranteed settlement through notation in the CCIL, trading in dematerialized form, and uniform accounting, valuation, and disclosure norms, it is expected that the market will deepen further (see also, Mohan and Prasad, 2005).

It is also being proposed to remove the provision for payment of interest to banks on the excess CRR maintained by the commercial banks, as this reduces the effectiveness of the CRR as a monetary policy tool.

There is finally the issue of ownership. Several studies including those of the World Bank (2001) and Barth, Caprio, and Levine (2001) indicate that private banks are more efficient. Given the public banks' large current share in intermediation, it will take time for new entrants to displace growth, although the capital markets provide an increasingly viable alternative for large listed companies. There is currently no credible proposal, however, to dilute public ownership in these banks to passive, minority status.

Assessment

Somewhat unexpectedly, financial sector reform can now be counted as one of the relative successes of India's economic reform program since 1991. Significant liberalization and (as will be discussed further below) significant international financial integration have occurred without, so far, a major financial crash. Yet, as Kletzer (2004) points out, the lack of coordination between fiscal adjustment and financial reform has had significant implications through the loss of revenue associated with financial repression. He further argues that funding of the government's high debt stock will become harder as the capital account liberalizes.

Positive surprises over the 15-year span have been the growth in assurance and professionalism of both the RBI and SEBI, as well as the beneficial impact of increased competition from some of the newly established domestic private sector banks. By contrast, so far the collective impact of foreign banks has not been significant. Yet, while the stability of the system is no doubt greater now than at the beginning of the process (Table 7.3), the contradictions between a still largely nationalized banking system and the needs of an increasingly sophisticated and rapidly growing economy are growing more serious and glaring. Unfortunately, denationalization is even less discussed than before. The fact that India emerged unscathed from contagion in the Asian crisis of 1997–98, the fact that China has succeeded in growing rapidly despite a largely publicly owned banking system, and the exigencies of domestic politics have all served to make bank privatization the "third rail" of Indian reform.

India has shown an impressive capacity to reform its financial system behind the protective barrier of a semi-closed (but gradually opening) capital account. The issue is whether this impetus is running out of steam. Reducing these protective barriers is one way to stimulate competition and domestic financial innovation, but to do so in the presence of widespread public ownership of banks and a large fiscal deficit raises additional challenges and risks. It is to an examination of these issues that the paper now turns.

International Financial Integration

Context

Global economic integration increased progressively during the 1980s and 1990s. World trade in goods and services increased from 37.9 percent of global GDP (at market prices and exchange rates) during 1981–85 to 48.0 percent during 2001–03 (Table 7.4). During the same period international flows of gross private capital (direct, portfolio, and other) increased from 7.4 percent to 22.9 percent and gross foreign direct investment increased from 2.3 percent to 11.1 percent of GDP. In low-income countries, trade increased from 23.6 percent to 43.7 percent, gross private capital flows from 2.4 percent to 4.4 percent, and gross foreign direct investment from 0.3 percent to 1.6 percent of GDP, respectively.

Global attitudes on the need for and priority of capital account convertibility (KAC) have evolved substantially since World War II. Certain countries (Canada, later Indonesia) were early adopters, largely because of the infeasibility of imposing capital controls given their proximity to major financial hubs. But, for most countries, the focus of domestic and international policy following the war was on liberalizing trade and ensuring a payments regime that was supportive of this more liberal trade. Free capital movements were considered potentially disruptive, and capital controls were not disallowed under the Articles of Agreement of the IMF. Capital mobility was, however, established as a goal for members of the Organization for Economic Cooperation and Development when it was founded in the early 1960s, although certain of the more recent members retain capital controls.

Many of the developed European countries only gradually dismantled their capital controls during the 1970s and 1980s. As private flows began

Table 7.3. Moody's Weighted Average Bank Financial Strength Index

	December 2002	December 2003	December 2004
China	10.0	10.0	10.0
Hong Kong SAR	62.3	62.3	62.3
India	27.5	27.5	24.2
Indonesia	3.0	3.0	7.3
Korea	16.7	18.3	18.3
Malaysia	31.7	33.3	35.2
Philippines	20.4	20.4	19.2
Singapore	74.7	74.7	74.7
Thailand	15.8	15.8	15.8
Argentina	0.0	0.0	0.0
Brazil	25.0	24.3	24.3
Chile	52.5	56.5	57.8
United Kingdom	83.8	83.3	83.3
Japan	12.9	12.0	20.6
United States	75.0	75.0	77.0

Source: World Bank, *Global Development Finance* (2005).

to dominate official flows in development finance, and as financial institutions in the developed countries regained interest in furnishing financial services to the individuals and companies of the developing world, KAC started to assume a larger place in international debate.

Financial Integration: Analytic Considerations

China and India are both being led toward greater KAC as an inevitable by-product of their desire for greater overall integration into the global economy, and as part of their effort to strengthen their domestic systems of financial intermediation and risk mitigation. Yet, unlike the case for trade liberalization, the academic community remains divided in its assessment of the benefits of accelerating KAC. Indeed, in contrast to trade in goods, there even remains confusion as to the definition of KAC. Arguments rage both on the importance (and priority) of KAC for long-term economic growth, as well as the balance between benefits and risks of approaching full KAC. The experience with financial crises in Asia in the late 1990s has clearly checked some of the earlier enthusiasm for a more rapid move toward KAC. In addition, issues of monetary management and autonomy in a world of capital movements have become more pressing. Below we review major arguments in the literature, for and against KAC, before assessing the current status of KAC in India and the relevance of these arguments for India at its present juncture.

Table 7.4. Selected Indicators of Global Integration and Domestic Financial Deepening

	World		High Income		Low Income		China		India	
	1981–85	2001–03	1981–85	2001–03	1981–85	2001–03	1981–85	2001–03	1981–85	2001–03
Trade in goods and services (percent of GDP)	37.9	48.0	38.8	45.7	36.6	43.7	18.4	56.5	14.2	29.6
Exports of goods and services (percent of GDP)	18.7	24.0	19.2	22.6	9.5	20.8	9.0	29.6	6.0	14.4
Gross FDI (percent of GDP)	1.3	5.5	1.4	5.9	0.3	1.6	0.5	4.7	0.0	0.9
Gross private capital flows (percent of GDP)	7.4	22.9	7.7	25.4	2.4	4.4	1.9	10.8	0.4	3.2
FDI, net inflows (percent of gross capital formation)	2.3	11.1	2.1	11.1	1.3	6.6	1.0	9.0	0.1	3.3
Share of FDI, net inflows (BoP, current US$)	100	100	77.9	76.9	2.3	2.1	1.7	7.1	0.1	0.6
Market capitalization of listed companies (percent of GDP)	57.9	84.7	106.0	95.6	8.6	26.5	5.70[1]	43.0	9.9	31.7
Money and quasi-money (M2) as percent of GDP	55.0	80.1	67.0	83.0	30.8	46.3	42.2	162.8	35.0	57.9
Share of services sector in GDP	57.4	67.9	60.6	71.3	40.6	47.8	23.3	33.6	38.3	50.4
Per capita GDP growth	0.9	0.8	2.0	1.0	1.3	3.3	9.3	7.6	3.1	4.3

Source: World Bank, *World Development Indicators, 2005.*
[1]Data pertain to 1991–95.
Notes: FDI: foreign direct investment; BoP: balance of payments.

Several theoretical studies have attempted a rigorous defense of the benefits of financial integration. In a continuous-time stochastic model, Obstfeld (1994) argues that growth depends on the availability of an ever-increasing array of specialized, and hence inherently risky, production inputs and that most countries could reap large steady-state welfare gains through the beneficial effects of consumption from enhanced financial integration and wider risk sharing.

As against this, other analyses, based on a neoclassical growth model with an exogenous capital account regime, find that the potential gains from mitigating inefficiency due to international credit rationing might be quite moderate as compared to the gains from upgrading domestic financial intermediation—for example, by relaxing domestic credit rationing (Gourinchas and Jeanne, 2006).

A key argument put forth by the advocates of international financial integration is that there are endogenous productivity gains from capital mobility. It is also argued that the superior efficiency of foreign banks in allocating domestic saving, or the competition they introduce in the domestic financial system, accelerates domestic financial development resulting in efficiency gains in the whole economy (Levine and Zervos, 1998). Prasad and others (2005) argues that financial globalization with good governance and good macroeconomic policies appears to be conducive for growth. In a more revealing empirical analysis of the relationship between financial openness and industrial growth, Vanassche (2004) finds evidence that financial openness has a positive effect on the growth of industrial sectors, regardless of their characteristics. Moreover, industries that rely relatively more on external finance grow disproportionately faster in countries with more integrated financial systems. The process is enhanced further by improving the functioning of the domestic financial system.

In contrast to this benign view of KAC, Rodrik (1998), Panagariya (1998), and Bhagwati (1998) vehemently oppose full capital account convertibility. They argue that financial and goods markets are fundamentally different; also that the irreversibility of KAC enjoins prudence and caution. Panagariya cites research that demonstrates that once a country lives with an open capital account it is impossible to return to effective capital controls because residents and banks are quickly able to devise channels that circumvent the control. Bhagwati (1998) further argues that substantial gains from "full" KAC have been asserted not demonstrated, and that the decision, once taken, is irreversible.

It may be remarked that these arguments are very much in the spirit of the founders of the IMF, notably Keynes, who felt that free capital movements were at best irrelevant and at worst harmful for liberal trade. It might also be noted that many developing countries (particularly India) were initially hostile to all forms of international engagement and that attitudes first to liberal trade and then to liberal direct investment have changed only slowly. The underlying mechanism by which liberalization of trade and foreign direct investments affects productivity is through increased competitive pressure. The issue is whether these gains are further enhanced by increasing the competitive pressure on the financial system, and, if so, at what cost and risk.

It is now abundantly clear that there are tight links between the growth of trade and exposure to foreign direct investment (FDI). Countries attracting a larger share of FDI are also likely to have a higher export percentage of GDP (Figure 7.1). Although the direction of causality is not clear, higher exports are typically associated with faster growth of productivity. As the Chinese experience itself suggests, though, it is possible, at least for a while, to attract substantial volumes of FDI without full financial liberalization, although few would hold up China as a model of efficient capital allocation.

At present, just about 3.3 percent India's capital formation is contributed by FDI; in the case of China, the FDI share capital formation is over 9 percent despite much higher investment rates. While China has made formidable inroads in the manufacturing sector, the Indian economy is driven by the services sector (see Table 4). In a recent speech, Prime Minister Manmohan Singh pointed out the need to strengthen India's comparative advantage in the services sector, arguing that in this area, unlike manufacturing, there may be tighter links between direct investment and financial integration in order to modernize technology and enhance productivity, while actively managing the risks involved (Singh, 2006).

These long term arguments for increased financial integration aside, fear of currency crisis is perhaps the single most important reason for resisting international financial integration. The so-called first-generation models of currency crises were developed to explain crises arising from current account and balance of payments deficits, and the depletion of foreign exchange reserves (Krugman, 1979). The so-called second-generation models (so-called capital account crises) are particularly useful in explaining self-fulfilling contagious currency crises (Obstfeld, 1986). This theoretical work suggests four factors that can influence the onset and magnitude of a currency crisis: domestic public debt, domestic private debt, expectations, and the state of financial markets. A common ingredient has typically also been the need to defend a currency peg.

Figure 7.1. Scatter Plot Between Gross FDI and Exports (2001–03)
(In percent of GDP)

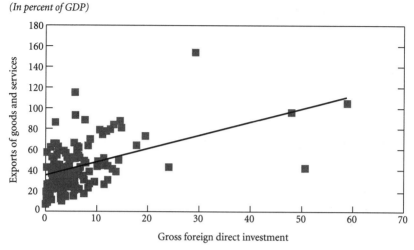

With regard to the first-generation models, it has been argued that open or (repressed) inflation is incompatible with convertibility and a stable exchange rate. Therefore, "easy money policies, budgetary deficits, [and] lax credit policies are all incompatible with convertibility and stability of the currency" (Haberler, 1954, p. 22). With the experience of so-called capital account crises in the 1990s, several other preconditions have been added, mostly in the nature of strengthening prudential and risk management practices in the domestic financial system.

The importance of fiscal discipline as a precondition for KAC can be traced to the Latin American debt crises of 1982, which unleashed an entire literature on over-borrowing in developing countries, placing the blame squarely on expansionary fiscal policies (and, in some countries, on inappropriate sequencing of liberalization). This literature is also known as the "Neo-Alejandrian" paradigm based on Diaz-Alejandro (1985), which relies on three problems associated with governments (Pesenti, 2001). The first one is the over-borrowing/over-lending/over-investment syndrome, wherein domestic and foreign creditors keep lending against future bailout revenue, unprofitable projects, excessively risky investments, and cash shortfalls being refinanced and rolled over. In the case of foreign borrowing, this translates into an unsustainable path of current account deficits. The second problem is public guarantees (explicit, implicit, or simply presumed) and expected bailouts. Whether or not depositors are explicitly insured, "the public expects governments to intervene to save most depositors from losses when financial intermediaries run into trouble.

Warnings that intervention will not be forthcoming appear to be simply not believable" (Diaz-Alejandro, 1985, p. 13). And, thirdly, even if public deficits may not be high before a crisis, when the government steps in and guarantees the stock of private liabilities, it must undertake complementary fiscal reforms. If these involve recourse to seigniorage revenue and money creation, expectations of inflationary financing may lead to speculation in the currency market. If the central bank intervenes to stabilize the domestic currency, it loses reserves that could otherwise be used to bail out insolvent private institutions, and vice versa. Thus, the parallel phenomenon of currency and banking crises appears. In many cases, currencies are pegged, which again amounts to a kind of guarantee, and the consequences are similar.

Such crises did not go away when governments became better behaved on the monetary and fiscal front. For example, the European Exchange Rate Mechanism (ERM) crisis in 1992 could not be blamed on lax monetary and fiscal policies in Europe, and therefore led to a new set of models with multiple equilibria (Rodrik, 1998).

International and Indian Practice

The IMF's *Annual Report on Exchange Arrangements and Exchange Restrictions* is the standard official source documenting controls on capital transactions imposed by its member countries. Controls and other provisions are broadly classified into 13 groups (Table 7.5), which are further classified as controls/provisions on inflows and outflows (see Appendix II). India is among the few countries that have controls and restrictions of one form or the other in all 13 groups.

IMF (1999) provides a comprehensive overview of the pervasiveness of exchange and capital controls during 1996. According to the indices reported there, even the East Asian countries involved in the 1997 crisis were not excessively open by international standards. Extensive exposure to intra-regional trade and currency trading were perhaps more important mechanisms for contagion.

India's balance of payments recovered surprisingly swiftly after the 1991 crisis, and as previously mentioned, current account convertibility was declared in 1993. Given the international intellectual support for capital account convertibility in emerging markets at that time, and despite the Mexican crisis of late 1994, a committee was constituted in 1996 by the RBI to review international experience and prepare a road map for liberalization of India's capital account. The committee was chaired by a former Deputy Governor of the RBI, Mr. S.S. Tarapore. Its report "Report of the Committee

Table 7.5. Features of Exchange Controls in Selected Countries

Capital Transactions	**	India	United States	Brazil	China
December 2001 Position					
Control on					
Capital market instruments	69	1	1	1	1
Money market instruments	60	1	1	1	1
Collective investment securities	55	1	1	1	1
Derivatives and other instruments	45	1		1	1
Commercial credits	59	1		1	1
Financial credits	61	1		1	1
Guarantees, sureties, and financial backup facilities	52	1		1	1
Direct investment	78	1	1	1	1
Liquidation of direct investment	31	1		1	1
Real estate transactions	74	1			1
Personal capital movements	50	1		1	1
Provisions specific to					
Commercial banks and other credit institutions	84	1		1	1
Institutional investors	45	1		1	
Proportion of controls		100	31	92	92
December 2004 Position					
Control on					
Capital market instruments	68	1	1	1	1
Money market instruments	55	1	1		1
Collective investment securities	52	1	1		1
Derivatives and other instruments	45	1		1	1
Commercial credits	53	1			1
Financial credits	59	1			1
Guarantees, sureties, and financial backup facilities	47	1		1	1
Direct investment	77	1	1	1	1
Liquidation of direct investment	29	1			1
Real estate transactions	73	1			1
Personal capital movements	52	1		1	1
Provisions specific to					
Commercial banks and other credit institutions	84	1			1
Institutional investors	49	1		1	
Proportion of controls		100	31	46	92

Source: IMF, *Annual Report on Exchange Arrangements and Exchange Controls* (2001, 2005).
Notes: **: proportion of member countries having a particular feature. A "1" means that the item is a feature of capital control in that country.

on Capital Account Convertibility" (henceforth, Tarapore Committee or TC) was finalized in 1997, on the eve of the Asian financial crisis.

As the committee had been asked to examine the positive case for KAC, it is not surprising that it accepted that there were several benefits that could be expected to flow from a more open capital account. These included mobilization of external capital for domestic investment, convergence between domestic and international interest rates, portfolio diversification by residents, and enhanced innovation in the domestic financial sector. The TC emphasized that capital controls progressively become ineffective, costly, and even distortionary. One could add that, like all other discretionary controls, restrictions on access to cheaper sources of overseas capital are also a potential source of both corruption and discrimination.

The TC further noted that domestic financial liberalization had already served to expose weaknesses in the domestic economy. The introduction of KAC could be even more damaging, so that "proactive policy action" would be needed to prepare the economy for KAC. But, on the whole, the committee believed that KAC would impose a strong (presumably positive) discipline on the financial system and would "expedite the early rectification of infirmities in the system and lead to widening/deepening of markets to enable the spreading distribution of risks" (RBI, 1997, para. 1.27). Thus the TC was commendably clear on the two-way links between domestic liberalization and KAC: the financial system had to be prepared for KAC, but, in turn, KAC would stimulate further development of the financial system for the greater benefit of both the government and the private sector.

At this point it is worth distinguishing between official capital account convertibility and de facto convertibility. With expanding trade, foreign investment, and travel, and given India's large overseas migrant population, it is increasingly difficult to make capital controls even partially effective. Opening trade without opening capital flows creates opportunities for under- or over-invoicing as export and import activity is used as a cover for capital exports and risks constraining the growth of trade as cumbersome controls are needed to enforce capital account restrictions (Krueger, 2004). In addition to such manipulated invoicing, there are legion other mechanisms of unauthorized capital flight. Evidence from China as well suggests that capital movements have been much more volatile than anything that could be suggested from having effective capital controls (Anderson, 2005).

In India, the distinction between remittance flows and capital movements is particularly blurred. India has historically been the hub of the so-called "hawala" market for informal financial flows between the subcontinent and the Persian Gulf. This market has been associated with smuggling, tax evasion, and illegal gold transactions (even allegedly the financing of terrorism, making this market a major focus for control of money laundering). But this market also serves legitimate cross-border payments needs of individuals efficiently, cheaply, and swiftly. India's ambivalence on the need for effective capital controls is exemplified by the numerous exemptions made for NRIs, a very broadly defined category of foreigners of Indian ethnic origin who are granted privileged access to Indian financial and physical assets as compared to other overseas natural persons.

KAC is not an unambiguous concept in the literature, and the concepts of capital account convertibility and currency convertibility are sometime intertwined and conflated. Bhalla (1999) follows the definition of the TC report, which defines KAC as "the freedom to convert local financial assets into foreign assets and vice-versa at market determined rate of exchange" (Reserve Bank of India, 1997, p. 339). India too has relaxed inflows of FDI and portfolio flows by foreign institutional investors but outflows by residents have been more strictly controlled. In fact, some feel that liberalization of inflows is almost complete (Bhalla, 1999). However, there remains a marked difference in treatment by type of entity. Differential restrictions are applied to residents vs. nonresidents and to individuals vs. corporates and financial institutions (Reddy, 2002). Nonresident corporates now have almost complete FDI access other than limits on FDI related to the financial and infrastructure sectors, and to retail trade.

Nonresident corporates and individuals are required to channel their portfolio investments through registered FIIs. FIIs are allowed to invest in Indian stocks and Indian corporates and are allowed to raise funds abroad through depositary receipts. They are also allowed to list in selected overseas stock exchanges. Domestic corporates require approval for ECB, equity issues, and overseas acquisitions, but these regulatory approvals are generally liberally provided. The regime for nonresident individuals discriminates between NRIs and other nonresidents. While NRIs are allowed direct access to onshore bank accounts, shares, and real estate, other nonresidents face restrictions in undertaking such investments. Following the budget announcements of 2002–03, NRI accounts have been made fully convertible. Transactions involving NRIs and Indian joint ventures abroad have been made more liberal for investment in fully convertible countries subject to specific limits.

While inflows have thus been liberalized for domestic and foreign corporates and for nonresident individuals of Indian origin on the outflow side, India continues to maintain a restrictive regime for capital outflows on individual accounts for domestic residents; such relaxations as have occurred are discretionary and easily reversed. With the recent marked improvement in external sector conditions, particularly the surge in foreign exchange reserves, cautious moves have been made in small steps to permit overseas bank accounts and portfolio investments by individuals. Most recently, some provisions have also been made to allow controlled outflows by Indian corporates. Companies can now offer all forms of guarantees subject to an overseas investment cap of 200 percent of their net worth, corporates can disinvest their stakes in wholly owned subsidiaries and joint ventures without RBI approval, and proprietary concerns can set up joint ventures and subsidiaries abroad without prior RBI approval.

The consolidated fiscal deficit position of the central and state governments has improved relatively little. Combined total net domestic public debt is around 76 percent of GDP. It is often noted that India's fiscal and debt indicators now are worse than many other emerging markets that have suffered crisis, and comparable to levels at the time of India's 1991 crisis (Ahluwalia, 2001a). Kletzer argues that the maintenance of capital controls has been critical to preventing the fiscal position from leading to crisis: "Capital controls are instrumental to financial repression in India in that they separate domestic financial intermediation from international financial markets and capture domestic savings for the financing of the public sector budget deficit" (Kletzer, 2004, p. 256).

Greater integration would increase pressure for fiscal reform, which would be growth enhancing in the long run. Empirical studies have shown that, if capital account liberalization were to be exogenously imposed, ceteris paribus, the government's budget deficit would be reduced by 2.275 percent of GDP (Kim, 2001). The disciplinary effect was also found to be stronger in the 1990s. With the Fiscal Responsibility and Budget Management (FRBM) Act, 2002 (in effect as of July 2005), the central government is bound to bring in fiscal discipline. Capital account liberalization will only add to the urgency with which such measures are implemented.

India has been faced with huge capital inflows since 2000. Like other Asian economies, India has chosen to accumulate foreign exchange reserves, rather than allow its nominal exchange rate to appreciate. In addition, India has chosen to sterilize the domestic counterpart of this intervention. On the whole, India's management of its exchange rate and its domestic monetary affairs has been well regarded, although the wedge between domestic and international monetary conditions has only been possible because of capital controls. One of India's successes has been to lengthen the maturity of its (relatively low) external debt. This may be difficult to maintain with convertibility. India's trade liberalization still has some way to go. Greater volatility in nominal and real exchange rates would make this harder to sell politically. The increased competitiveness of the corporate sector, however, and a large and diversified economy, are positives. Given its competitive private sector, India stands to reap substantial benefits from the more efficient resource allocation that would likely flow under a liberalized capital account.

Conclusion

International financial integration offers significant economic gains for countries, but it also carries the possibility of crises. The history of international financial market growth and economic development suggests that financial crises cannot be avoided, just as India's domestic financial liberalization has been punctuated by politically painful but economically salutary scams. Many officials and some researchers fear that premature liberalization of the capital account could be so damaging as to jeopardize the whole reform effort. In our view, this is too risk-averse a position to take. The banking system has demonstrated stability and strength over recent years. Similarly, an open capital account would supplement the transparency provided by the FRBM Act to get on with promised fiscal adjustment. The strength of the international and domestic economies and India's strong reserves position are other propitious factors. Monetary and financial integration sooner or later must accompany the real integration that is under way (and desired) in South Asia and East Asia and would facilitate India's desire to develop as a regional financial center. Many less sophisticated economies have had open capital accounts for a long time; others, in Southern Europe, for example, moved to integration with Europe even before the euro. It is interesting that Mr. Tarapore has been called upon once again, in 2006, to examine the case for full convertibility. Given the progress that India's financial system has made, and the natural caution of our bureaucracy, it is unlikely that India will do anything reckless.

Appendix I

The Tarapore Committee (TC) recommended that India achieve the following benchmarks as preconditions for capital account convertibility.
1. Consolidate public finances to achieve a sustainable position (defined as a deficit of the central government of 3.5 percent of GDP or less, accompanied by a reduction in the deficit of the states and the quasi-fiscal deficit). The fiscal deficit in 2005–06 is 4.1 percent of GDP.

2. Reduce inflation, to 3–5 percent annually. Average inflation for last three years (2003–04 is 5.5 percent; 2004–05 is 6.5 percent; 2005–06 is 4.4 percent).
3. Strengthen the financial system, including by:
   a. taking steps to reduce the net nonperforming asset ratio to 5 percent in 1999–2000; achieved 5.2 percent in 2004–05.
   b. reducing the cash reserve requirement to 3 percent over the same period.
   c. leveling the playing field between banks and nonbanks.
   d. harmonizing the cash reserve requirement on domestic liabilities with those on overseas and nonresident liabilities (with a possibly higher cash reserve requirement on nonresident liabilities including overseas borrowing by banks).
   e. improving risk management by financial institutions (marking to market, monitoring currency and maturity mismatches, internal control systems, accounting and disclosure, capital adequacy to cover market risk, and training in best practices techniques with the adoption of corresponding technology).
   f. improving prudential supervision (effective off-site surveillance, more stringent capital adequacy norms than the Basel minimums, tighter income recognition, and asset clarification norms).
   g. increasing the autonomy of public sector banks and financial institutions to deal with increased competition from foreign banks and the growing private sector.
   h. strengthening legal framework for loan recovery and execution of collateral to deter default.
4. Establish a monitoring band for real exchange rate developments (+/–5 percent around an estimate of a neutral real exchange rate).
5. Adopt macroeconomic policies consistent with a current account deficit that can be sustainability covered by normal capital inflows and, consistent with this, trade and external financing policies that would allow the debt service ratio to decline. The current account surplus (+)/deficit (–) positions for the last three years are as follows (percentage of GDP):

2003–04	2.3 percent (surplus)
2004–05	0.8 percent (deficit)
2005–06 (April–December)	1.7 percent (deficit)

6. Maintain adequate foreign exchange reserves (at least six months of imports) and legally required reserves to currency ratio of at least 40 percent.

Appendix II

Types of Capital Transactions Possibly Subject to Control

		Restrictions on Inflow	Restrictions on Outflow
Controls on capital market instruments	Shares or other securities of a participatory nature	Purchase locally by nonresidents Sale or issue abroad by residents	Sale or issue locally by nonresidents Purchase abroad by residents
	Bonds or other debt securities	Purchase locally by nonresidents Sale or issue abroad by residents	Sale or issue locally by nonresidents Purchase abroad by residents
Controls on money market instruments		Purchase locally by nonresidents Sale or issue abroad by residents	Sale or issue locally by nonresidents Purchase abroad by residents
Controls on collective investment securities		Purchase locally by nonresidents Sale or issue abroad by residents	Sale or issue locally by nonresidents Purchase abroad by residents
Controls on derivatives and other instruments		Purchase locally by nonresidents Sale or issue abroad by residents	Sale or issue locally by nonresidents Purchase abroad by residents
Controls on credit operations	Commercial credits	To residents from nonresidents	By residents to nonresidents
	Financial credits	To residents from nonresidents	By residents to nonresidents
	Guarantees, sureties, and financial backup facilities	To residents from nonresidents	By residents to nonresidents
Controls on direct investment		Inward direct investment	Outward direct investment Controls on liquidation of direct investment
Controls on real estate transactions		Purchase locally by nonresidents	Purchase abroad by residents Sale locally by nonresidents

Appendix II (*concluded*)

	Restrictions on Inflow	Restrictions on Outflow
Controls on personal capital movements		
Loans	To residents from nonresidents	By residents to nonresidents
Gifts, endowments, inheritances and legacies	To residents from nonresidents	By residents to nonresidents
Settlements of debts abroad by immigrants; transfer of assets	Transfer into the country by immigrants	Transfer abroad by emigrants
Provisions specific to banks and other credit institutions	Borrowing abroad	Maintenance of accounts abroad; Lending to nonresidents
Provisions specific to institutional investors	None	Limits (maximum) on securities issued by nonresidents and on portfolio invested abroad; Limits (maximum) on portfolio invested locally

Source: IMF (1999, Table 5).

Appendix III

Indices of Exchange Controls, 1996

	Exchange and Capital Controls (ECI)	Current Payment and Transfers (CCI)	Capital Controls (KCI)
Netherlands	0.03	0.05	0.01
Norway	0.03	0.01	0.05
United Kingdom	0.05	0.03	0.07
Denmark	0.05	0.02	0.07
Germany	0.05	0.04	0.07
New Zealand	0.05	0.02	0.01
Greece	0.06	0.06	0.06
Canada	0.07	0.09	0.06
Italy	0.08	0.10	0.06
Spain	0.08	0.04	0.11
United States	0.09	0.05	0.13
France	0.10	0.04	0.16
Latvia	0.10	0.10	0.10
Kenya	0.11	0.05	0.17
Uruguay	0.11	0.09	0.13
Argentina	0.11	0.03	0.19
Australia	0.12	0.04	0.20
Saudi Arabia	0.12	0.03	0.21
Japan	0.12	0.09	0.16
Czech Republic	0.19	0.04	0.33
Mexico	0.21	0.05	0.36
Egypt	0.21	0.12	0.30
Turkey	0.26	0.16	0.36
Philippines	0.32	0.16	0.47
Hungary	0.33	0.10	0.57
Indonesia	0.34	0.18	0.50
Israel	0.35	0.16	0.54
Thailand	0.40	0.17	0.63
Poland	0.40	0.12	0.69
Korea	0.40	0.10	0.70
South Africa	0.43	0.29	0.56
Brazil	0.46	0.31	0.60
Pakistan	0.48	0.31	0.66
Morocco	0.49	0.27	0.72
Tunisia	0.51	0.21	0.81
China	0.53	0.33	0.73
India	0.55	0.22	0.87
Chile	0.56	0.22	0.89
Côte d'Ivoire	0.58	0.34	0.82
Russia	0.59	0.27	0.91
Kazakhstan	0.62	0.30	0.95
Summary statistics			
Mean	0.39	0.26	0.13
Standard Deviation	0.30	0.20	0.10
Minimum	0.01	0.03	0.01
Maximum	0.62	0.34	0.95

Source: IMF (1999).

References

Ahluwalia, Montek S., 2002a, "India's Vulnerability to External Crises: An Assessment," in *Macroeconomics and Monetary Policy: Issues for a Reforming Economy*, ed. by Montek S. Ahluwalia, Y.V. Reddy, and S.S. Tarapore (New Delhi: Oxford University Press).

————, 2002b, "Economic Reforms in India Since 1991: Has Gradualism Worked?" *Journal of Economic Perspectives*, Vol. 16, No. 3, pp. 67–88.

Anderson, Jonathan, 2005, "Capital Account Controls and Liberalization: Lessons for India and China," in *India's and China's Recent Experience with Reform and Growth*, ed. by Wanda S. Tseng and David Cowen (Basingstoke: Palgrave Macmillan).

Barth, James, G. Caprio, and Ross Levine, 2001, "Banking Systems Around the Globe: Do Regulation and Ownership Affect Performance and Stability?" in *Prudential Supervision: What Works and What Doesn't*, ed. by Frederic S. Mishkin (Chicago: University of Chicago Press).

Bhagwati, Jagdish N., 1998, "The Capital Myth: The Difference Between Trade in Widgets and Dollars," *Foreign Affairs*, Vol. 77 (May/June), pp. 7–12.

Bhalla, Surjit S., 1999, "Eureka: Capital Account Convertibility and the Law of Flotation," in *India: A Financial Sector for the Twenty-First Century*, ed. by James A. Hanson and Sanjay Kathuria (New Delhi: Oxford University Press).

Diaz-Alejandro, F. Carlos., 1985, "Good-Bye Financial Repression, Hello Financial Crash," *Journal of Development Economics*, Vol. 19, pp. 1–24.

Financial Stability Forum, 2000, "Report of the Working Group on Capital Flows: Meeting of the Financial Stability Forum, March 25–26" (Washington).

Gourinchas, Pierre-Olivier, and Olivier Jeanne, 2006, "The Elusive Gains from International Financial Integration," *Review of Economic Studies* (forthcoming). Available via the Internet: http://www.restud.com/PDF/01_2006/9687_3_paper_text.pdf

Haberler, Gottfried, 1954, *Currency Convertibility* (Washington: American Enterprise Institute).

Hanson, James A., 1994, "An Open Capital Account: A Brief Survey of the Issues and the Results," in *Financial Reforms: Theory and Experience*, ed. by Gerard Caprio, Izak Atiyas, and James A. Hanson (New York: Cambridge University Press).

International Monetary Fund, 1999, "Exchange Rate Arrangements and Currency Convertibility: Developments and Issues." Available via the Internet: http://www.imf.org/external/pubs/cat/longres.cfm?sk=3215.0.

Jadhav, Narendra, 2005, "Capital Account Liberalization: The Indian Experience," in *India's and China's Recent Experience with Reform and Growth*, ed. by Wanda S. Tseng and David Cowen (Basingstoke: Palgrave Macmillan).

Joshi, Vijay, 2003, "India and the Impossible Trinity," *The World Economy*, Vol. 26, No. 4, pp. 555–83.

————, and Sanjeev Sanyal, 2004, "Foreign Inflows and Macroeconomic Policy in India," in *India Policy Forum 2004 (Volume 1)*, ed. by Suman Bery, Barry

Bosworth, and Arvind Panagariya (New Delhi: National Council of Applied Economic Reasearch; and Washington: Brookings Institution).

Kim, Woochan, 2001, "Does Capital Account Liberalization Discipline Budget Deficit?" (unpublished; Cambridge, Massachusetts: Harvard University).

Kletzer, Kenneth M., 2004, "Liberalizing Capital Flows in India: Financial Repression, Macroeconomic Policy, and Gradual Reforms," in *India Policy Forum 2004 (Volume 1)*, ed. by Suman Bery, Barry Bosworth, and Arvind Panagariya (New Delhi: National Council of Applied Economic Reasearch; and Washington: Brookings Institution).

Krueger, Anne O., 2004, "An Intolerable Surge," address to the National Institute for Bank Management, Pune, India, January 21.

Krugman, Paul, 1979, "A Model of Balance of Payment Crises," *Journal of Money, Credit and Banking*, Vol. 11, pp. 311–25.

Lal, Deepak, Suman Bery, and Devendra Pant, 2003, "The Real Exchange Rate, Fiscal Deficits, and Capital Flows: India, 1981–2000," *Economic and Political Weekly*, Vol. 38, No. 47, pp. 4965–76.

Levine, Ross, and Sara J. Zervos, 1998, "Capital Control Liberalization and Stock Market Development," *World Development*, Vol. 26, pp. 1169–83.

Mathieson, Donald J., and Lilliana Rojas-Suárez, 1993, *Liberalization of the Capital Account: Experience and Issues*, IMF Occasional Paper No. 103 (Washington: International Monetary Fund).

Mohan, Rakesh, and Anantakrishnan Prasad, 2005, "India's Experience with Financial Sector Development," in *India's Financial Sector: Recent Reforms, Future Challenges*, ed. by Priya Basu (New Delhi: Macmillan).

Obstfeld, Maurice, 1986, "Rational and Self-Fulfilling Balance-of-Payments Crises," *American Economic Review*, Vol. 76, No. 1, pp. 72–81.

———, 1994, "Risk Sharing, Global Diversification, and Growth," *American Economic Review*, Vol. 84, No. 5, pp. 1310–29.

Panagariya, Arvind, 1998, "Full Convertibility: Must We Have It?" *Economic Times*, October 26 (New Delhi).

Patnaik, Ila, 2004, "India's Experience with a Pegged Exchange Rate," in *India Policy Forum 2004 (Volume 1)*, ed. by Suman Bery, Barry Bosworth, and Arvind Panagariya (New Delhi: National Council of Applied Economic Research; and Washington: Brookings Institution).

Pesenti, Paolo, 2001, "Domestic Bank Regulation and Financial Crises: Theory and Empirical Evidence from East Asia: Comment" (New York: Federal Reserve Bank of New York and National Bureau of Economic Research).

Prasad, Eswar, Kenneth Rogoff, Shang-Jin Wei, and Ayhan M. Kose, 2005, "Effects of Financial Globalization on Developing Countries: Some Empirical Evidence," in *India's and China's Recent Experience with Reform and Growth*, ed. by Wanda S. Tseng and David Cowen (Basingstoke: Palgrave Macmillan).

Quirk, Peter J., and Owen Evans, 1995, *Capital Account Convertibility: Review of Experience and Implications for IMF Policies*, IMF Occasional Paper No. 131 (Washington: International Monetary Fund).

Reserve Bank of India (RBI), 1985, *Report of the Committee to Review the Working of the Monetary System (Chairman, S. Chakravarty)* (Mumbai).

———, 1997, *Report of the Committee on Capital Account Convertibility (Chairman, S.S. Tarapore)* (Mumbai).

———, 1998, "Report of the Committee On Banking Sector Reforms—A Summary," *Reserve Bank of India Bulletin*, July, pp. 561–80.

———, 2004, *Report on Trend and Progress of Banking in India* (Mumbai).

———, 2005a, *Annual Report* (Mumbai).

———, 2005b, *Report on Currency and Finance 2004–05* (Mumbai).

Reddy, Y.V., 1999, "Financial Sector Reform: Review and Prospects," *Reserve Bank of India Bulletin*, Vol. LIII, No. 1, pp. 33–94.

———, 2002, "India's Foreign Exchange Reserves: Policy, Status and Issues," *Reserve Bank of India Bulletin* (July), pp. 433–51.

Rodrik, Dani, 1998, "Who Needs Capital-Account Convertibility?" Available via the Internet: http://ksghome.harvard.edu/~drodrik/essay.PDF.

Singh, Kanhaiya, and Suman Bery, 2005, "India's Growth Experience," in *India's and China's Recent Experience with Reform and Growth*, ed. by Wanda S. Tseng and David Cowen (Basingstoke: Palgrave Macmillan).

Singh, Manmohan, 2006, speech on the occasion of the release of the "Third Volume of the History of the Reserve Bank of India," Mumbai.

Vanassche, Ellen, 2004, "The Impact of International Financial Integration on Industry Growth," lecture delivered at the Center for Financial Studies, Frankfurt. Available via the Internet: http://www.econ.kuleuven.be/CES/discussionpapers/DPS04/Dps0412.pdf.

World Bank, 2001, *Finance For Growth: Policy Choices in a Volatile World* (Washington).

8

Putting the Cart Before the Horse? Capital Account Liberalization and Exchange Rate Flexibility in China

Eswar Prasad, Thomas Rumbaugh, and Qing Wang*

L ike their counterparts in many other emerging market economies, Chinese policymakers are facing a complex set of questions related to the desirability and appropriate mode of implementing exchange rate flexibility and capital account liberalization. The Chinese authorities have stated publicly that both exchange rate flexibility and capital account convertibility are their medium-term objectives, but they have resisted recent calls from the international community for an early move toward more flexibility.

The issue has come to the fore in the context of discussions about the appropriateness of maintaining the current exchange rate regime—wherein the renminbi is effectively linked to the U.S. dollar—given the rapid pace of China's reserve accumulation. Many observers have interpreted this surge in reserve accumulation over the past two years, which has reflected a rapid expansion of China's exports as well as large inflows

*Eswar Prasad was Chief of the China Division in the IMF's Asia and Pacific Department (APD) when this paper was written. He is currently Chief of the Financial Studies Division in the IMF's Research Department. Thomas Rumbaugh was Deputy Chief of the China Division when this paper was written. He is now an Advisor in APD. Qing Wang was an Economist in the China Division when this paper was written. He is now with the Bank of America. We are grateful to Ray Brooks, Steven Dunaway, Gauti Eggertsson, Cem Karacadag, and numerous other colleagues for their helpful comments and advice. The analysis in this paper draws extensively upon work by other members of the IMF's China team, whose input and suggestions we gratefully acknowledge.

of foreign direct investment (FDI), as clear evidence of undervaluation of the renminbi. However, it also reflects large speculative capital inflows, suggesting that the evidence on whether the renminbi is substantially undervalued in terms of fundamentals is far from conclusive.[1] A more important reason for recommending exchange rate flexibility is that it is in China's own interest. As its economy matures and becomes closely integrated with the global economy, China will inevitably become more exposed to different types of macroeconomic shocks, both internal and external. It would therefore benefit from having some flexibility in the exchange rate and, by extension, a more independent monetary policy to help the economy better adjust to such shocks. Thus, a strong argument can be made for an early move toward greater exchange rate flexibility in China, irrespective of whether or not the renminbi is substantially undervalued. A corollary to this argument is that it is a move toward flexibility rather than a revaluation of the rate that is desirable.[2] As experiences of other countries have shown, rapid economic growth and a strong external position constitute relatively favorable circumstances for making such a move.

An interesting point in this public discussion is that the Chinese authorities as well as a number of observers on both sides of the exchange rate flexibility debate have conflated the issue of exchange rate flexibility with that of capital account liberalization.[3] One of the main points of this

---

[1]On the one hand, IMF (2004) and Funke and Rahn (2005) conclude that there is no strong evidence that the renminbi is substantially undervalued. Goldstein (2004) and Frankel (2004), on the other hand, argue that the renminbi is undervalued by at least 30–35 percent. Market analysts have a similarly diverse range of views. The role of speculative capital inflows in accounting for pressures on China's exchange rate appears to have increased substantially since 2001. For instance, about half of the increase in international reserves in 2003 can be accounted for by non-FDI capital inflows (for more details, see IMF, 2004; and Prasad and Wei, 2005).

[2]See Prasad (2004b) for a further discussion of this point. Goldstein and Lardy (2003) argue for a two-step approach to exchange rate reform in China—a revaluation followed by a widening of the trading band. At the other end of the spectrum, the most prominent proponents of the view that China should not alter its current exchange rate regime include McKinnon and Schnabl (2003) and Mundell (2003).

[3]To cite a prominent example, Alan Greenspan has been quoted as saying that, "Many in China fear that removal of capital controls that restrict the ability of domestic investors to invest abroad and to sell or to purchase foreign currency—which is a necessary step to allow a currency to float freely—could cause an outflow of deposits from Chinese banks, destabilizing the system" (Ip, 2004). News reports interpreted his statement as indicating "...that before floating its exchange rate China should fix its banking system" (Ip, 2004). Standard & Poor's has also said, in their evaluations of China, that "risk control systems are ill prepared to deal with rapid liberalization of the exchange rate and capital controls," suggesting that the two issues are linked (S&P, 2003).

paper is that these are related, but distinct, issues. They do not necessarily have to be implemented simultaneously, and neither one necessarily implies the other.

The juxtaposition of these issues appears to have come about in the context of the notion that exchange rate flexibility could pose major problems for the financial sector. Indeed, a number of observers—and the Chinese authorities themselves—have argued that the weaknesses in China's banking system are a reason to defer making a move toward greater exchange rate flexibility. The logic appears to be that such flexibility could expose the financial system's vulnerabilities by facilitating outflows from the banking system as domestic economic agents take advantage of investment opportunities abroad.

We argue that with existing capital controls in place—even if these are somewhat porous—the banking system is unlikely to be subject to substantial stress simply as a result of greater exchange rate flexibility. Domestic banks do not have a large net exposure to currency risk, and exchange rate flexibility by itself is unlikely to create strong incentives (or channels) to take deposits out of the Chinese banking system. Furthermore, the introduction of greater flexibility would create stronger incentives for developing the foreign exchange market and for currency risk management, including developing the hedging instruments and forward markets that are currently absent. In this way, the introduction of exchange rate flexibility could, in fact, facilitate capital account liberalization by better preparing the economy to deal with the impact of increased capital flows.

Capital controls do, however, tend to become less effective over time. Expanding trade and the increasing sophistication of domestic and international investors invariably generate new ways to get around capital controls. In addition, the experiences of numerous emerging market countries have shown the risks associated with maintaining a fixed exchange rate in tandem with a capital account that is open in either de jure or de facto terms, especially if there are weaknesses in the domestic financial system. Thus, the authorities' recent efforts to gradually liberalize capital outflows in the context of the current exchange rate regime could well prove counterproductive. Moreover, these factors suggest that delaying a move toward greater exchange flexibility could precipitate the need for an adjustment in the future under far less desirable circumstances.

At the same time, given the weaknesses in China's banking system, a cautious and gradual approach to capital account liberalization would, indeed, be appropriate. There are substantial risks associated with exposure to capital flows in the absence of sufficient institutional development, especially in the financial sector. The liberalization of capital flows should be sequenced in a manner that reinforces domestic financial liberalization and allows for institutional capacity building to manage the additional risks. A more stable financial system and experience over time with greater flexibility in the exchange rate should, in fact, be regarded as prerequisites to fully opening the capital account.[4]

But what does it mean to have exchange rate flexibility if the country's currency is not convertible on the capital account? The exchange rate can still be allowed to fluctuate in response to the evolution of supply and demand for foreign exchange, even though there may be constraints on capital flows. A move toward more flexibility also does not necessarily mean immediate adoption of a free float.[5] In fact, a period of "learning to float" can be advisable to overcome "fear of floating," a term used to characterize policymakers' initial aversion, upon exiting a fixed exchange rate regime, to allow the nominal exchange rate to move significantly. At the same time, the maintenance of capital controls can, to some degree, support this process by providing protection from potential instability arising from capital flows while institutional arrangements needed to support capital account convertibility are allowed to develop.

The remainder of this paper develops the case for two key points: that a move toward greater exchange rate flexibility is in China's own interest and that it should precede capital account liberalization (Eichengreen, 2004, reaches similar conclusions). It does not deal with a whole host of related (and equally important) issues, including how the move toward greater exchange rate flexibility should be managed, what the best alternative exchange rate regime would be, what form an alternative monetary anchor could take, or how much financial sector and institutional development is adequate to minimize the risks of capital account liberalization.

The Case for Exchange Rate Flexibility

With China's increasing integration into the global economy, its exposure to external shocks has increased. This has heightened the need for an autonomous monetary policy and greater use of market-oriented instruments such as interest rate changes to control economic activity. Indeed, the constraints on the use of such instruments have been highlighted by

---

[4]Yu (2004) has argued that it would be optimal for gradual capital account liberalization and moves toward greater exchange rate flexibility to proceed simultaneously.

[5]IMF (2004) notes that an initial move toward flexibility could take the form of a widening of the renminbi trading band, a peg to a currency basket, or some combination of these.

the capital inflows since 2001 that have increased liquidity in the banking system and complicated domestic monetary management. During this period, rapid growth of bank credit has contributed to a surge in investment growth, leading to the possible buildup of excess capacity and associated nonperforming loans in several sectors of the economy, as well as potential problems of more generalized overheating. Increases in interest rates to control these problems have perforce been limited by the increased incentives for capital inflows that would result.

In this context, it is worth reiterating that the Chinese authorities themselves have clearly articulated the desirability of having a more flexible exchange rate and independent monetary policy; the main focus of the recent debate has been about the appropriate timing for such a move. It is useful to set the stage for the case for an early move to flexibility by reviewing the economic concerns that could be inhibiting it.

Concerns About Greater Exchange Rate Flexibility

China's export growth is widely regarded as playing an important role in catalyzing overall economic and employment growth. Thus, a key concern about allowing more flexibility is that an appreciation of the renminbi could hurt China's external competitiveness, thereby reducing export growth and weakening prospects for continued FDI inflows (see Mundell, 2003). However, the direct impact on exports of a moderate appreciation of the exchange rate is likely to be considerably muted by the high import content of China's exports, as well as China's strong productivity growth and low labor costs. Indeed, during the period 1999–2002, China's total exports (in value terms) rose by 37 percent despite a 7 percent real effective appreciation. Trade data show that more than 50 percent of Chinese export operations involve the final assembly of products using intermediate inputs produced by other countries. Despite the high gross value of Chinese exports, the domestic value-added content of these exports to the rest of the world in general, and to the United States in particular, is only about 30 percent and 20 percent, respectively (Lau, 2003). An appreciation of the renminbi, while raising the cost of processing and assembly in China, would also lower the cost of imported intermediate inputs. Hence, an appreciation of the renminbi may not put much of a dent in China's external competitiveness.[6]

---

[6]Anderson (2004) makes a similar point. Lau (2003) estimates that a 10 percent real appreciation of the renminbi would increase the cost of Chinese exports to the United States by only about 2 percent.

Another concern is that an exchange rate appreciation could adversely affect the agricultural sector. There is believed to be a large amount of surplus labor in the rural areas—about 150 million workers by the Chinese authorities' own estimates. This, in conjunction with the notion that the Chinese agricultural sector is not internationally competitive, has raised considerable concerns among policymakers that a fall in domestic prices of food imports that would result from an appreciation of the renminbi could have significant adverse consequences. Although this is a plausible and relevant concern, there is as yet little empirical evidence to support it. In addition, recent research suggests that the competitiveness of China's agricultural sector has improved significantly in recent years, making it less sensitive to external shocks (see Rosen, Rozelle, and Huang, 2004).[7]

As noted earlier, a greater concern is that exchange rate flexibility could imperil the health of the banking system. Indeed, this is a typical problem in countries in which a devaluation imposes a large burden on firms and banks that have large amounts of debt denominated in foreign currencies. The situation in China is of course quite the opposite because current pressures are for an appreciation, but the fact that domestic banks have a positive net foreign asset position implies that there could still be costs to the banking sector.

The current overall exposure of the corporate sector and banks in China to foreign exchange risks appears to be low; however, there are some indications that the degree of exposure has been on the rise in recent years. In 2003, banks' net foreign assets accounted for 3 percent of broad money and 6 percent of GDP, and foreign currency lending constituted about 5 percent of domestic credit and 9 percent of GDP. These indicators seem relatively innocuous when compared with those of other countries. Their recent evolution, however, points to a trend that bears watching closely: during 2001–03, banks' foreign currency loans to domestic residents have increased by more than 60 percent, net foreign currency liabilities are up by nearly 50 percent, and total short-term external debt (which is denominated in foreign currencies) has risen by more than 50 percent. These are trends that are likely to continue with China's increasing global integration and the opening of the financial system as part of the terms of World Trade Organization (WTO) accession.

There are some caveats to be borne in mind in interpreting the aggregate figures discussed above. Detailed information on exposures of large

---

[7]This study notes that, contrary to expectations, the agricultural sector was able to cope quite well with the opening up of China's agricultural markets that resulted from WTO accession commitments.

financial institutions, including the currency composition and maturity of foreign currency assets and liabilities, would have to be analyzed to determine the exposure of specific institutions and any possible systemic spillovers that could result from the effects of an exchange rate appreciation on any of these institutions. Moreover, there is currently little information available on hedging practices in the corporate sector. Anecdotal evidence suggests that the use of hedging instruments is limited; however, other forms of hedging—particularly "natural" hedges (for example, denomination of processing imports and related exports in the same currency)—may be more prevalent.

A more general concern is that nominal exchange rate volatility under a more flexible exchange rate regime could affect trade flows and FDI inflows, both of which have been important to China's growth. On the former, recent studies find little evidence that exchange rate volatility has a significant adverse effect on trade flows (see Clark, Tamirisa, and Wei, 2004). It is also worth noting that, by maintaining an effective peg to the dollar, China's currency is stable relative to its major trading partner—the United States—but it still fluctuates relative to most of China's other trading partners. This does not appear to have hurt China's trade expansion in other industrial country markets.

There is also little evidence in the literature that exchange rate volatility has a significant role in determining the level of FDI a country receives. The most important factors affecting FDI include market size, GDP growth, productivity growth, political and macroeconomic stability, the regulatory environment, and the ability to repatriate profits (Lim, 2001). Nevertheless, some recent papers have suggested that China's maintenance of an undervalued exchange rate is crucial for its ability to attract strong FDI inflows.[8] Our view is that, given China's strong productivity growth, increasing access to world markets, and rapidly expanding domestic demand, there is little reason to believe that an exchange rate appreciation would have a substantial negative effect on FDI inflows. Indeed, the prospects of greater macroeconomic stability that could result from exchange rate flexibility could well offset any negative effects from an appreciation.

In summary, our assessment is that the net adverse effects on the Chinese economy of any appreciation in the renminbi resulting from a move toward greater flexibility would be quite modest. There could,

---

[8]For instance, this is implicitly suggested by the work of Dooley, Folkerts-Landau, and Garber (2004), although it is not their central thesis.

however, be significant distributional effects, with some sectors such as agriculture potentially facing larger adjustment costs.

All of these potential costs would, in any case, depend on the persistence of any appreciation of the currency. Under current circumstances, a near-term appreciation of the renminbi is widely regarded as a sure thing. Over the medium term, however, the trend in the real exchange rate is much harder to predict because it will depend on a number of additional factors with potentially offsetting effects. Forces for appreciation include the continuing strong productivity growth in China's traded goods sector, aided by structural reforms and further improvement in access to world markets. Forces for depreciation include the further liberalization of China's domestic market that will take place as part of WTO accession commitments, and the expected gradual liberalization of the capital account, which could lead to more outflows if domestic agents sought to undertake some international diversification of their portfolios. Moreover, as noted earlier, recent upward pressure on the exchange rate reflects strong capital inflows that in large part appear to be driven by speculative inflows in anticipation of a currency appreciation. Such inflows are likely to be transitory and could easily reverse. Thus, it is far from obvious that greater flexibility will result in a persistent appreciation of the renminbi.

The Potential Costs of Not Having Exchange Rate Flexibility

We now turn to a discussion of the costs of delaying a move toward exchange rate flexibility. In this context, it is first worth reviewing why countries adopt fixed exchange rate systems in the first place. A crucial consideration for developing economies is that such regimes provide a well-defined nominal anchor and, in principle, impose discipline on macroeconomic policies. This discipline can be useful for countries with institutional and policy weaknesses that tend to manifest themselves in higher inflation, problems of debt sustainability, fragile banking systems, and other sources of macro volatility. Empirical studies have shown that fixed or relatively rigid exchange rate regimes have indeed provided some benefits in terms of macroeconomic stability, especially to low-income countries where financial market development is limited and the capital market closed (see, for example, Rogoff and others, 2004). But these benefits tend to erode over time whereas exchange rate flexibility becomes more valuable as economies mature and become integrated with global markets.

In fact, maintenance of a fixed exchange rate regime can often mask underlying policy and institutional weaknesses and result in the buildup of various sorts of imbalances. These problems can be exacerbated by an open capital account. For instance, governments may accumulate external debt in order to get around constraints to domestic financing of budget deficits. Domestic firms and financial institutions may also react to the perception of limited foreign exchange risk by taking on foreign currency debt. Given the relative riskiness of lending to emerging markets as perceived by international investors, much of this debt tends to be short term. The presence of large amounts of short-term external debt denominated in foreign currencies is now widely recognized as being a key risk factor in precipitating balance of payments crises.

In addition to these general considerations, the particular circumstances that China faces also generate some specific costs of maintaining a fixed exchange rate. The sterilization of capital inflows has been facilitated by the fact that domestic interest rates related to the main sterilization instrument (central bank bills) have been lower than interest rates on medium- and long-term industrial country treasury bonds, which is where much of China's reserves are presumed to be held. Thus, the traditional net costs of sterilization are absent in this case. However, maintaining such low domestic interest rates, which have recently been negative in real terms, requires domestic financial repression, which in turn creates large distortions and efficiency losses (see Prasad and Rajan, 2005a).

Moreover, the depreciation of the U.S. dollar since 2003 suggests that the terms of trade for China have worsened. This effectively acts as an implicit tax on consumption and, although such costs are difficult to detect directly, they are likely to be significant in terms of potential welfare losses, especially in view of China's high level of trade openness.

Furthermore, if fundamental factors such as relative productivity growth create persistent pressures for real exchange appreciation, these pressures eventually tend to force adjustment through one channel or another. Even in an economy with capital controls and a repressed domestic financial sector, these pressures can be bottled up for only so long (Rajan and Subramanian, 2004). It is typically better to allow the required adjustment to take place through changes in the nominal exchange rate rather than through inflation. Particularly in a developing economy, such inflationary dynamics can pose serious risks because expectations of rising inflation can feed on themselves and become entrenched.

For an independent monetary policy (with exchange rate flexibility) to be most effective, further institutional and operational improvements would be needed to establish a credible monetary policy framework and improve the monetary policy transmission mechanism. However, the movement toward an independent monetary policy regime should not be delayed. Although it may indeed be possible to maintain China's present exchange rate regime for a long period, the explicit and implicit costs of maintaining this regime are potentially large and likely to grow over time, especially in view of China's increasing integration with global markets and the authorities' stated objective to gradually liberalize the capital account.

Capital Account Liberalization

Benefits and Risks in Theory and Practice

The financial crises experienced by many emerging markets in the past two decades have led to an intense debate about the benefits and risks of capital account liberalization for developing countries. In theory, capital account liberalization should have unambiguous benefits in terms of promoting more efficient international allocation of capital, boosting growth in developing countries through a variety of channels, and allowing countries to reduce their consumption volatility by offering opportunities for sharing income risk. The reality, however, is far more sobering. There is little conclusive evidence of a strong and robust causal relationship between financial integration and growth. Moreover, there is evidence that financial integration could actually increase the relative volatility of consumption growth for emerging markets (see Prasad and others, 2003).

Opening the capital account while maintaining an inflexible exchange rate regime, especially when domestic macroeconomic policies are not consistent with the requirements of the regime, has proven to be a precursor of crisis in many countries. Recent episodes involving emerging market economies, from the "tequila crisis" of 1995 through the Asian, Russian, and Brazilian crises of 1997–98, have added to the evidence that a fixed exchange rate regime with an open capital account provides a fertile ground for crises. By contrast, emerging market economies that maintained greater flexibility in their exchange rate regimes have generally fared much better when faced with external pressures. For example, Chile, Mexico, Peru, South Africa, and Turkey all seem to have benefited from the flexibility of their exchange rates during periods of instability in emerging markets. China and India were less affected by the Asian crisis of 1997–98, and their relatively closed capital account regimes have been credited with helping to limit vulnerability to financial contagion, although other factors may have played a role as well, including comfortable foreign reserves positions (see Krugman, 1998; and Fernald and Babson, 1999).

As noted earlier, capital account liberalization can also aggravate risks associated with imprudent fiscal policies. Moreover, in the presence of weak and inadequately supervised banking systems and other distortions in domestic capital markets, inflows of foreign capital could be misallocated and create a host of problems, including currency, maturity, and duration mismatches on the balance sheets of financial and corporate sectors, as well as unsustainable levels and maturity structures of external debt (Ishii and Habermeier, 2002).

All of this suggests that China would do well to adopt a cautious approach to capital account liberalization. Indeed, China's approach of opening up to FDI rather than other types of capital inflows has helped insulate it from many of the risks associated with capital account liberalization. But, as discussed below, the dominance of FDI in China's total capital inflows has declined markedly in recent years, implying that the composition of inflows is likely to be increasingly driven by market forces rather than the desires of policymakers.[9]

Capital Controls and Their Inevitable Erosion Over Time

Growing awareness about the potential pitfalls of capital account liberalization has refocused attention on the usefulness of capital controls in managing the process of integration with the global economy. Capital controls do provide a degree of protection from the vagaries of international capital flows and can help control the risks posed by a weak financial sector. However, they can often perpetuate inefficiencies and distortions in domestic financial systems, with consequences for long-term growth and stability.

In countries with weak financial systems, capital controls can prevent the corporate sector as well as domestic banks—whose operations may not entirely be run on a commercial basis and that may have inadequate risk assessment capacity—from excessive external borrowing. In countries with an inflexible exchange rate regime, capital controls are also used to preserve a degree of monetary policy autonomy. Some countries resort to capital controls to reduce both exchange rate volatility generated by swings in short-run capital flows as well as exposure to balance of payments crises. At the same time, capital controls can also support policies of domestic financial repression that can be used to ensure that domestic

---

[9]Prasad and Wei (2005) document changes over time in the relative importance of FDI in China's total capital inflows and discuss various hypotheses about why China's inflows have been largely tilted toward FDI.

savings are used to finance the government budget and sectors deemed as priorities by policymakers.

In practice, capital controls tend to be far from watertight. A number of channels can be used to evade capital controls. One of the most frequently used channels has been under- and over-invoicing of export and import contracts (Gulati, 1987; Kamin, 1988; and Patnaik and Vasudevan, 2000). Multinational companies can also use transfer pricing schemes to evade capital controls. Another trade-related channel for unrecorded capital flows is associated with the leads and lags in the settlement of commercial transactions or variation in the terms offered on short-term trade credits. Remittances of savings by foreign workers in the domestic economy and by domestic nationals working abroad, family remittances, and tourist expenditures—although typically regarded as current account transactions—have also been used as vehicles for the acquisition or repatriation of foreign assets.

There is by now considerable evidence that the effectiveness of capital controls tends to diminish over time, especially when strong exchange rate pressures are resisted by official intervention. Japan's experience in the wake of the collapse of Bretton Woods system in the 1970s and the experiences of Latin American countries during the debt crisis of the 1980s demonstrate that capital controls have generally not been very effective in restricting capital outflows (inflows) when there is strong downward (upward) pressure on the exchange rate.

Capital controls in China are extensive and appear to have been reasonably effective in the past. However, recent experience suggests that their efficiency may be waning. It is widely cited that China's capital controls were one reason the country withstood the Asian financial crisis (for example, Gruenwald and Aziz, 2003), but it should be noted that the capital flight from China during the Asian crisis was triggered by external shocks, whereas public confidence in the domestic financial system remained basically intact. In this sense, China's capital controls have not really been tested in a crisis context.

Despite the existence of controls on capital outflows, sizable amounts of financial capital still appear to have flown out of China during the Asian crisis and its aftermath.[10] Since 2001, expectations of an appreciation of the renminbi, coupled with a positive Chinese-U.S. interest differen-

---

[10]Gunter (2004) estimates that capital flight from China exceeded US$100 billion a year during 1997–2000. He also notes that, during this period, stricter controls on cross-border currency and investment flows were largely offset by increasing use of trade mis-invoicing.

tial, have resulted in substantial net inflows of non-FDI capital despite the extensive controls on non-FDI inflows (see Prasad and Wei, 2005). Moreover, these expectations have also been reflected in recorded capital account transactions. Foreign currency loans from domestic banks to residents increased by almost 30 percent during 2003, whereas residents' foreign currency deposits declined slightly. At the same time, anecdotal evidence of early collection of export receipts and increased use of trade credit for imports are also consistent with general expectations of an appreciation of the renminbi.

These experiences, corroborated by more formal empirical work (for example, Cheung, Chinn, and Fujii, 2003), suggest that the capital controls have become less effective over time, increasingly limiting the room for an independent monetary policy. China's continued rapid trade expansion also creates a growing scope for getting around capital account restrictions. As China becomes increasingly integrated into the global economy in the context of its WTO accession, with commitments to further liberalization of trade and the opening up of the financial sector, its capital controls are likely to become even more porous.

The Foreign Exchange Market

Some commentators have argued that the absence of a well-functioning foreign exchange market will inhibit any move toward greater exchange rate flexibility. Furthermore, it has been argued that, so long as controls on capital account transactions are in place, there will not be a fully functioning foreign exchange market in China, because much of the potential demand for foreign exchange in China is still excluded from the market (for example, Lau, 2003). The latter is a valid point. However, although liberalizing the capital account can expand the sources and uses of foreign exchange, an open capital account is not a necessary condition for deepening the foreign exchange market. Because China has a large volume of trade transactions and few restrictions on convertibility on current account transactions, there is clearly potential for a deep and well-functioning foreign exchange market even without a fully open capital account.[11]

---

[11]Duttagupta, Fernandez, and Karacadag (2004) also discuss the potential to develop the foreign exchange market in these circumstances and show that it is difficult to establish a strong positive relationship between capital account liberalization and depth of foreign exchange markets.

Furthermore, the notion of needing to first perfect the foreign exchange market before moving toward greater flexibility is, in our view, a red herring. In fact, the functioning of the foreign exchange market can be greatly improved even within the context of the present exchange rate regime.[12] A phased approach toward flexibility should not pose any major risks even if existing financial instruments to hedge foreign exchange risks are limited, and would give economic agents stronger incentives to hedge foreign exchange risks that have so far been borne entirely by the monetary authorities. This would itself be an important factor nurturing the development of a deeper and more sophisticated foreign exchange market.

Considerations of Timing

International experiences have varied considerably in terms of the order in which countries have adopted policies to open up to global integration. Some countries have liberalized capital flows without exchange rate flexibility—an approach that entails considerable risks if financial markets are not sufficiently developed—whereas others have introduced exchange rate flexibility well in advance of capital account liberalization. In general, countries appear to have better medium-term outcomes if they introduce exchange rate flexibility before fully liberalizing their capital account, especially if there are weaknesses in the financial sector.[13]

The Chinese authorities have attempted to alleviate recent appreciation pressures by easing controls on capital as well as current account transactions in order to provide more channels for capital outflows.[14] These measures, although broadly in the direction of the authorities' long-term objective of full capital account convertibility, run the risk of getting the sequencing wrong. As discussed above, an increasingly open capital account without exchange rate flexibility has been the root cause of many recent emerging market financial crises.

---

[12]For instance, allowing enterprises access to the China Foreign Exchange Trading System through a licensed broker system would increase trading volume and reduce the dominant role of official intervention in the market. Even within a narrow band of a de facto peg, relaxing bid-offer spreads could encourage participants to take positions on both sides. Foreign exchange surrender requirements could also be further reduced. Easing the requirement that enterprises need "real commercial demand" to enter forward contracts would allow them to hedge based on future needs (see Lin, 2004; Luo, 2004; and Ma, 2004).

[13]Selected international experiences are discussed in Annex I of the fuller version of this paper (Prasad and Rajan, 2005b). India is one example of a country that has recently introduced some exchange rate flexibility while only gradually easing capital account restrictions.

[14]See Annex II of Prasad and Rajan (2005b) for a detailed description of recent measures taken to ease restrictions on cross-border foreign exchange transactions.

Moreover, easing controls on capital outflows may end up being counter-productive because this could stimulate further inflows. The removal of controls on outflows, by making it easier to take capital out of a country when desired, tends to make investors more willing to invest in a country (Labán and Larraín, 1993). In addition, to the extent that an easing of controls on outflows is perceived as a commitment to sound domestic macroeconomic policies, more capital could be induced to flow in (Bartolini and Drazen, 1997). A number of countries that have removed controls on outflows (for example, Uruguay in 1970, Italy in 1984, New Zealand in 1984, and Spain in 1986) have experienced rapid and massive inflows soon after.

Although capital controls provide some degree of protection to the domestic financial system, these controls are likely to become less effective over time. It would, therefore, be in China's best interest to consider an early move toward exchange rate flexibility, while the existing capital account controls are still relatively effective and the underlying structural problems manageable. The current strength and stability of the economy, together with existing capital account controls, have contributed to a reasonably high level of confidence in the banking system despite its weak financial position. But domestic banks are likely to come under increasing competitive pressure, especially once foreign banks are allowed to enter the Chinese market under WTO accession commitments.

In principle, an orderly exit from a fixed exchange rate regime to greater flexibility can best be accomplished during a period of relative tranquility in exchange markets. Because such periods are rare and fleeting, however, experiences of other countries suggest that a next-best set of circumstances is when the domestic economy is strong and pressures are for an appreciation of the currency (Eichengreen and others, 1998; and Agénor, 2004). Such circumstances provide a useful window of opportunity that should be taken full advantage of. History is replete with examples of countries that, having passed up such opportunities, had to change their exchange rate regimes in far less ideal circumstances and with much less desirable macroeconomic outcomes during the adjustment to the new regime.

Concluding Remarks

China is firmly on the path of greater integration with the global economy—a path that has provided great benefits for China and for the world in general (see Prasad, 2004a). The Chinese authorities clearly intend to continue on this path, undertaking more trade integration and a gradual liberalization of capital controls. In view of these objectives, gaining experience over time with greater flexibility in the exchange rate and achieving a more stable financial system should be prerequisites to fully opening the capital account.

Introducing more flexibility in the exchange rate would help to improve macroeconomic control and reduce vulnerabilities to shocks. Steps toward more flexibility in the exchange rate need not be deferred until all of the prerequisites for full capital account convertibility have been achieved. The exchange rate can be allowed to move in response to the evolution of supply and demand for foreign exchange, even though these forces may be constrained by restrictions on capital flows.

Historical experiences of other countries highlight the risks associated with capital account liberalization in the absence of exchange rate flexibility. Easing controls on capital outflows in order to alleviate pressures on the exchange rate could, in fact, be counterproductive and induce even larger inflows. Thus, capital account liberalization should be given a lower priority and should not be regarded as a substitute for greater exchange rate flexibility.

This paper has also argued that greater flexibility can be introduced without creating disruptions in the financial sector. Maintenance of capital controls can, to some degree, support this process by providing protection from potential instability arising from capital flows while institutional arrangements needed to support capital account convertibility, including a stronger domestic banking sector, are allowed to develop. A movement toward more exchange rate flexibility also does not necessarily mean immediate adoption of a free float. In fact, a period of "learning to float" can be useful in overcoming "fear of floating."

However, capital controls will become increasingly ineffective as integration with the global economy continues. Furthermore, historical experiences of other countries clearly show the merits of making a move toward flexibility when the domestic economy is growing rapidly and the external position is strong. All of these factors lead to the conclusions that a relatively early move toward greater exchange rate flexibility would be in China's best interest and that there could be significant costs associated with long delays in making such a move.

Bibliography

Agénor, Pierre-Richard, 2004, "Orderly Exits from Adjustable Pegs and Exchange Rate Bands: Policy Issues and the Role of Capital Flows," background study for *Global Development Finance 2004* (Washington: World Bank).

Anderson, Jonathan, 2004, "How I Learned to Stop Worrying and Forget the Yuan," *Far Eastern Economic Review*, Vol. 168 (December), pp. 37–42.

Bank for International Settlements (BIS), 2003, "China's Capital Account Liberalisation: International Perspective," BIS Paper No. 15 (Basel).

Bartolini, Leonardo, and Allan Drazen, 1997, "Capital Account Liberalization as a Signal," *American Economic Review*, Vol. 87 (March), pp. 138–54.

Cheung, Yin-Wong, Menzie D. Chinn, and Eiji Fujii, 2003, "The Chinese Economies in Global Context: The Integration Process and Its Determinants," NBER Working Paper No. 10047 (Cambridge, Massachusetts: National Bureau of Economic Research).

Clark, Peter B., Natalia Tamirisa, and Shang-Jin Wei, 2004, *A New Look at Exchange Rate Volatility and Trade Flows*, IMF Occasional Paper No. 235 (Washington: International Monetary Fund).

Dooley, Michael P., David Folkerts-Landau, and Peter Garber, 2004, "Direct Investment, Rising Real Wages and the Absorption of Excess Labor in the Periphery," NBER Working Paper No. 10626 (Cambridge, Massachusetts: National Bureau of Economic Research).

Duttagupta, Rupa, Gilda Fernandez, and Cem Karacadag, 2004, "From Fixed to Float: Operational Aspects of Moving Towards Exchange Rate Flexibility," IMF Working Paper 04/126 (Washington: International Monetary Fund).

Eichengreen, Barry, 2004, "Chinese Currency Controversies," CEPR Discussion Paper No. 4375 (London: Centre for Economic Policy Research).

———, and others, 1998, *Exit Strategies: Policy Options for Countries Seeking Exchange Rate Flexibility*, IMF Occasional Paper No. 168 (Washington: International Monetary Fund).

Fernald, John, and Oliver D. Babson, 1999, "Why Has China Survived the Asian Crisis So Well? What Risks Remain?" International Finance Discussion Paper No. 633 (Washington: Board of Governors of the Federal Reserve System).

Frankel, Jeffrey A., 2004, "On the Renminbi: The Choice between Adjustment under a Fixed Exchange Rate and Adjustment under a Flexible Rate" (unpublished; Cambridge, Massachusetts: Harvard University, Kennedy School of Government). Available via the Internet: http://ksghome.harvard.edu/~jfrankel/On%20the%20Renminbi.pdf

Funke, Michael, and Jörg Rahn, 2005, "Just How Undervalued Is the Chinese Renminbi," *The World Economy*, Vol. 28 (April), pp. 465–90.

Goldstein, Morris, 2004, "Adjusting China's Exchange Rate Policies," Working Paper 04/1 (Washington: Institute for International Economics).

———, and Nicholas Lardy, 2003, "Two-Stage Currency Reform For China," *Asian Wall Street Journal*, September 12.

Gruenwald, Paul, and Jahangir Aziz, 2003, "China and the Asian Crisis," in *China: Competing in the Global Economy*, ed. by W. Tseng and M. Rodlauer (Washington: International Monetary Fund).

Gulati, Sunil, 1987, "A Note on Trade Misinvoicing," in *Capital Flight and Third World Debt*, ed. by D. Lessard and J. Williamson (Washington: Institute for International Economics).

Gunter, Frank R., 2004, "Capital Flight from China: 1984–2001," *China Economic Review*, Vol. 15, No. 1, pp. 63–85.

International Monetary Fund, 2004, "People's Republic of China: Staff Report for the Article IV Consultation" (Washington). Available via the Internet: http://www.imf.org/external/pubs/cat/longres.cfm?sk=17828.0

Ip, Greg, 2004, "The Economy: Greenspan Warns About Yuan Float," *Wall Street Journal*, March 2, p. A2.

Ishii, Shogo, and Karl Habermeier, 2002, *Capital Account Liberalization and Financial Sector Stability*, IMF Occasional Paper No. 211 (Washington: International Monetary Fund).

Kamin, Steven, 1988, "Devaluation, Exchange Controls, and Black Markets for Foreign Exchange in Developing Countries," International Finance Discussion Paper No. 334 (Washington: Board of Governors of the Federal Reserve System).

Krugman, Paul, 1998, "Saving Asia: It's Time to Get Radical," *Fortune* (September).

Labán, Raul, and Felipe Larraín, 1993, "Can a Liberalization of Capital Outflows Increase Net Capital Inflows?" Working Paper No. 155 (Santiago: Pontifica Universidad Catolica de Chile).

Lau, Lawrence, 2003, "Is China Playing By the Rules? Free Trade, Fair Trade, and the WTO," testimony at a hearing of the Congressional-Executive Commission on China, Washington, September 24.

Lim, Ewe-Ghee, 2001, "Determinants of, and the Relation Between, Foreign Direct Investment and Growth: A Summary of the Recent Literature," IMF Working Paper 01/175 (Washington: International Monetary Fund).

Lin, Yuli, 2004, "Welcoming a New Era in the Development of China's FX Market," *China Money*, No. 2 (Shanghai: China Foreign Exchange Trading System). Available via the Internet: http://202.108.40.100/content/online2002/english/finance2.html

Luo, Xi, 2004, "Options and Measures for Further Development of China's FX Market," *China Money*, No. 2 (Shanghai: China Foreign Exchange Trading System). Available via the Internet: http://202.108.40.100/content/online2002/english/finance2.html

Ma, Guonan, 2004, "China's FX Market, An International Perspective," *China Money*, No. 1 (Shanghai: China Foreign Exchange Trading System).

McKinnon, Ronald, and Gunther Schnabl, 2003, "China: A Stabilizing or Deflationary Influence in East Asia? The Problem of Conflicted Virtue." Available via the Internet: http://www.stanford.edu/~mckinnon/papers/China.pdf

Mundell, Robert, 2003, "Globalization and RMB Exchange Rate," presentation at Renmin University of China, Beijing, October 31.

Patnaik, Ila, and Deepa Vasudevan, 2000, "Trade Misinvoicing and Capital Flight from India," *Journal of International Economic Studies*, Vol. 14, pp. 99–108.

Prasad, Eswar, 2004a, *China's Growth and Integration into the World Economy: Prospects and Challenges*, IMF Occasional Paper No. 232 (Washington: International Monetary Fund).

———, ed., 2004b, "Growth and Stability in China: Prospects and Challenges," remarks at the Harvard China Review Annual Conference, Cambridge, Massachusetts, April 17. Available via the Internet: http://www.imf.org/external/np/speeches/2004/041704.htm

———, and Raghuram Rajan, 2005a, "China's Financial-Sector Challenge," *Financial Times* (London), May 10.

———, 2005b, "Controlled Capital Account Liberalization: A Proposal," IMF Policy Discussion Paper No. 05/7 (Washington: International Monetary Fund). Available via the Internet: http://www.imf.org/external/pubs/cat/longres.cfm?sk=18632.0

Prasad, Eswar, Kenneth Rogoff, Shang-Jin Wei, and M. Ayhan Kose, 2003, *Effects of Financial Globalization on Developing Countries: Some Empirical Evidence*, IMF Occasional Paper No. 220 (Washington: International Monetary Fund).

Prasad, Eswar, and Shang-Jin Wei, 2005, "The Chinese Approach to Capital Inflows: Patterns and Possible Explanations," IMF Working Paper 05/79 (Washington: International Monetary Fund). Forthcoming in an NBER volume on capital flows edited by Sebastian Edwards (Chicago: University of Chicago Press).

Rajan, Raghuram, and Arvind Subramanian, 2004, "Exchange Rate Flexibility Is in Asia's Interest," *Financial Times* (London), September 27.

Rogoff, Kenneth, Aasim M. Husain, Ashoka Mody, Robin Brooks, and Nienke Oomes, 2004, *Evolution and Performance of Exchange Rate Regimes*, IMF Occasional Paper No. 229 (Washington: International Monetary Fund).

Rosen, Dan, Scott Rozelle, and Jikun Huang, 2004, *Roots of Competitiveness: China's Evolving Agricultural Interests*, Policy Analyses in International Economics No. 72 (Washington: Institute for International Economics).

Standard & Poor's (S&P), 2003, "Risky Move to Float China's Exchange Rate," September 13.

Yu, Yongding, 2004, "China's Capital Flow Liberalization and Reform of Exchange Rate Regime" (unpublished; Beijing: Chinese Academy of Social Sciences).

PART IV

OTHER POLICIES FOR SUSTAINING GROWTH

9

Some Apparent Puzzles for Contemporary Monetary Policy

Rakesh Mohan*

I feel very honored to have been invited to deliver this dinner address to this distinguished audience. We have had a long day of intensive discussions centered on issues related to the Indian and Chinese economies. I thought that, given the timing of this address and the fact that we have experts present here on both these economies, it would be more advisable to talk about some general issues that are engaging economic and monetary policymakers today all over the world. This is perhaps safer since there are no clear answers and hence one is free to speculate!

We are living in interesting times. Oil prices have been rising at a fast pace over the past two years. The IMF, in September 2004, had used an implicit projection of oil prices at US$37.25 per barrel in 2004. Now, however, the forecast for international crude prices—which could pose the biggest risk to global growth—has been revised upward by 20.5 percent from the April 2005 projections, and the projection for growth in world

*Keynote address by the Deputy Governor, Reserve Bank of India, at the conference, "China's and India's Changing Economic Structures: Domestic and Regional Implications," organized by the IMF, the China Society of Finance and Banking, and the Stanford Center for International Development, in Beijing, October 27–28, 2005. The assistance of M.D. Patra, Sanjay Hansda, and Partha Ray in the preparation of this paper is gratefully acknowledged. The author also wishes to thank, without implicating, T.N. Srinivasan, Raghuram Rajan, and Ashoka Mody for their comments on an earlier version of the paper.

trade has been cut by half a percent. Unlike earlier forecasts, when the oil price rise was expected to be relatively temporary, international opinion now is that it is more permanent than temporary. Yet the IMF's September 2005 *World Economic Outlook* (*WEO*) has retained the global output growth forecast at 4.3 percent, a level higher than average world output growth through the 1990s and until 2004, though it admits that risks are still slanted to the downside. In our own two countries there is, as yet, no sign of a slowdown; in fact, just earlier this week, we at the Reserve Bank of India revised our growth forecast for 2005–06 (that is, April 2005–March 2006) for policy purposes from "around 7 percent" in April 2005 to "7.0 percent–7.5 percent" now. And we are among the countries that are said to be more energy inefficient and dependent on oil imports.

One also sees little impact of the current oil price episode on global financial markets. Undisturbed by the somewhat slowing global growth scenario, financial markets have remained generally benign, with low interest rates and healthy stock markets. Moreover, corporate balance sheets in most countries have been exhibiting continuous improvement with no pause in the determined efforts observed toward restructuring and productivity-promoting cost-cutting activities. This is certainly true in India and presumably in China as well. In fact, this financial strengthening of the real corporate sector is perhaps underpinning the continued health of the financial system and is emerging as a cushion against medium-term risks and uncertainties. I am saying all this against the backdrop of the difficulties that we all went through in the previous oil price shock episodes of 1973–74, 1979–80, and 1989–90.

Besides, the macroeconomic imbalances—a key risk to global growth—have actually increased, with the current account deficit of the United States poised to cross 6 percent of GDP and its fiscal deficit 3.7 percent of GDP in 2005; surpluses are correspondingly set to rise in Japan, China, oil exporters in the Middle East, emerging Asia (excluding India, where current account deficits have returned), and the Commonwealth of Independent States countries. Yet financial conditions have enabled a smooth financing of these imbalances, with growth and interest rate differentials continuing to fuel investors' appetite for the United States markets.

At the same time, the same favorable financial developments have caused large imbalances to grow inward, particularly in the form of household debt and increases in housing prices, and this is seen as heightening risks for the future. Low bond yields and flat yield curves have triggered an ever-widening search for yields, aided by the compression of credit risk spreads. This has, perhaps, increased the risks embedded in the financial system, and financial markets could become vulnerable to corrections.

Questions regarding the sustainability of current global growth, overall credit quality, and the state of the household sector's finances have begun to arise. The same set of factors, however, have improved the access of emerging market economies to financial markets, with the low spreads of their bond yields enabling the financing of strong growth with moderate inflation, strengthening of fiscal and balance of payments positions, and the accumulation of foreign exchange reserves.

Perhaps the greatest puzzle in current global developments is the coexistence of abundant liquidity and low consumer inflation.[1] Despite the prolonged period over which monetary policy all over the world has remained accommodative, inflation has been unusually benign, relatively impervious to soaring crude prices and the elevated levels of prices of nonfuel commodities. This phenomenon is unique in recent history.

These are not out-of-this-world paradoxes, and many explanations have been offered. Indeed, they may be characterized as puzzles only because they are in conflict with conventional wisdom, or because the traditional models that calibrated our thinking are no longer valid. It is in this context that I shall focus on some of these apparent puzzles and their explanations in the present lecture. I am particularly concerned with possible erosion of the efficacy of traditional price-related policy measures, that is, the exchange rate and interest rate mechanisms, in restoring macroeconomic balances.

Some Apparent Puzzles

From the various puzzles that monetary policymakers routinely face, let me focus on six issues, namely, (1) the dollar's appreciation despite increasing U.S. twin deficits, (2) soaring oil prices accompanied by strong global growth, (3) long-term bond yields falling in the presence of Federal Fund rate hikes, (4) low consumer inflation in the presence of abundant liquidity and increasing asset prices, (5) strong global growth accompanied by a slowdown in global saving and investment rates, and (6) the phenomenon of low inflation despite currency depreciation.

---

[1]As per McKinsey's Global Survey of Business Executives for the quarter ending December 2005, "Nearly half of the surveyed executives around the world expect the inflation rate in their countries to rise by at least one percentage point over the next year, while more than half say they won't be able to raise prices" (McKinsey & Company, 2005).

Increasing U.S. Twin Deficits and the Appreciating Dollar

Over the past two decades, the United States has transformed itself from the world's largest creditor into the world's largest debtor nation. At the end of 2004, U.S. debt to the rest of the world exceeded its assets by about US$2.5 trillion, that is, 21 percent of its GDP. Driving this massive mismatch is the quantum jump in the current account deficit during 2000–04 from the level during 1995–99, largely resulting from the mounting fiscal deficit and falling private savings. The U.S. macro imbalances are set to increase following the disaster brought by Hurricanes Katrina and Rita. The IMF's September 2005 *WEO* projects the U.S. current account deficit will rise to over 6 percent of GDP in 2005, driven by higher oil prices and strong domestic demand (Table 9.1).

What is the solution to these persistent and mounting imbalances? Conventional wisdom would suggest that the existence of these twin deficits and little expectation of improvement at present would have led to a sizable market-led adjustment of the dollar against other major currencies. The dollar, which did encounter depreciation in terms of the nominal effective exchange rate in the first half of the 1990s, appreciated in the second half of that decade and did so even in terms of the real effective exchange rate during 2000–04. The process has also continued during the first eight months of 2005 despite the sustained rise in the U.S. current account deficit, offset primarily by depreciation of the euro, pound sterling, and yen. The weakening of the euro against the dollar in recent months possibly reflects the increasingly unfavorable short-term interest rate differentials and growing political uncertainties in Europe following the rejection of the European Union's (EU's) constitution in France and the Netherlands, and post-election problems in Germany. Except in the ASEAN-4, the trade-weighted exchange rates of the U.S. have generally appreciated in emerging markets, particularly in Latin America.[2] Following the Chinese exchange rate reform on July 21, 2005—including a 2.1 percent revaluation, the adoption of a reference basket of currencies, and a 0.3 percent daily fluctuation range against the dollar—the renminbi has remained broadly unchanged against the dollar. Clearly, the steady/appreciating dollar despite the rising current account deficit constitutes a daunting paradox of the day.

---

[2]ASEAN-4 (Association of Southeast Asian Nations—Brunei Darussalam, Cambodia, Indonesia, Lao People's Democratic Republic, Malaysia, Myanmar, Philippines, Singapore, Thailand, and Vietnam).

Table 9.1. U.S. Twin Deficits, NEER, and REER

	Current Account Balance/GDP (Percent per annum)	General Government Fiscal Balance/GDP (Percent per annum)	NEER (2000 = 100)	REER (2000 = 100)
1990–94	−1.00	−4.88	85.80	87.80
1995–99	−2.06	−1.24	89.78	86.33
2000–04	−4.63	−2.39	97.13	98.09
2005	−6.0[1]	−3.7[1]	83.13[2]	87.73[2]

Sources: IMF, *World Economic Outlook (WEO)*, and *International Financial Statistics (IFS)*; and World Bank, World Development Indicators Online.

[1] *WEO*'s projection.

[2] Pertains to August 2005.

Strong Global Growth Despite Soaring Oil Prices

After the oil shocks of the 1970s, the first half of the 1990s witnessed deflationary pressures in terms of real oil prices. However, the lull in oil prices turned out to be short-lived. Soaring oil prices have since characterized the 2000–04 period. While the IMF's real oil price index at 277 in 2005 so far remains below the peak of 452 witnessed in 1980, oil prices are scaling new heights every day, driven mainly by growing or unchanged demand, low inventories, lack of spare capacity, and geopolitical tensions and uncertainties. Although the accommodating global monetary conditions have placed oil futures in the class of sought-after financial assets, the persisting high levels of oil prices increasingly indicate that a large part of the oil price hike has become permanent (Table 9.2).

The worrisome news on oil continues to project the image of a world besieged with higher oil prices, bringing painful memories of the oil shocks of the 1970s to the fore. Yet global growth remains remarkably on track. Indeed, the growth momentum has only improved from the second half of the 1990s to the first half of this decade. The growth in world trade volume (goods and services) has also recovered after some slowdown in 2001 and 2002. The September 2005 *WEO* has, thus, retained its April estimate for 2005 global growth at 4.30 percent. What is all the more surprising is the increasing business confidence (for example, in the United States) coupled with high corporate profit growth during 2002–05, much higher than in the roaring 1990s.

Falling Long-Term Bond Yields in the Presence of Fed Fund Rate Hikes

With the economic expansion continuing strongly and risks shifting toward possible inflationary pressures, the U.S. Federal Reserve

Table 9.2. **Global Growth, Business Confidence, Corporate Profit Growth, and Oil Price Inflation**

	World Economic Growth (Percent per annum)	Growth in World Trade Volume (Goods and services) (Percent per annum)	U.S. Business Confidence Index	U.S. Corporate Profit Growth (Percent per annum)	WTI Oil Prices (US$ per barrel)
1990–94	2.62	5.57	—	7.15	20.44 (–1.86)
1995–99	3.69	7.46	54.63[1]	7.57	18.95 (4.67)
2000–04	3.84	6.34	60.50[1]	6.88	30.97 (19.36)
2000	4.71	12.44	51.66	–3.91	30.32 (58.17)
2001	2.44	0.08	43.91	–6.19	25.87 (–14.67)
2002	2.95	3.41	52.37	15.49	26.12 (0.95)
2003	3.97	5.44	53.31	16.42	31.10 (19.07)
2004	5.13	10.33	60.50	12.57	41.45 (33.29)
2005	4.30[2]	7.00[2]	54.45[3]	16.00[4]	56.01 (35.14)[2]

Sources: IMF, *WEO*, and *IFS*, IMF; U.S. Federal Reserve; and Bureau of Economic Analysis, U.S.

Notes: The overall U.S. Business Confidence Index, referred to as the U.S. Business Conditions Index, ranges between 0 and 100. An index greater than 50 indicates an expansionary economy over the course of the next three to six months. (Taken from *WEO*, originally compiled by the Institute for Supply Management, U.S.) Figures in parentheses are annual percentage changes.

[1] Pertains to the year 1999 and 2004, respectively.
[2] *WEO*'s projection for 2005 over 2004.
[3] August 2005.
[4] 2005-Q2, year-on-year.

Board (Fed) has started reducing the degree of policy accommodation and raised the policy rate 11 times since June 2004 by a "measured" 25 basis points each time, with indications of further such hikes. While the prime lending rate of banks in the United States has responded to every hike in the target federal fund rate, the long-term interest rates that are set by financial markets continue to remain unusually low—what former Federal Reserve Chairman Alan Greenspan has referred to as a "conundrum." The best way to summarize this issue is to quote from Greenspan:

> In this environment, long-term interest rates have trended lower in recent months even as the Federal Reserve has raised the level of the target federal funds rate by 150 basis points. This development contrasts with most experience, which suggests that, other things being equal, increasing short-term interest rates are normally accompanied by a rise in longer-term yields. For the moment, the broadly unanticipated behavior of world bond markets remains a conundrum. Bond price movements may be a short-term aberration, but it will be some time before we are able to better judge the forces underlying recent experience. (Greenspan, 2005b)

Table 9.3. Federal Funds Rate, Private Lending Rates (PLR), and U.S. Government Securities (GSec) Yield

(In percent)

		Federal Funds Rate	U.S. PLR	10-Yr. GSec Yield
2004	May	1.00	4.00	4.72
	Jun	1.03	4.01	4.73
	Jul	1.26	4.25	4.50
	Aug	1.43	4.43	4.28
	Sep	1.61	4.58	4.13
	Oct	1.76	4.75	4.10
	Nov	1.93	4.93	4.19
	Dec	2.16	5.15	4.23
2005	Jan	2.28	5.25	4.22
	Feb	2.50	5.49	4.17
	Mar	2.63	5.58	4.50
	Apr	2.79	5.75	4.34
	May	3.00	5.98	4.14
	Jun	3.04	6.01	4.00
	Jul	3.26	6.25	4.18
	Aug	3.50	6.44	4.26
	Sep	3.62	6.59	4.20

Source: U.S. Federal Reserve.

Note: U.S. PLR is the rate posted by a majority of top 25 (by assets in domestic offices) insured U.S.-chartered commercial banks. It is one of several base rates used by banks to price short-term business loans.

Given the understanding that the long-term yield tracks the behavior of current and expected inflation (Fama, 1986) along with expected growth performance of the economy in terms of productivity of capital (Mishkin, 1991), the current behavior of yield defies conventional wisdom (Table 9.3).

A host of hypotheses have been put forward as an explanation for the conundrum, among other things: easy liquidity conditions; a glut in global savings over investment (Bernanke, 2005); the foreign exchange reserves buildup in the Asian economies; the gradual expected pace of U.S. tightening made possible by a high level of monetary credibility; the fact that markets may have become deeper, thereby improving their risk-bearing capacity; and low expected inflation, low term/risk premiums, and a flight to quality after the dot-com crash in 2000. Meanwhile, the low bond yields and flat yield curves have triggered an ever-widening search for yields, aided by the compression of credit risk spreads. The behavior of long-term rates to the short-term policy rates is, thus, posing a threat to the traditional transmission channels of monetary policy, looming large on the efficacy of monetary management worldwide.

Low Consumer Inflation in the Presence of Abundant Liquidity and Increasing Asset Prices

The global economy is currently awash with liquidity. Exactly seven years ago, the U.S. Fed responded to the "low probability but highly adverse events" (Blinder and Reis, 2005) leading up to the Russian debt default and the Long-Term Capital Management collapse with an emergency cut in interest rates in September, October, and November 1998. Even though the reduction was just 25 basis points each month, it shifted the monetary policy stance to accommodation. Once again, prompted by a deflation scare, the federal funds rate was cut over a 42-month stretch from December 2000 to June 2003, to a 45-year low of 1 percent, taking the real federal funds rate into negative territory. Thus, real policy rates were effectively zero or negative until very recently in the United States and remain below the "Wicksellian" long-term neutral rate. Real policy rates in the United Kingdom and euro area are also generally hovering around zero. Coupled with benign policy rates, money supply growth, which increased in the second half of the 1990s in the United Kingdom, continued at the elevated level during 2000–04. Similarly, money supply growth went up in the euro area in 2000–04, from a lower level in 1995–99. Even in the United States, where money supply has lost much of its charm as an information variable, there has been accelerated money supply growth during 1995–99, which has largely been sustained during 2000–04 (Table 9.4).

The policy accommodation pursued until recently by the United States has had a global impact, flooding the rest of the world with an abundance of liquidity (Table 9.5). Low interest rates in the United States have encouraged capital to flow into emerging market economies. For the countries that prefer some form of managed parity against the dollar, this inflow of capital has resulted in a large buildup of foreign exchange reserves and excessive domestic liquidity, amplifying the Fed's policy stance. Yet, the global supply of dollars reflected in the so-called super money (that is, the sum of cash and banks' reserve holdings at the Fed plus foreign reserves held by central banks around the world) is estimated to have grown by about 25 percent a year in the past couple of years.

The global glut of liquidity has facilitated highly leveraged positions, debt-financed consumption, and booming credit growth, raising financial stability concerns. Although equity prices shot up in the second half of the 1990s, they came down subsequently in the wake of the dot-com crash. Facilitated by the policy accommodation in the United States and the subsequent easing in the rest of the world, housing prices have now witnessed a boom during 2000–04 all over the world.

Table 9.4. Policy Rates and Growth in Money Supply, Credit, Asset Prices, Consumer Prices, and Producer Prices
(In percent)

	Variable	1990–94	1995–99	2000–04
United States	Policy rate	4.9	5.4	2.8
	Money supply	1.4	8.5	7.6
	Reserve money	7.8	8.6	3.7
	Credit	3.0	7.5	7.0
	Equity prices (Dow Jones)	7.2	24.7	−0.3
	Housing prices	−1.9	1.9	5.8
	Producer prices	1.4	0.8	3.2
	Consumer prices	3.6	2.4	2.6
United Kingdom	Policy rate	9.1	6.3	4.6
	Money supply	5.9	7.6	7.6
	Reserve money	4.1	4.6	5.3
	Credit	5.7	7.4	10.3
	Equity prices (FTSE 100)	5.8	17.8	−5.9
	Housing prices	−1.8	4.3	15.3
	Producer prices	4.2	1.6	1.1
	Consumer prices	4.6	2.8	2.4
Euro area	Policy rate		2.8 (1999)	3.0
	Money supply	7.1	4.7	6.9
	Credit		7.9 (1998–99)	5.9
	Equity prices (Xetra DAX)	12.6 (1991–94)	27.8	−5.4
	Housing prices	4.0 (1991–95)	3.5 (1996–2000)	6.8 (2001–04)
	Producer prices	2.3 (1991–95)	1.1 (1996–2000)	1.4 (2001–04)
	Consumer prices	3.2 (1991–95)	1.6 (1996–2000)	2.2 (2001–04)
World	Consumer prices	22.3	8.3	3.8
	Consumer prices— advanced countries	3.8	2.0	1.9
	Consumer prices— emerging markets	12.9	7.6	4.3
	Non-oil commodity prices	−6.1	−4.0	1.9

Sources: IMF, *WEO*, and *IFS*; and relevant central banks' websites.
Note: Policy rates are in percent, and growth rates are annual average growth (in percent).

Perhaps the greatest puzzle in current global developments is the coexistence of abundant liquidity and low consumer inflation.[3] Despite the prolonged period over which monetary policy worldwide has remained accommodative, inflation has been unusually benign, impervious to

---

[3]Yet another puzzle that remains to be resolved is why liquidity is chasing financial assets rather than consumption.

Table 9.5. Policy Rates, Money Supply Growth, and Producer and Consumer Inflations in Select Emerging Asian Countries

(In percent per annum)

		1990–94	1995–99	2000–04
China	Bank rate	8.5	7.2	3.0
	Money supply	27.6	19.1	16.2
	Reserve money	28.8	15.5	12.4
	Consumer prices	10.4	5.2	1.0
	Credit	26.5	20.0	16.5
India	Policy rate	11.4	10.6	5.9
	Money supply	18.0	13.3	14.0
	Reserve money	16.9	11.4	11.5
	Producer prices	10.5	5.5	5.2
	Consumer prices	10.2	8.9	3.9
	Credit	13.3	14.9	14.3
Thailand	Discount rate	10.5	10.0	3.5
	Money supply	20.4	9.1	4.6
	Reserve money	16.1	20.4	8.1
	Producer prices	2.8	4.5	3.8
	Consumer prices	4.8	5.1	1.7
	Credit	24.2	8.5	0.8
Malaysia	Money market rate	6.5	6.4	2.7
	Money supply	17.9	14.6	7.3
	Reserve money	21.9	10.9	2.1
	Producer prices	2.5	3.6	3.5
	Consumer prices	3.8	3.5	1.5
	Credit	12.7	16.4	5.9
		(1993–94)		
Korea	Discount rate	6.2	4.2	2.5
	Money supply	18.2	7.2	9.2
	Reserve money	14.7	4.2	6.7
	Producer prices	3.1	4.4	1.9
	Consumer prices	7.0	4.4	3.2
	Credit	18.1	17.3	12.0
Philippines	Discount rate	12.0	11.5	8.0
	Money supply	14.6	20.3	7.8
	Reserve money	13.8	15.5	1.6
	Producer prices	4.1	6.0	9.6
		(1994)		
	Consumer prices	11.1	7.0	4.6
	Credit	40.2	19.8	6.5
Indonesia	Discount rate	14.4	19.6	12.2
	Money supply	16.0	22.5	17.0
	Reserve money	16.9	41.7	15.3
	Producer prices	5.9	28.1	8.0
	Consumer prices	8.6	20.5	8.0
	Credit	27.4	29.0	10.6

Source: IMF, *IFS*.

Note: Policy rates are in percent, and growth rates are annual average growth (in percent).

soaring oil prices and the elevated prices of nonfuel commodities, particularly ferrous and nonferrous metals. Whereas the industrial countries have maintained inflation pressures at low and stable levels during both 1995–99 and 2000–04, there has been a noticeable decline in inflation during 2000–04 in emerging market economies. Such low levels of inflation have not been witnessed since the pre–war period when the discipline of fixed exchange rates under the gold standard ensured that prices were roughly stable and episodes of deflation were not uncommon. The current phenomenon is unique in recent history, prompting some to visualize the death of inflation, though there have been some signs of its resurrection in the current year.

Slowdown in Global Saving and Investment Versus Strong Global Growth

Global saving and investment rates have declined in recent years. Global saving increased by a fraction in 1995–99, from its 1990–94 level, before declining in 2000–04 (Table 9.6). Although saving as a percentage of GDP declined in the United States, United Kingdom, and European Monetary Union (EMU) in 2000–04, from the 1995–99 level, it increased in China and India. The decline of savings in the industrial countries could have its demographic roots in an aging population weighted against higher saving (Mohan, 2004c).

Meanwhile, the world investment rate declined steadily during the period, ignoring the signals of softening interest rates. Investment in the United States, United Kingdom, and EMU fell during 2000–04 with increasing risk aversion on the part of the corporates in the wake of the dot-com and other financial crises in 1990s. The investment rate improved in China during 2000–04, whereas it declined in India during 2000–03.

Notwithstanding the declining saving and investment rates, global growth has continued its surge from period to period. Although consumption has arguably played a critical role in the industrial countries' growth momentum, exports might have played a similar role in the emerging markets. The sustenance of consumption as opposed to investment-led growth has thus given rise to new controversies on present versus future allocation of resources and also on the relevance of overlapping generation outlooks.

Low Inflation Despite Currency Depreciations

Traditionally, the degree of exchange rate pass-through, that is, the speed and extent of transmission of exchange rate movements into domes-

Table 9.6. Global Savings and Investment

	1990–94	1995–99	2000–04
GDP growth (percent)			
World	2.6	3.7	3.8
European Monetary Union (EMU)	1.9	2.4	1.7
United States	2.4	3.9	2.8
United Kingdom	1.3	3.0	2.6
India	4.9	6.5	5.7
China	10.7	8.8	8.5
Savings (as percent of GDP)			
World	22.0	22.3	21.4
EMU	22.5	22.8	22.5
			(up to 2003)
United States	16.2	17.6	15.2
			(up to 2002)
United Kingdom	15.8	16.6	14.2
			(up to 2003)
India	22.4	21.7	22.2
China	39.7	42.1	43.6
Investment (as percent of GDP)			
World	23.0	22.7	21.6
EMU	22.0	20.8	20.7
			(up to 2003)
United States	17.1	19.3	19.1
			(up to 2002)
United Kingdom	17.1	17.3	16.9
			(up to 2003)
India	22.9	23.2	22.7
			(up to 2003)
China	38.0	38.8	40.8

Sources: IMF, *WEO*; and World Bank, World Development Indicators Online.

tic prices, used to be an important consideration for the conduct of monetary policy, leading to the alleged "fear of floating" on the part of the emerging economies (Calvo and Reinhart, 2002). However, there is now increasing evidence that exchange rate pass-through to domestic inflation has tended to decline since the 1990s across a number of countries. For example, inflation turned out to be largely immune and insensitive—barring the sole exception of Indonesia—to the wild volatility and currency depreciation witnessed in Korea, Thailand, the Philippines, and Malaysia in the aftermath of the Asian financial crisis (Table 9.7).

Similarly, the dollar's substantial depreciation against the euro during 2002–04 has not led to inflationary pressures in the United States. With inflation standing rock steady even in the face of exchange rate volatility, the traditional channels of current account adjustment have failed to work toward restoring the external balances in a sustainable manner. Further,

Table 9.7. Exchange Rates and Consumer Price Inflation—Select Asian Countries During the Crisis

	Year	1996	1997	1998	1999	2000
Korea	Exchange rate	805	951	1,401	1,189	1,131
		(4.3)	(18.3)	(47.3)	(−15.2)	(−4.9)
	CPI inflation	4.98	4.40	7.54	0.83	2.25
Thailand	Exchange rate	25	31	41	38	40
		(1.7)	(23.8)	(31.9)	(−8.6)	(6.1)
	CPI inflation	5.83	5.60	8.07	0.30	1.57
Philippines	Exchange rate	26	29	41	39	44
		(1.9)	(12.4)	(38.8)	(−4.4)	(13.1)
	CPI inflation	7.51	5.59	9.27	5.95	3.95
Malaysia	Exchange rate	2.52	2.81	3.92	3.80	3.80
		(0.5)	(11.8)	(39.5)	(−3.2)	(0.0)
	CPI inflation	3.49	2.66	5.27	2.75	1.54
Indonesia	Exchange rate	2,342	2,909	10,014	7,855	8,422
		(4.2)	(24.2)	(244.2)	(−21.6)	(7.2)
	CPI inflation	7.97	6.23	58.39	20.49	3.72

Sources: IMF, *WEO* and *IFS*.
Notes: Exchange rates are national currencies per U.S. dollar. Figures in parentheses are the percentage changes over the previous year. CPI inflation rates are annual percentage changes.

the weakening of the dollar against the euro has not brought about substantial changes in the trade pattern between the United States and the euro area. On the contrary, U.S. imports from the euro area surged ahead during the phase of the dollar's depreciation against the euro while U.S. exports to the euro area did not increase, at least initially (Table 9.8).

Possible Explanations

What factors explain these seeming puzzles and counterintuitive relationships across a large set of variables? What really explains the divergence between the producer price index (PPI) and consumer price index (CPI) and the imperviousness of consumer prices to liquidity conditions? Is the received wisdom on the relationship between money, output, and prices undergoing yet another paradigm shift? Has the inflation process changed at its core? Country experiences present a wide diversity of circumstances, producing a variety of outcomes. This makes generalizations difficult and even adventurous. Central bankers are not known to be adventurous, but this opportunity of delivering a dinner speech has emboldened me.

Table 9.8. Exchange Rate, Trade, and Consumer Price Inflation—Recent Trends in the United States

Year	2000	2001	2002	2003	2004
NEER (2000 = 100)	100	105.94	104.28	91.46	83.97
REER (2000 = 100)	100	103.61	105.18	95.56	86.1
Exchange rate (US$ per euro)	0.924	0.896	0.944	1.131	1.243
	(−13.4)	(−3.0)	(5.4)	(19.8)	(9.9)
CPI inflation (percent)	3.38	2.83	1.59	2.27	2.68
Imports from euro area (US$ million)	226,901	226,568	232,313	253,042	281,959
	(13.42)	(−0.15)	(2.54)	(8.92)	(11.43)
Exports to euro area (US$ million)	168,181	161,931	146,621	155,170	172,622
	(8.63)	(−3.72)	(-9.45)	(5.83)	(11.25)

Sources: IMF, *WEO* and *IFS*; and U.S. Census Bureau.
Note: Figures in parentheses are the percentage changes over the previous year.

As a central banker, I would like to subscribe to the objective of low and stable inflation in the conduct of monetary policy. Reforms in the manner in which monetary policy is set currently, and the institutional changes that have occurred in the 1990s, have undoubtedly enhanced the reputation of monetary authorities in terms of delivering price stability. The current trend of increasingly independent central banks, enhanced transparency, and greater accountability has, in fact, improved public credibility in these institutions. The institutional strengthening of central banks has coincided with the worldwide thrust on fiscal consolidation and structural reforms in the labor and product markets, which have also worked toward attaining price stability. Specified fiscal rules such as those under the Maastricht Treaty and the Stability and Growth Pact in the euro area have been emulated the world over, charting out explicit road maps for fiscal consolidation. Thus, fiscal deficits in emerging market economies are now less than half of their levels in the 1970s and 1980s. It has been estimated that inflation could have declined by 5–15 percentage points on account of lower fiscal deficits in emerging market economies (IMF, 2002). So there are some broad structural fiscal reasons for the worldwide decline in inflation.

Globalization has arguably unleashed the most significant anti-inflationary forces. Lower trade barriers, increased deregulation, innovation, and competition all over the world have led to exponential growth in cross-border trade, with world trade racing ahead of output. With the rapid expansion in tradables, domestic economies are, therefore, increasingly exposed to the rigors of international competition and comparative advantage, reducing unwarranted price markups (Greenspan, 2004a). The competition among nations to attract and retain factors of production has also induced governments to reduce entry barriers for new productive activities. Intensified competition in the domestic economy, which has now become part of the global marketplace, has rendered prices more flexible, containing the impact of unanticipated inflation on output. This has reduced the incentive for monetary authorities to raise output above the potential (Rogoff, 2003). Increasingly, a firm or country that can produce for global markets, with the greatest cost efficiency, sets global prices. Currently, China is perhaps in such a position but other competitors are not far behind. It needs to be recognized, however, that globalization may not continue to maintain its tempo indefinitely into the future.[4]

An important contributor to low inflation has also been the productivity growth in a number of sectors, partly owing to information technology (IT) investments combined with restructuring. Even the services sector, which was otherwise believed to lag in productivity vis-à-vis industry in view of its "cost disease" syndrome (à la Baumol), has witnessed impressive productivity growth with increased penetration of IT in most services activities. Productivity growth has been particularly discernible in the United States from the mid-1990s, with continuing signs of sustenance in the next decade (Oliner and Sichel, 2002). Although productivity growth in the euro area may not have been as high as in the United States, the disinflationary effects of productivity growth in one region get transmitted across borders through increased competition in a globalized world (Table 9.9).

The impact of cross-country integration is also at work in the labor market. An economy that is open to migrant labor exhibits a different inflationary process from one that is not. An increase in spending raises the pressure of demand on supply and leads to upward pressure on wages and prices. But if the increased demand for labor generates its own supply in the form of immigrant labor, then the link between demand and prices is broken, or at least altered. Indeed, in an economy that can call

---

[4]It is instructive to turn to former Chairman Greenspan, who said, "We have not experienced a sufficient number of economic turning points to judge the causal linkages among increased globalization, improved monetary policy, significant disinflation and greater economic stability" (Greenspan, 2004a).

Table 9.9. Productivity in Manufacturing
(Annual percentage change)

	1987–96	1997–99	2000–04
Advanced economies	3.1	3.37	3.76
United States	2.8	3.97	4.96
United Kingdom	3.4	3.47	4.42
Euro area	. . .	4.13	2.88
Japan	2.7	1.57	3.62

Source: IMF, *WEO*.
Note: Productivity in manufacturing refers to labor productivity, measured as the ratio of hourly compensation to unit labor costs.

on unlimited supplies of migrant labor or can outsource, the concept of output gap may not be that meaningful (King, 2005). The inflow of immigrant labor in both the United States and the United Kingdom has arguably led to a diminution of inflationary pressure in the labor market in these countries (Table 9.10).

The expanding canvas of knowledge has also had its impact in the form of low and stable inflation. The technological advances in architecture and engineering as well as the development of lighter but stronger materials have resulted in "downsized" output, evident in the huge expansion of the money value of output and trade but not in tonnage. As a consequence, material intensity of production has declined, reflecting "the substitution, in effect, of ideas for physical matter in the creation of economic value" (Greenspan, 1998). This has contributed to the secular decline in commodity prices, notwithstanding short spells of spikes in these prices. The increasing commodity price volatility around the declining trend has, however, engaged monetary policy attention in the short run (Mohan, 2004a). The declining share of commodity prices in final goods prices has been an important factor, leading to a divergence between PPI and CPI. Thus even substantial increases in input prices no longer lead to corresponding increases in output prices and are further muted by the forces of global competition.

Thus the persistence of low and stable inflation worldwide despite considerable monetary accommodation in recent years can be explained by invoking these new economic developments in the real economy. The role of central banks in the recent containment of inflation can, at best, be seen to have limited applicability.

For industrial countries, the exchange rate pass-through to consumer price inflation has been found to have almost halved in the 1990s compared to the pre-1990s period (McCarthy, 2000; and Gagnon and Ihrig,

Table 9.10. Net Immigration to the United States and the United Kingdom

	1985–90	1990–95	1995–2000
United States	3,775,000	5,200,000	6,200,000
United Kingdom	104,310	380,840	574,470

Source: World Bank, World Development Indicators Online.

Note: Net immigration is the number of immigrants less the number of emigrants, including both citizens and noncitizens.

2001).[5] Furthermore, the pass-through has reportedly declined more in developing countries in the 1990s than in the advanced economies (Frankel, Parsley, and Wei, 2005). Financial innovations such as the availability of hedging products have also lowered the degree of pass-through by enabling exporters and importers to ignore temporary shocks and set stable product prices despite large currency fluctuations—witness the lack of price change in BMWs, Mercedes, and Porsches in the United States despite substantial dollar depreciation with respect to the euro. The import composition of the industrial countries is found to have shifted in favor of sectors with low pass-through, such as the manufacturing sector. There is also a view that, in some cases, the low observed pass-through might be due to the disappearance of expensive goods from consumption and their replacement by inferior local substitutes (Burstein, Eichenbaum, and Rebelo, 2003)—that is, no more Mercedes and BMWs!

The increasing share of nontradables in GDP has also worked toward containing the exchange rate pass-through. Nontradables generally approximated by services have increased their share in all major industrial countries, as well as in China and India. As populations age, demand moves more in favor of services than for goods. Thus, the aging population in industrial countries has provided much of the growth impetus for services. With the shift in demand composition in favor of services, it is no wonder the extent of exchange rate pass-through, which works primarily through tradables, has been limited (Table 9.11).

The role of exchange rate movements or policy-induced adjustments in influencing the behavior of economic agents through the domestic price

---

[5]Banik and Biswas (2006) have estimated that for a 100 percent appreciation of the Japanese yen against the U.S. dollar, Japanese exporters increase their local currency price by about 13 percent for small automobiles, and around 39 percent for medium-size automobiles, whereas Korean exporters increase their price approximately by 30.37 percent for medium-size automobiles in response to 100 percent appreciation of Korean currency against the U.S. dollar.

Table 9.11. Share of Services in GDP
(In percent)

Country	1990–94	1995–99	2000–04
United States	71.71	72.89	74.65[1]
United Kingdom	65.55	67.91	71.62[2]
Japan	60.26	64.92	67.45[3]
Euro area	64.25	67.24	69.21[2]
China	32.74	31.36	33.72
India	42.16	45.14	50.44

Source: World Bank, World Development Indicators Online.
[1]Up to 2001.
[2]Up to 2003.
[3]Up to 2002.

mechanism appears to have been significantly truncated. If an exchange rate depreciation (appreciation) does not appreciably increase (decrease) domestic prices of imported goods, there would be little reason to expect a reduction (increase) in demand for imported products. Hence, small exchange rate changes can scarcely be expected to help significantly in effecting changes in the current account.

There has been reduced volatility of GDP growth in most G-7 countries over the past three decades, coinciding with growing integration and synchronization of business cycles (Mohan, 2004a). The standard deviation of U.S. GDP growth during 1984–2002 was two-thirds of that during 1960–83. This could have also contributed to lowering inflation (Stock and Watson, 2003). The growing share of services (a sector less susceptible to volatility), better inventory management, and easy access to credit with financial deepening have also brought down the volatility of GDP growth and, therefore, expectations of future inflation.

The global financial landscape has undergone a sea change over the past couple of decades, characterized by increasing liberalization and growing completeness of markets and institutions. The pursuit of flexible exchange rates for the major currencies since the 1970s has made the spot and forward foreign exchange markets strikingly efficient in tracking the expectations of economic agents. Also, the broadening and deepening of the secondary and derivatives markets for government and other fixed income securities has added to the flows of market information. With the onset of demystification and decomposition of risks, there has been a deluge of new financial products, enabling economic agents to manage, hedge, or lay off risks. Simultaneously, there has been discernible improvement in the institutional infrastructure—legal or informational—providing a durable basis for efficient functioning of the financial markets. With the arrival of options pricing in the early 1970s, more and more complex financial products are hitting the market every day. Financial markets—at least in the industrial countries—have, thus, transformed themselves into super-efficient vehicles for allocating resources and spreading risks across sectors, time, and space. The lower costs of financial intermediation, the greater scope for risk spreading, and the reduced reliance on any individual institution or market channel for the intermediation of savings and investment have spurred financial activities undertaken by households, businesses, and governments. Thus, the global financial system appears to be more robust and resilient to financial shocks emanating from individual countries. Certainly, the increasing confidence of the financial system has its reflection in the sustained global growth and taming of inflation all over world (Blinder and Reis, 2005). The growing sophistication of financial markets has therefore, paradoxically, reduced the power of the price mechanism in bringing about changes in a desired policy direction.

It is, therefore, possible that such developments in financial markets have had the effect of reducing risks across the board, both spatially and temporally. Such developments have received further support from the increased focus of central banks on inflation containment and stability, along with overall financial stability. The accompanying institutional changes, mainly the increased acceptance of central bank autonomy, have probably contributed to enhancement of their credibility. Thus there could be a secular decline in risk perception and in medium- and long-term inflationary expectations, thereby reducing the neutral real interest rate. If these conjectures have some element of validity, the effect of changes in short-term policy rates on long-term yields would be muted, as seems to have happened in the United States. Paradoxically then, the central banks' own success could have blunted the efficacy of their most powerful policy instrument: the short-term interest rate.

As regards the muted impact of soaring oil prices on the general price level and economic activities, it needs to be recognized that, unlike in the past when oil price surges were driven by supply shocks, the current bull market in oil is mainly the result of a perceived secular increase in demand emanating from accelerated growth in our countries, which, moreover, is expected to continue in the foreseeable future. The sharp rise in oil prices is perceived to have been triggered by sustained global growth (particularly in the United States) among developed countries, and by increasing contributions from the emerging market economies that tend to demand relatively more oil than the developed world for a similar expansion in output. The higher oil prices of the 1970s brought to an abrupt end the extraordinary period of growth in U.S. oil consumption. Between 1945 and 1973, consumption of petroleum products in the United States rose at a startling 4.5 percent average annual rate, well in excess of real GDP growth. However, between 1973 and 2004, oil consumption in the United States grew, on an average, only 0.5 percent a year, far short of the rise in real GDP (Greenspan, 2005a). The mandated fuel-efficiency standards for cars and light trucks coupled with the imports of small, fuel-efficient Japanese cars and the increasing share of the services sector in GDP induced slower growth of gasoline demand in the United States. Thus, while the oil intensity of output has fallen in the industrial countries—for example, from the peak of 0.19 kg per real dollar in the United States in 1970 to 0.09 kg per real dollar in 2000—the relatively slower decline for developing countries such as China and India has been neutralized by the pace of the rise in incomes (Table 9.12).

Unlike the oil shocks of the 1970s, when the oil surplus with the oil-exporting countries mainly found its way out into conspicuous consumption, this time around, the oil-exporting countries seem to be doing a much better job of recycling the oil surpluses into the global economy. For example, the OPEC countries are running only a marginal trade surplus with China because they are importing a range of goods from China, which is using more oil to manufacture those goods. Oil-exporting countries have also been active in the international investment arena, using their export revenue to buy stocks and bonds in various countries, thereby keeping the global cost of capital low.

Furthermore, the self-equilibrating demand-supply mechanism in the face of rising oil prices has been kept in abeyance in a number of countries. Although the current oil cycle has witnessed a doubling in the price of oil over the past three years, on average only a third of the price increase has been passed on to end users. While Europe and Japan have cut down high taxes on oil consumption to cushion the impact of higher oil prices, governments in many developing countries are subsidizing oil prices in recognition of the lower resilience of low-income people to sudden price shocks. Greenspan (2005a) notes, "But if history is any guide, should higher prices persist, energy use will over time continue to decline, relative to GDP. Long-term demand elasticities have proved noticeably higher than those that are evident in the short term." Nevertheless, since oil use is only two-thirds as important an input into world GDP as it was three decades ago, the effect of the current surge in oil prices, though noticeable, is likely to prove significantly less than in 1970s.

The entry into the world economy of the erstwhile centrally planned economies, in general, and China, in particular, has arguably constituted

Table 9.12. Oil Intensity in Select Countries (Using Constant US$ GDP)
(In kilograms of oil per real US$)

	1970	1980	1990	2000	2003
World	0.18	0.17	0.13	0.11	0.11
United States	0.19	0.15	0.11	0.09	0.09
United Kingdom	0.14	0.09	0.07	0.05	0.05
Japan	0.11	0.09	0.06	0.05	0.05
France	0.15	0.13	0.08	0.07	0.07
Germany	0.15	0.12	0.08	0.07	0.07
India	0.17	0.21	0.22	0.23	0.21
China	0.30	0.52	0.27	0.21	0.19
Malaysia	0.24	0.32	0.29	0.23	0.22
Indonesia	0.27	0.37	0.30	0.33	0.32
Philippines	0.27	0.23	0.20	0.22	0.18
Korea	0.14	0.20	0.17	0.20	0.18
Thailand	0.27	0.31	0.25	0.28	0.28
Brazil	0.14	0.14	0.13	0.14	0.13
Mexico	0.11	0.14	0.16	0.15	0.14

Sources: British Petroleum, *Statistical Review of World Energy*; and World Bank, World Development Indicators Online.

a massive positive supply shock, raising the world's potential growth, holding down inflation, and triggering changes in the relative prices of labor, capital, goods, and assets (BIS, 2005). In this context, the desirability of positive inflation rates has been questioned in certain circles. In other words, are central banks targeting too high a rate of inflation now that China has joined the global market economy?

During the era of rapid globalization in the late nineteenth century, falling average prices were quite common. This "good deflation," which was accompanied by robust growth, was very different from the bad deflation experienced in the 1930s depression. Today, we could have been in yet another phase of "good deflation," but central banks have favored low but positive interest rates while setting and meeting their inflation targets. Furthermore, China's entry into the global economy has raised the worldwide return on capital. That, in turn, should imply an increase in the equilibrium level of real interest rates. However, central banks are holding real rates at historically low levels and one finds scenarios of excessive credit growth, mortgage borrowing, and housing investment. In this context, however, some estimates suggest that the impact of Chinese exports on global inflation has been fairly modest. China's exports could have reduced (1) global inflation by 30 basis points a year, (2) U.S. import price inflation by 80 basis points (but in view of the United States being a relatively closed economy, the impact on producer and consumer prices has likely been quite small), and (3) import unit values inflation by 10–25 basis points in the Organization for Economic Cooperation and Development countries (Kamin, Marazzi, and Schindler, 2004). These estimates should be treated as upper bounds, because they ignore the fact that China's rapid export growth has also been associated with equally rapid import growth and China is, therefore, contributing not only to global supply but also global demand. This is also reflected in the sharp rise in global commodity prices beginning in early 2003.

The Way Ahead

Measured by the growth in global credit or property prices, some parts of the world are currently experiencing strong asset price inflation. As with traditional inflation, the surging asset prices distort relative prices and cause a misallocation of resources. For instance, because households think they are wealthier, they spend more and save and invest less. The risk is that as interest rates rise, the fragility of the economic recovery would be exposed and decisions based on cheap credit would look less than wise.

Whereas there is no question about the desirability of maintaining financial stability, monetary policy is often considered to be too blunt an instrument to achieve financial stability, especially to counter threats from asset price misalignments. Indeed, it is often difficult to judge ex ante whether asset price misalignments are bubbles or not. Second, even if the bubble is identified on a real time basis, the typical monetary tightening measures such as an increase in interest rates may not be effective in deflating asset price bubbles.

In view of such limitations of monetary policy actions and also the fact that inflationary pressures take more than the usual time to surface in conditions of low inflation, central banks need to be cognizant of emerging financial imbalances by lengthening their monetary policy horizons beyond the usual two-year framework. More important, in view of the possibility of the role of prices becoming muted as an equilibrating mechanism, whether in terms of changes in exchange rates, interest rates, or commodity prices, central banks will have to contribute to financial stability more through prudential regulation and supervision to address the emergence of financial sector excesses or imbalances arising from excess liquidity or other economic imbalances. Indeed, greater transparency and cooperation between monetary policy and supervision is being increasingly recognized, and many central banks are exploring alternatives to traditional monetary policy instruments.

Given the fact that the defining characteristic of the monetary policy landscape is "uncertainty," no *simple* rule could possibly describe the policy action to be taken in every contingency (Greenspan, 2004b). As a consequence, the conduct of monetary policy has come to involve, at its core, crucial elements of risk management. This conceptual framework emphasizes understanding as much as possible the many sources of risk and uncertainty that policymakers face, quantifying those risks when possible, and assessing the costs associated with each of the risks.

Under these conditions, the separation of the function of financial regulation and supervision from central banking has come up for critical reappraisal. Even though a formal separation of functions may have become more common than in the past, there remains a question of whether that change would make much difference to the practical realities (Goodhart, 1995).[6] In their quest for financial stability, central banks worldwide have exhibited a variety of responses. Several central banks have been given an explicit mandate to promote financial stability. Another broad category of response has been the constitution of independent departments to oversee financial stability. Illustratively, at the Reserve Bank of New Zealand, the banking supervision department and financial markets department were merged into a Financial Stability Department, headed by a Deputy Governor. In the Netherlands, the newly established Financial Stability Division concentrates experienced staff members from monetary policy, supervision, financial markets, oversight, and research departments. At the European Central Bank, the area concerned with financial stability matters (Prudential Supervision Division) was upgraded to a Directorate (Financial Stability and Supervision), which reports to a member of the Executive Board, and plays a coordination role for euro area/EU financial stability monitoring. Finally, the Bank of England has recently constituted a dedicated Financial Stability Department for oversight of financial stability matters. The transfer of supervisory responsibilities outside the central bank in several countries has also led central banks to focus their attention on systemic issues as reflected in a reorientation of organizational arrangements.

The traditional signals, such as inflation, interest rates, and exchange rates, are today overly anchored whereas the global economy is on a long leash supported by easy finance. However, the increasing potential for

---

[6]Although the central bank as the lender of last resort needs to play a critical role in avoiding a meltdown in the wake of unexpected "catastrophic" events, there is no consensus on the role of the central bank in dealing with the state of the financial sector and ensuring its efficient and prudent performance.

sharp corrections in the medium term needs to be contained by following a twofold strategy: consumption needs to give way smoothly to investment, with the withdrawal of policy accommodation in industrial countries, and the locus of domestic demand needs to shift from countries running deficits to ones with surpluses so as to reduce the current account imbalances. Obviously, coordinated policy initiatives have to be high on the agenda of the global community for ensuring a smooth transition.

If it is indeed true that the efficacy of price-based indirect monetary policy instruments has become blunted because of central banks' own success in containing inflation and muting expectations, along with the increasing sophistication of financial markets, what alternatives do we now have to address the emerging global imbalances? Ironically, the answer perhaps is that we may need to return to more quantity-based instruments, through either micro actions by central banks or structural actions by the fiscal authorities. Central banks would perhaps have to again resort to activating more detailed prudential, regulatory, and supervisory roles aimed at disciplining different segments of the financial markets. Similarly, if external imbalances are perceived to arise because of fiscal imbalances, they will have to be attacked directly, rather than through increasingly ineffective exchange rate signals.

This finally gives me an opportunity to provide some illustrations from recent monetary management actions in China and India.

The People's Bank of China (PBC) has been trying to contain the possible downside risks by way of a range of direct and indirect instruments. Required reserve ratios have been lifted several times, within the context of a newly differentiated reserve requirement system aimed at better aligning the degree of restraint with the degree of excess credit expansion, institution by institution. Moral suasion has been used with "window guidance" and "credit policy advice" in relation to credit allocation, including warnings on the riskiness of increasing exposures to certain overheated sectors. Benchmark interest rates were increased by about 0.3 percentage points in October 2004. At the same time, the upper limit on interest rates charged by commercial banks was abolished, and the limits for urban and rural cooperatives were increased to 2.3 times the benchmark rate. The interest rates that the PBC charges for providing short-term liquidity support were increased by between 0.3 and 0.6 percentage points, and the PBC was given additional room to adjust these rates according to economic and financial conditions. PBC has also continued its sterilization operations by way of changes in reserve ratios, open market operations, and issuance of central bank bills in the wake of strong foreign exchange inflows. China has also revalued its currency and the renminbi now floats against a basket of currencies. This policy of having greater flexibility in the exchange rate would allow monetary authorities to guard against the risk of any further increase in inflation in both product and asset markets. Thus, as I understand it, China has used a judicious mix of traditional monetary instruments, along with a selection of detailed prudential and regulatory instruments, to deal with the possibility of overheating in the economy.

In India, monetary management has had to contend with testing challenges on several fronts—an increase in domestic prices in the first half of 2004 driven largely by a sustained increase in international commodity prices including fuel, a large overhang of domestic liquidity generated by capital inflows, and the upturn in the international interest rate cycle. The Reserve Bank of India (RBI) has, therefore, had to strike a fine balance between reining in inflationary expectations, encouraging the impulses of growth, and ensuring financial stability. In early 2004, it was recognized that the finite stock of government paper with the RBI could potentially circumscribe the scope of outright open market operations for sterilizing capital flows that were last carried out in January 2004. The RBI cannot issue its own paper under the extant provisions of the Reserve Bank of India Act, 1934, and such an option has generally not been favored in India. Central bank bills/bonds would impose the entire cost of sterilization on the RBI's balance sheet. Besides, the existence of two sets of risk-free paper—gilts and central bank securities—tends to fragment the market. Accordingly, the liquidity adjustment facility, which operates through repurchases of government paper to create a corridor for overnight interest rates and thereby functions as an instrument of day-to-day liquidity management, had to be relied upon for sterilization as well. Under these circumstances, the Market Stabilization Scheme (MSS) was introduced in April 2004 to provide the monetary authority an additional instrument of liquidity management and sterilization. Under the MSS, the government issues treasury bills and dated government securities to mop up domestic liquidity and parks the proceeds in a ring-fenced deposit account with the RBI. The funds can be appropriated only for redemption and/or buyback of paper issued under the MSS. In addition to an increase in the MSS ceiling; raising of the cash reserve ratio (CRR); lowering of the rate of remuneration on the eligible CRR balances; and hikes in the reverse repurchase rate by 25 basis points each in October 2004, April 2005, and October 2005, several measures were also initiated to maintain asset quality of the banking system at a time of rapid credit growth.

The runaway oil prices riding on the back of growing demand in a cyclical upturn are currently looming large on the pace and pattern of the growth performance in both the economies. Although the economies have so far absorbed the oil shocks in stride and with surprising resilience, continuing uncertainties on the oil front pose a question mark on their sustained performance. Paradoxically, the reserves buildup with the Asian central banks, with its attendant cost implications, has started slowing down of late with soaring oil prices, cutting into the oil importers' trade and current account surpluses. However, the growing transfer on account of oil portends yet another risk in terms of the sustenance of current accounts. Besides, foreign direct investment and portfolio inflows are also showing signs of fatigue in several Asian countries with the hardening of the rates in the United States. With sudden reversals of expectations, the Asian economies thus run the risk of disruption in their financial and real markets.

Several countries in Asia have followed a relatively flexible exchange rate policy to ensure smooth adjustment along with corrections in the world economy. Such flexibility has served these countries well. However, the world has to guard against any new risks arising out of any large corrections in the exchange rates of the world's major currencies accompanied by rising inflation and interest rates (Mohan, 2004c). First, protectionist tendencies need to be curbed in keeping with the multilateral spirit of trade negotiations. Second, we need to work collectively toward developing a sound international financial architecture, the lack of which, it may be recalled, has led to excessive caution on the part of developing countries in building large reserves. Third, given the need for financial stability alongside monetary stability, central banks need to be cautious before joining the recent trend of separating the monetary and supervisory authorities, particularly in view of the muted responses to the pricing channels of monetary policy. In the recent past, faced with an unprecedented rise in housing credit, the Reserve Bank of India has raised the risk weight of housing loans as a countercyclical action for maintaining the capital-to-risk assets ratio. It is felt that availability of prudential instruments at the disposal of a central bank facilitates its twin tasks of monetary and financial stability.

Bibliography

Banik, N., and B. Biswas, 2006, "Exchange Rate Pass-Through in the U.S. Automobile Market: A Cointegration Approach," *International Review of Economics and Finance* (forthcoming).

Bank for International Settlements (BIS), 2005, *Annual Report, 2004–05* (Basel, Switzerland).

Bernanke, Ben S., 2005, "The Global Saving Glut and the U.S. Current Account Deficit," Sandridge Lecture, Virginia Association of Economics, Richmond, Virginia, March 10.

Blinder, Alan S., and Ricardo Reis, 2005, "Understanding the Greenspan Standard," paper prepared for the Federal Reserve Bank of Kansas City symposium, Jackson Hole, Wyoming, August 25–27.

Burstein, Ariel, Martin Eichenbaum, and Sérgio Rebelo, 2003, "Why Is Inflation So Low After Large Devaluations?" Discussion Paper 2003/8 (Budapest: Institute of Economics, Hungarian Academy of Sciences).

Calvo, Guillermo A., and Carmen M. Reinhart, 2002, "Fear of Floating," *Quarterly Journal of Economics*, Vol. 117 (May), pp. 379–408.

Fama, E.F., 1986, "Term-Structure Forecasts of Interest Rates, Inflation and Real Returns," *Journal of Monetary Economics*, Vol. 25, No. 1, pp. 59–76.

Faruqee, Hamid, 2004, "Exchange Rate Pass-Through in the Euro Area: The Role of Asymmetric Pricing Behavior," IMF Working Paper 04/14 (Washington: International Monetary Fund).

Frankel, Jeffrey, David Parsley, and Shang-Jin Wei, 2005, "Slow Pass-Through Around the World: A New Import for Developing Countries?" NBER Working Paper No. 11199 (Cambridge, Massachusetts: National Bureau of Economic Research).

Gagnon, J.E., and J. Ihrig, 2001, "Monetary Policy and Exchange Rate Pass-Through," International Finance Discussion Paper No. 704 (Washington: Board of Governors of the Federal Reserve System, July).

Goodhart, C., 1995, *The Central Bank and the Financial System* (Cambridge, Massachusetts: MIT Press).

Greenspan, Alan, 1998, "The Implications of Technological Changes," remarks before the Charlotte Chamber of Commerce, Charlotte, North Carolina, July 10.

———, 2004a, "Current Account," remarks before the Economic Club of New York, New York, January 13.

———, 2004b, "Risk and Uncertainty in Monetary Policy," remarks at the Meetings of the American Economic Association, San Diego, California, January 3.

———, 2005a, "Energy," remarks before the Japanese Business Federation, the Japan Chamber of Commerce and Industry, and the Japan Association of Corporate Executives, Tokyo, October 17.

———, 2005b, Testimony before the Committee on Banking, Housing, and Urban Affairs, United States Senate, Washington, February 16.

International Monetary Fund, 2002, *World Economic Outlook*, World Economic and Financial Surveys (Washington).

———, 2005, *World Economic Outlook*, World Economic and Financial Surveys (Washington).

Kamin, Steven B., Mario Marazzi, and John W. Schindler, 2004, "Is China 'Exporting Deflation'?" International Finance Discussion Paper No. 791 (Washington: Board of Governors of the Federal Reserve System).

King, Mervyn, 2005, "The Governor's Speech Salt Mills, Bradford," *Bank of England Quarterly Bulletin* (Autumn).

McCarthy, Jonathan, 2000, "Pass-Through of Exchange Rates and Import Prices to Domestic Inflation in Some Industrialized Economies," Staff Report No. 111 (New York: Federal Reserve Bank of New York).

McKinsey & Company, 2005, "Global Survey of Business Executives: Inflation and Pricing," *McKinsey Quarterly* (December).

Mishkin, F.S., 1991, "A Multi-Country Study of the Information in the Shorter Maturity Term Structure About Future Inflation," *Journal of International Money and Finance*, Vol. 10 (March), pp. 2–22.

Mohan, Rakesh, 2004a, "Challenges to Monetary Policy in a Globalizing Context," *RBI Bulletin* (January).

———, 2004b, "Fiscal Challenges of Population Aging: The Asian Experience," paper delivered at the Federal Reserve Bank of Kansas City symposium, Jackson Hole, Wyoming, August 26–28.

———, 2004c, "Orderly Global Economic Recovery: Are Exchange Rate Adjustments Effective Any More?" speech at the G-20 Deputies Meeting, Leipzig, Germany, March 3–4, *RBI Bulletin* (April 16).

Oliner, S., and D. Sichel, 2002, "Information Technology and Productivity: Where Are We Now and Where Are We Going?" Federal Reserve Bank of Atlanta *Economic Review*, Vol. 87 (Summer), pp. 15–44.

Rogoff, Kenneth, 2003, "Globalization and Global Disinflation," Federal Reserve Bank of Kansas City *Economic Review* (Fourth Quarter), pp. 45–78.

Stock, James H., and Mark W. Watson, 2003, "Has the Business Cycle Changed?" paper presented at the Federal Reserve Bank of Kansas City symposium, Jackson Hole, Wyoming, August 28–30.

The Economist, September 30, 2004.

10

Fiscal Policy in China

STEVEN DUNAWAY AND ANNALISA FEDELINO*

In recent years, fiscal policy in China has been prudent. Fiscal deficits have been lower than budgeted, because revenue overperformances relative to the budget targets were not fully spent and the stock of government debt has remained low and even declined in 2004 and 2005 (Figure 10.1). Fiscal policy has largely been guided by the government's medium-term focus on fiscal consolidation aimed at making room for likely future expenditures on contingent liabilities, such as the banking sector's large nonperforming loans, and a need for higher social spending as the population ages.

Fiscal policy has also been used, albeit less frequently, for short-term macroeconomic management. For example, as concerns about possible overheating and excessive investment in some sectors emerged in early 2003, fiscal policy was used to contain demand. In the future, as the authorities aim to direct growth away from investment, fiscal policy has an important role to play—for example, by reprioritizing spending in favor of programs that would boost household incomes, including spending on social safety nets and education. To make greater use of fiscal policy for demand management, broader coverage of fiscal accounts and a better assessment of the impact of budget operations on current macroeconomic conditions would be helpful, as well as improvements in cash management to better coordinate fiscal and monetary policies.

---

*Steven Dunaway is Deputy Director, IMF's Asia and Pacific Department, and is also the IMF's mission chief for China. Annalisa Fedelino is Senior Economist, IMF's Fiscal Affairs Department.

Figure 10.1. Fiscal Developments

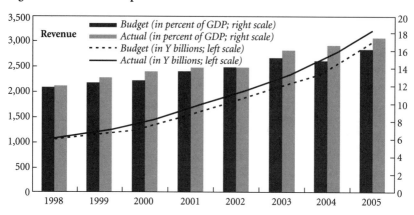

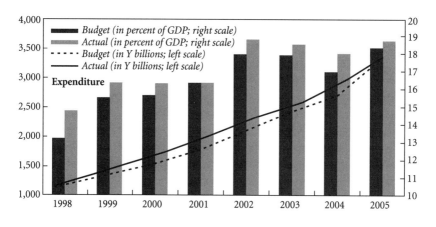

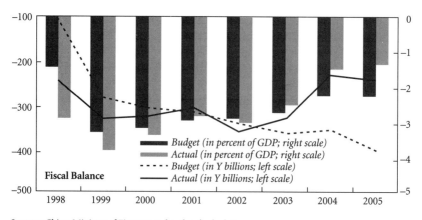

Sources: China, Ministry of Finance; and authors' calculations.

Table 10.1. Government Revenue[1]

	1998	1999	2000	2001	2002	2003	2004	2005
	(In percent of GDP)							
Total revenue	12.1	13.1	13.8	15.1	15.9	16.2	16.6	17.3
Tax revenue	11.0	11.9	12.7	13.9	14.6	14.7	15.1	15.8
of which: taxes on income and profits	1.9	2.1	2.6	3.6	3.9	3.5	3.7	4.2
Value-added tax (VAT) on domestic goods	4.3	4.3	4.6	4.9	5.1	5.3	5.6	5.8
VAT and excises on imports	0.7	1.1	1.5	1.5	1.6	2.1	2.3	2.3
Nontax revenue	1.1	1.2	1.1	1.2	1.3	1.4	1.5	1.5
	(As a share of total revenue)							
Tax revenue	90.7	91.0	92.0	92.4	92.0	91.2	90.7	91.3
of which: taxes on income and profits	15.4	16.4	19.2	23.6	24.6	21.7	22.3	24.4
VAT on domestic goods	35.5	33.1	33.3	32.4	32.2	33.0	33.9	33.7
VAT and excises on imports	5.4	8.7	10.9	10.0	9.8	12.7	13.9	13.4
Nontax revenue	9.3	9.0	8.0	7.7	8.0	8.8	9.3	8.7

Source: China Ministry of Finance.
[1]The coverage of this data includes the central government, provinces, municipalities, and counties.

Overview of the Budget

The budget deficit has declined from a peak of 3.7 percent of GDP in 1999 to 1.3 percent of GDP in 2005. This consolidation was achieved through revenue increases of more than 5 percent of GDP during this period; strong growth in tax collections, in particular income taxes and value-added taxes, was driven by both buoyant economic activity and improvements in tax administration (Table 10.1). At the same time, spending grew by about 3.5 percent of GDP, mostly in the areas targeted by the government's development policies. For example, capital expenditures expanded by about 3.5 percent of GDP over the period; expenditures on pension and social welfare programs increased by almost 2 percent of GDP, reflecting the transfer of some social expenditure mandates previously assigned to state-owned enterprises back to the government (Table 10.2).[1]

Fiscal consolidation over the past few years contrasts sharply with the performance in the years immediately following the Asian financial crisis. At that time, the Chinese authorities attempted to boost domestic demand by stimulating the economy; as a result, the budget deficit widened by

---

[1]The current budget classification, which is being upgraded, does not provide an accurate description of expenditures by economic and functional types. Hence, it is difficult to explain past trends in expenditure programs.

Table 10.2. Government Expenditure[1]

	1998	1999	2000	2001	2002	2003	2004	2005
	(In percent of GDP)							
Total expenditure and net lending	14.9	16.8	17.0	17.9	18.9	18.6	18.1	18.5
Current expenditure	11.7	12.5	12.7	13.7	14.5	14.4	14.4	14.9
of which: Administration								
and defense	3.5	3.8	4.0	4.4	4.8	4.8	4.8	4.8
Culture, education, public								
health, science	2.5	2.8	2.9	3.2	3.5	3.5	3.4	3.5
Pensions and social welfare relief	0.2	0.9	1.5	1.8	2.2	2.0	1.9	1.9
Capital expenditure	2.4	3.2	3.6	3.8	4.0	4.0	3.6	3.6
Unrecorded expenditure	0.9	1.1	0.8	0.4	0.3	0.3	0.2	0.2
Memo item: primary expenditure	14.0	16.1	16.3	17.1	18.3	17.9	17.7	18.1
	(As a share of total expenditure)							
Current expenditure	78.3	74.7	74.6	76.6	76.9	77.2	79.3	80.5
of which: Administration								
and defense	23.5	22.6	23.4	24.6	25.4	25.9	26.4	26.0
Culture, education, public								
health, science	16.9	16.7	16.9	17.9	18.3	18.6	18.5	19.1
Pensions and social welfare relief	1.4	5.5	9.1	9.9	11.6	10.5	10.7	10.4
Capital expenditure	15.9	18.8	20.9	21.2	21.3	21.3	19.6	19.5
Unrecorded expenditure	5.8	6.5	4.4	2.2	1.8	1.5	1.1	0.9
Memo item: primary expenditure	94.2	96.0	95.7	95.9	97.0	96.3	97.4	97.6

Source: China Ministry of Finance.
[1]The coverage of this data includes the central government, provinces, municipalities, and counties.

about 1.3 percentage points in 1998 and by 1 percentage point of GDP in 1999—the largest consecutive deficit increases recorded in the past two decades.

By and large, both revenue and expenditures have deviated by significant amounts from budget targets (Figure 10.2). Deviations were more sizable for expenditures in the earlier years (with a peak of almost 12 percent, relative to the budget, in 1998), when the government focused on stimulating the economy. This trend reversed in later years, when revenue overperformances relative to the budget (reaching a sizable 12 percent of the budget in 2004) were larger.

Assessing the Stance of Fiscal Policy

The Chinese authorities have described their post–Asian crisis fiscal policy as being "proactive." In addition to significant and deliberate

Figure 10.2. Overshooting in Revenue and Expenditure
(Outturn less budget, as percent of budget)

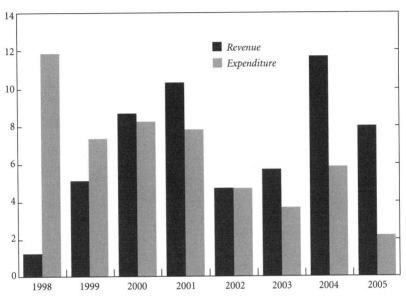

Sources: China, Ministry of Finance; and authors' calculations.

spending overruns, special bonds (referred to as "construction bonds") were issued beginning in 1998. The proceeds of these bond issues were largely on-lent to local governments to be spent on capital projects.

In the 2005 budget, the authorities portray a shift in the fiscal policy stance from "proactive" to "neutral." The targeted budget deficit was lowered in nominal terms to Y 300 billion—about Y 20 billion lower than the medium-term target announced in 2004—and the issuance of construction bonds was reduced to Y 80 billion (0.5 percent of GDP, about one-third the average annual issuance during 1998–2004).

However, the impact of fiscal policy on the economy was not only the result of changes in spending. Indeed, although spending exceeded budgeted amounts in every year since 1998, revenue was also much stronger. Thus, while the authorities were injecting stimulus from the spending side, they were also withdrawing it from the revenue side through higher taxes.

An assessment of the stance of China's fiscal policy using the conventional analysis of fiscal impulses takes account of the changes in both

Figure 10.3. Fiscal Impulse
(In percent of GDP)

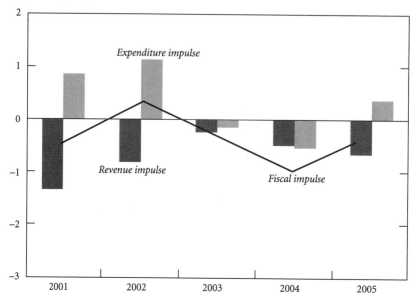

Source: Authors' calculations.

spending and revenue. The fiscal impulse is a simple indicator of the impact of fiscal policy on aggregate demand. Its main purpose is to provide a measure of fiscal policy that is adjusted for changes induced by cyclical movements in economic activity.[2] The measure can be used only as a guide, because a number of uncertainties surround the analysis, such as major structural changes and incomplete data; results are also sensitive to the choice of assumptions, particularly with respect to trend growth.[3] Based on estimates of the fiscal impulse, fiscal policy was broadly contractionary during 2004 and 2005 (Figure 10.3). As expected, spending was expansionary in the earlier years, whereas revenue has systematically exerted a contractionary impact.

---

[2]A positive fiscal stance indicates that the budget deficit (surplus) is larger (smaller) than it would be, given the cyclical position of the economy; similarly, a negative fiscal stance indicates that the fiscal deficit (surplus) is smaller (larger) than it would be, given the cyclical position of the economy. The fiscal impulse measures the change in the fiscal stance and indicates the direction and amount of fiscal stimulus.

[3]For simplicity, it is assumed that annual trend growth is 8 percent.

Figure 10.4. Implications of Fiscal Policy Execution for Liquidity Management

Uneven expenditure execution . . .

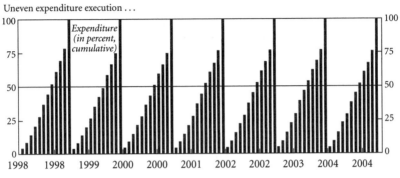

. . . leads to a cumulative deficit at the very end of the year . . .

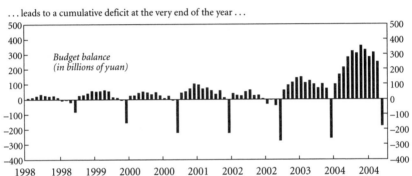

. . . and a sharp fall in government deposits at the PBC every December

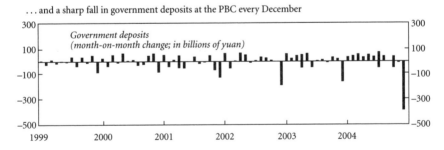

Sources: China, Ministry of Finance; and authors' calculations.

Strengthening the government's liquidity management is also important for improving macroeconomic policy operations. In China, government spending takes place unevenly during the year (Figure 10.4). Generally, it takes about 8 to 9 months to execute half of annual expenditures, and about 20 percent of recorded expenditures take place in December alone.

This leads to accumulation of fiscal surpluses during most of the year, with a sharp reversal in December. The associated large swings in government deposits significantly complicate the conduct of monetary policy over the course of a year.

China's New Fiscal Priorities and Their Impact on the Budget Balance

The Chinese authorities intend to shift spending away from capital projects to social programs. These policy intentions are reflected in a number of official statements and documents, including the 2005 budget speech by the minister of finance and the recently approved 11th Five-Year Plan. Because additional spending in health and education may require the construction of related infrastructure, this shift should not be seen as necessarily implying lower capital expenditures and higher current spending but rather as a move away from "construction of physical infrastructure to social infrastructure."[4]

Although these policy intentions are sound, spending increases should be weighed against a number of uncertainties and rigidities. The following are some key considerations:

- *The budget classification is inadequate.* Current classification of government expenditures—which is based more on functions and administration than on economic concepts—does not allow proper identification of programs or a clear-cut distinction between current and capital expenditures.
- *The budget classification is not consistent across the various levels of government.* Differences in expenditure and revenue classifications undermine coordination of budget formulation and implementation and hamper the consolidation of various budgetary items—a necessary requirement for consistency across various government programs. This is more of a problem in the context of social programs because most of this spending is delivered at the local level. For

---

[4]This will also reflect the model chosen by the authorities for the provision of the related services. For example, social infrastructure services may be provided by the private sector, as is the case in a number of countries, under concession contracts or public-private partnerships. This option is not without risks to the government, though, because shifting costs to the private sector may mean significant obligations later on. On the positive side, efficiency gains would be expected to stem from private sector participation. These (and other) issues will be explored in a forthcoming selected issue paper on social programs and policy options in China.

example, 94 percent of total health spending and 97 percent of total education spending were undertaken by local governments in 2004.
- *There is insufficient monitoring and lack of accountability.* Although the central government provides funding for most spending via transfers, thereby serving as an instrument to control and influence spending,[5] evidence suggests that monitoring mechanisms and accountability are lacking.
- *Political economy constraints are likely to play a role.* The model of development implemented so far in China has rewarded local authorities, promoting investment in fixed capital at the expense of other types of spending, including social programs. The planned shift in spending may actually meet with some resistance.
- *Spending is recorded on a cash basis.* Operations that would normally be treated as financing items (such as clearance of arrears or amortization of debt) are included in spending when the corresponding cash payments are made. This has biased spending upward when liabilities were paid back (for example, in 2004, when a large amount of arrears on value-added tax refunds to exporters was cleared) and has biased spending downward when the corresponding liabilities were incurred but not recorded. Hence, care should be taken when looking at spending patterns in China because there is not sufficient information to properly classify and record all government outlays.

Ongoing public financial management reforms would help address these weaknesses, and their implementation should buttress any significant increase in overall spending. This would provide assurance that policy intentions are translated into appropriate actions and that value for money is guaranteed. A new budget classification and chart of account should be promptly implemented, and the single treasury account should continue to be extended nationwide. Over time, the experience with pilots on performance-based budgeting of capital projects may also prove useful.

Significant increases in social spending might be achieved without major cuts in other expenditures or a substantial rise in the budget deficit, if recent history is any guide. Spending has risen significantly over the past several years, even when the budget dictated expenditure cuts. Over the period 1998–2005, the Chinese authorities intended to reduce spending relative to GDP more often than they intended to increase it

---

[5]Transfers from the center represent almost half of local governments' total resources on average, but this share varies significantly across provinces. For example, in 2002 this share ranged from about 20 percent in Beijing and Guangdong to about 60 percent in Inner Mongolia and Guizhou, and 85 percent in Tibet.

Table 10.3. China: Budgeted and Actual Spending
(In percent of GDP)

	1998	1999	2000	2001	2002	2003	2004	2005
Expenditure								
Actual	14.9	16.8	17.0	17.9	18.9	18.6	18.1	18.8
Budget	13.3	15.6	15.7	16.6	18.0	17.9	17.1	18.0
Difference	1.6	1.2	1.3	1.3	0.8	0.7	1.0	0.8
Memorandum items:								
Budgeted change		0.7	−1.0	−0.5	0.2	−0.9	−1.5	−0.1
Actual change		1.9	0.3	0.8	1.0	−0.3	−0.5	0.7

Source: China Ministry of Finance; and authors' calculations.

Figure 10.5. China: Deviations Between Outturn and Budget, 1998–2005
(In percent of budgeted level)

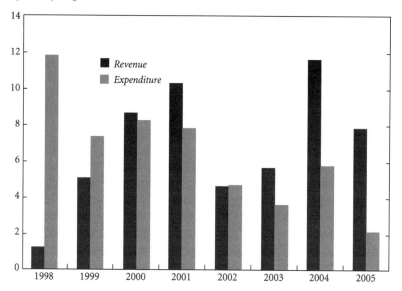

Sources: China, Ministry of Finance; and authors' calculations.

(Table 10.3 and Figure 10.5 show how budgeted spending in a year compared with actual spending in the preceding year). However, regardless of original intentions, spending has consistently exceeded budget targets. At the same time, these higher levels of spending have not led to a systematic deterioration in the fiscal position because revenue overperformance relative to the budget exceeded the increase in expenditure.

11

Labor Mobility in China and India: The Role of Hukou, Caste, and Community

ARVINDER SINGH*

Major debates on the industrialization of agrarian economies view labor mobility—sectoral and spatial, from agriculture to industry and from villages and small towns to cities—as central to understanding the pace and nature of industrialization. Many see labor mobility as the result of the commercialization and capitalization of agriculture, which leads to an increasing number of peasants who are alienated from the land and must be absorbed by the expanding urban and industrial sector. Indeed, industrialization is seen as hinging on the successful, rapid, and smooth transfer of the so-called surplus labor from agriculture to nonagriculture. Land and labor productivity rises in agriculture as a result of the labor transfer, which enables it to contribute more capital resources to the developing industrial sector through terms of trade (TOT) favorable to industry. The labor transfer mobilizes the savings of the rural households directly or through taxes and provides a ready "home market" for industrial sector goods. Speedy development of the industrial sector itself, along with rural industrialization and increasing urbanization, takes care of the transferred labor from agriculture.

Not only do the two sectoral, artificially neat distinctions present problems, but these models of the movement of labor and capital from agri-

*Arvinder Singh is a fellow at the Centre for the Study of Developing Societies, Delhi, India. An earlier version of this paper was presented at the China-India Roundtable at the Centre for Asian Studies, University of Hong Kong, September 22–23, 2005.

culture to the nonagricultural sectors are extremely state-centered. It is invariably the state that is seen as restricting, facilitating, or regulating the transfer of labor according to the needs of industrialization. In fact, neither the commercialization and capitalization of agriculture alone, which may indeed alienate peasants from the land and compel them to seek a livelihood elsewhere, nor the might or the policies of the state may explain why peasants are known to "irrationally" cling to the land (or, for that matter, to be too eager to move out even when the state intends to "keep" them in agriculture). Peasants often cling to the land despite the pressures of destitution. They may refuse to join the ranks of the factory proletariat even when they are made to give up the land.

Because states and state-centered theories are so preoccupied with extracting capital and food grains from agriculture for the supposed nascent industrial sector, labor is virtually treated as a residual issue. For one thing, by the time the state intervenes to "develop" agriculture for the sake of industry (a typical postcolonial developing-economy endeavor, modeled on Soviet-type planning), the industrial sector may already be fairly developed, generating its own surpluses and working on its own specific needs for skilled and unskilled labor. By this time, the industrial sector may not be short of capital in a blanket sense nor in need of help by cheap labor from agriculture. For this reason, planners should take into account simultaneous developments in agriculture and nonagriculture.

In addition, because of an aversion to depending on food imports, states may attempt to force peasantries to produce and deliver food grains for the national economies. These efforts can affect the retention or displacement of labor from agriculture. It would be better to recognize the ways that specific state policies affect labor in agriculture than to ascribe results vaguely to the "state."

The TOT, or the price scissors, so central in the literature on the rural-urban interface, fail to see beyond financial surplus from the agricultural sector.[1] The fact is that adverse TOT could depress agriculture and make more labor redundant. Policies on urbanization, on rural industrialization, and on raising incomes of agricultural households through investments in agriculture, which are often interrelated, would slow or hasten the movement of labor from agriculture. Equally important, labor's exo-

---

[1]See the section entitled "Agricultural Surplus, Industrialisation and Social Structure" in Singh (1999, pp. 1–29) for a discussion of the centrality of price scissors in debates on industrialization in contemporary developing agrarian economies. The article also discusses the desirability, feasibility, and efficiency of this tool in extracting surplus resources from agriculture.

dus from agriculture, whether on account of state policies or otherwise, might influence rural incomes, rural industry, and urbanization. It would help if the literature on rural nonfarm activities and employment and rural industry, and the demographic work on urbanization and migration, were linked more meaningfully with the economic literature on industrialization and labor mobility. The city studies as such, though interesting and growing in number, would be more useful if they would come out of the city limits and start looking at wider local economies of which the city is a part or with which it is linked.

Notwithstanding the occasional admission that the process of land alienation (or that of agriculture's dwindling relative importance in contributing to income or in engaging or supporting labor) is a long one, spread over generations, the models remain static by and large. Besides, a persisting or thriving agriculture is possible, is compatible with industrialization,[2] and has implications for rural-urban labor mobility. Even the role of differing forms of agrarian structures—land organization, ownership, and rights—and the size of holdings in rural-urban labor transfers has hardly been adequately captured in the literature.

Also, a wider class framework and a better appreciation of social differentiation in the economy than that suggested by the two-class polarization/pauperization framework—labor versus capital—would help in better understanding the dynamics of labor movement, both forced and voluntary, from agriculture to nonagriculture or from the rural to the urban sector. The polarization thesis is questionable in both agriculture and industry.[3] The thesis is simplistic. It is not the best way to analyze agrarian transformation and the way it links to the wider process of industrialization in the economy through sectoral movement of labor, capital, and enterprise. Creating a labor market, or a working class, in an industrializing agrarian economy is not all about conflict between labor and capital. The creation of a labor market would be better understood in the context of the wider social structure and institutions in which the developing economy is embedded. Also, not all peasants who leave the land will become part of the manual labor workforce. Some will become white-collar workers and entrepreneurs. Besides, there are also nonpeasant sections of the agricultural population to consider, such as artisans

---

[2]See "Agricultural Surplus, Industrialisation and Social Structure" in Singh (1999, pp. 1–29).

[3]See "Agricultural Surplus, Industrialisation and Social Structure" in Singh (1999, pp. 1–29). See also "Feasibility of High Accumulation in Peasant Agriculture" in Singh (1999, pp. 30–57).

and traders. The social and economic transition of artisans and traders is more difficult to capture in the polarization/pauperization perspective.[4] Then there is also the question of social and class relationships among land-owning peasants, landless labor, artisans, merchants, and industrialists; the relative social mobility of these classes should be considered.

Industrialization and Social Structure

Developing economies may be structured strongly around social and communal identities—for example, around caste and religion in India. Different social groups or communities provide different aspects of production in the economy. Land may belong to certain caste groups or religious communities; landless agricultural labor is provided by another caste group (usually lower menial castes); industrial capital may be in the hands of still others—traditionally the elite urban castes; and trade usually involves the traditional merchant communities (like *Baniyas*).

The following tables show how this is indeed the case in Punjab, a northern province in India, which also happens to be a classic Green Revolution site and is known for its rapid economic development over the past three to four decades. In fact, Punjab is a site of very large-scale labor migration—both into and out of the province. The data presented here make it clear that production and exchange in Punjab are almost neatly compartmentalized along religious and caste lines. The peasants are Sikhs (*Jats*), whereas merchants are Hindus (*Khatris/Aroras/Baniyas*). Sikhs cultivate and organize agricultural production, Hindus trade. Peasants live in villages, merchants live in towns. The occupational barriers between agriculture and nonagriculture are clear and strong.

Table 11.1 shows that the rural population in Punjab is predominantly Sikh and the urban population is predominantly Hindu. Of the rural households, 70 percent are Sikh whereas 65 percent of the urban households are Hindu.[5] The dominance of Sikh households in rural areas is greatest in the districts of Amritsar, Faridkot, Ludhiana, Bathinda, and Sangrur; while the

---

[4]See "Merchant Capital and Accumulation in Normal Commercialisation" in Singh (1999, pp. 58–82).

[5]The data in Tables 11.1 and 11.2 were obtained from the census of 1981, the time around which the Green Revolution was at its height. Punjab's population in 1981 was 16,788,915 and in 1991 it was 20,281,969. In 1981, 36.93% of the population were Hindus, 60.70% were Sikhs, and 2.37% were others. In 1991, Hindus were 34.46% of the population, Sikhs were 62.95%, and others were 2.59%. In the 1981 census, information on religion was collected according to the religion of the head of the household.

Table 11.1. **Rural and Urban Population in Different Districts in the Indian Punjab by Religion of the Head of the Household**

(In percent)

District	Rural		Urban	
	Sikhs	Hindus	Sikhs	Hindus
Punjab	**70.08**	27.74	32.25	**65.24**
Gurdaspur	**50.80**	40.70	19.73	**77.21**
Amritsar	**90.82**	7.01	41.60	**56.96**
Firozpur	**64.06**	34.79	20.85	**76.72**
Ludhiana	**87.20**	11.94	35.04	**63.21**
Jalandhar	**52.73**	46.21	20.62	**77.71**
Kapurthala	**70.27**	28.71	33.05	**65.92**
Hoshiarpur	**41.66**	57.06	22.93	**75.58**
Rupnagar	**58.19**	40.41	35.55	**62.03**
Patiala	**62.67**	35.33	34.06	**64.72**
Sangrur	**79.58**	16.49	34.79	**50.48**
Bathinda	**86.76**	12.54	36.59	**62.40**
Faridkot	**89.79**	9.60	42.75	**56.29**

Source: Singh (1999, p. 193).

dominance of Hindu households in urban areas is most pronounced in the districts of Jalandhar, Hoshiarpur, Gurdaspur, and Firozpur.

Table 11.2 makes it even clearer that the Sikhs in Punjab are concentrated heavily in rural areas. The table shows that 84 percent of the Sikhs live in rural areas and only 16 percent in urban areas. The occupational structure and religious composition of towns in Punjab make it clear that most merchants are Hindu and live in towns.

The towns in Punjab in which trading is predominant are precisely the ones where Hindus compose the majority of the population. Table 11.3 presents the percentage of the Hindu population that is engaged in trade in 42 towns the census has classified as primarily trading towns.[6] The names of the towns are arranged in descending order by population size.

The *mandi* towns are more striking. They owe their very existence to trade in agricultural goods. These towns are more prominent in the *Malwa* region, which comprises the southern districts of Bathinda, Sangrur, Faridkot, and Firozpur. Trade in these towns (including Abohar, Kot Kapura, Malout, Mansa, Sunam, Dhuri, Samana, Rampura Phul, Ahmedgarh, Budhlada, Patran, and Bhucho Mandi) has been conventionally handled by Baniyas.[7]

---

[6]The information, both on religion and on workers engaged in trade and commerce in towns, was obtained from the 1991 census.

[7]Otherwise, Tarn Taran in the district of Amritsar seems to be the only exception. In the Amritsar district/Majha, Sikhs have a more marked presence than they do in towns in *Doaba*, as in the districts of Jalandhar and Hoshiarpur.

Table 11.2. Percentage of Sikh Households in Different Districts in the Indian
Punjab According to Residence (Rural/Urban)

District	Sikhs	
	Rural	Urban
Punjab	83.80	16.20
Gurdaspur	89.43	10.57
Amritsar	79.98	20.02
Firozpur	90.75	9.25
Ludhiana	75.42	24.58
Jalandhar	82.20	17.80
Kapurthala	81.98	18.02
Hoshiarpur	90.74	9.26
Rupnagar	82.41	17.59
Patiala	78.80	21.20
Sangrur	87.83	12.17
Bathinda	87.50	12.50
Faridkot	86.44	13.56

Source: Singh (1999, p. 193).

The existing industrial capital in Punjab is primarily owned by the urban trading castes, the high-caste Hindu elite—Khatris, Aroras, and Baniyas—all of whom have trading backgrounds; however, artisans (Ramgarhias), who set up the small engineering goods workshops and factories that are connected with Green-Revolution technology, also own industrial capital. The religion and caste of the owners of the top 10 corporations in Punjab are telling (see Table 11.4 for religion and caste/subcaste of the chairperson and see Table 11.5 for the religion and caste of the members of the boards of directors of these companies). As these tables show, these companies are owned predominantly by Hindus. Of the 10 chairpersons, 9 are Hindu—3 are Khatri, 5 are Baniya, and 1 is Arora. The chairperson of the remaining company, Ranbaxy, is an Arora Sikh. Out of the 80 members of the boards of directors of these companies, as many as 70 are Hindus, 45 of them being Khatri, Baniya, or Arora.

At the top of the corporate ladder in Punjab, Khatris are represented by *Thapars*, Aroras by *Munjals*, and Baniyas by *Oswals*. Artisans are mainly Ramgarhias. Thapars represent the old Khatri industrial elite, whereas Munjals are newcomers, having emerged from the refugee middle class. The line that divides Baniya and Khatri in commerce seems to extend to industry too, where there is also a caste distinction. While the Baniya are rice shellers, the Khatris are more likely to enter the kind of modern industry not really related to agriculture.[8]

---

[8]Khatris have a strong taboo against working on iron or metals, which they consider to be the domain of the artisanal castes, mainly blacksmiths.

Table 11.3. Percentage of Hindu Population and of Main Workers Engaged in Trade
in Primarily Trading Towns in the Indian Punjab
(In percent)

Town	Hindus	Main Workers in Trade
Abohar	83.70	30
Ahmedgarh	56.28	35
Amloh	52.73	28
Banga	70.19	29
Bassi	51.42	29
Batala	66.67	31
Bhogpur	65.85	34
Bhucho Mandi	67.17	37
Budhlada	71.83	41
Dasua	68.92	32
Dhuri	63.51	36
Dinanagar	86.50	34
Doraha	47.63	30
Fatehgarh Churian	45.87	34
Garhdiwala	72.36	37
Giddarbaha	61.71	32
Goniana	63.25	46
Guru Har Sahai	74.82	38
Jagraon	43.32	33
Jaitu	57.52	28
Khanna	61.58	33
Kot Kapura	50.53	30
Lehragaga	71.52	40
Malout	71.84	33
Mansa	55.52	31
Morinda	51.87	28
Mukerian	77.78	43
Nabha	64.77	31
Nawanshahr	75.05	31
Patran	72.42	48
Qadian	56.89	38
Raman	64.65	33
Rampura Phul	55.74	31
Samana	68.93	41
Samrala	48.09	29
Shahkot	59.45	38
Sirhind	50.17	27
Sunam	60.01	33
Talwandi Bhai	45.11	35
Tapa	59.09	36
Tarn Taran	25.28	30
Urmar Tanda	55.39	29

Source: Singh (1999, p. 194).

Notice how the lower castes are almost completely missing from industry and trade. As Tables 11.6 through 11.9 show, the *Dalits*, or the *scheduled
castes*, play an extremely marginal role in trade in Punjab; commodity

Table 11.4. Religion and Caste of the Owners of the Top Ten Corporate Companies
in the Indian Punjab

Name of Company	Religious Affiliation of Chairman	Sub-Caste of the Chairman	Caste Group
Ranbaxy, Mohali	Sikh	1	Arora
JCT, Hoshiarpur	Hindu	Thapar	Khatri
Hero Cycles, Ludhiana	Hindu	Munjal	Arora
Mahavir Spinning, Ludhiana	Hindu	Oswal	Baniya
Jagatjit, Kapurthala	Hindu	Jaiswal	Baniya
Oswal Agro, Ludhiana	Hindu	Oswal	Baniya
Vardhman, Ludhiana	Hindu	Oswal	Baniya
JCT, Mohali	Hindu	Thapar	Khatri
Malwa Cotton, Ludhiana	Hindu	Oswal	Baniya
JCT Fibres, Hoshiarpur	Hindu	Thapar	Khatri

Source: Constructed by the author from a list of the names of the chairpersons and the members of
the boards of directors of the top corporate companies in Punjab. The list was provided in a report by
the Centre for Monitoring Indian Economy (January 1995). The table also appeared in Singh (1999,
p. 153).
Note: The companies have been arranged in descending order according to sales in 1994.
[1]Could not be ascertained.

trade there is predominantly in the hands of the higher castes. Scheduled
caste traders seem to be catering to the lower end of the markets. Fixed
costs, working capital, and turnover show that scheduled caste traders
operate at a much lower level than higher caste traders (see Table 11.6).
Interestingly, scheduled caste traders operate self-reliantly, with a low
frequency of loans.

Scheduled castes are more evident in trade in rural areas. One-fourth of
the trading enterprises located in rural areas in Punjab are owned by scheduled castes, whereas in towns, they account for only 8 percent of firms (see
Tables 11.7 and 11.8).[9] However, trade based in rural areas is itself of small
quantitative importance in Punjab (see Tables 11.7 and 11.9).[10]

I have argued elsewhere that such a peculiarly "communal" organization
of basic economic activities, along religious and caste lines, in which agricultural land and organization of its cultivation is almost exclusively in the
hands of one community whereas trading and industrial capital is owned
primarily by the other community, may not be incidental to the nature
and process of capital formation in the economy. Economic growth stem-
ming from a particular socioeconomic scenario and benefiting different

---

[9]The data pertain to 1990–91 and were obtained from the Government of India's
National Sample Survey Organisation (NSSO, 1996). See Singh (1999, pp. 147–48).

[10]The data pertain to 1985–86 and were obtained from the Government of India's
National Sample Survey Organisation (NSSO, 1989). See Singh (1999, p. 147).

Table 11.5. Religious and Caste Composition of the Board of Directors of the Top Ten Corporate Companies in the Indian Punjab

Name of Company	Total Size of the Board of Directors	Religion of the Members			Members of the Board Belonging to the Same Sub-Caste as Chairman (Number includes chairman)	Khatris (Hindu)	Aroras (Hindu)	Baniyas[1]	Others
		Sikhs	Hindus	Others					
Ranbaxy, Mohali	9	2	7	—	1	3	—	—	6
JCT, Hoshiarpur	9	1	8	—	3	5	1	—	3
Hero Cycles, Ludhiana	9	—	8	1	7	—	7	—	2
Mahavir Spinning, Ludhiana	9	1	7	1	1	2	1	1	5
Jagatjit, Kapurthala	8	2	6	—	3	1	1	3	3
Oswal Agro, Ludhiana	6	—	6	—	1	1	—	2	3
Vardhman, Ludhiana	9	1	8	1	2	—	—	4	5
JCT, Mohali	9	1	8	—	2	3	—	1	5
Malwa Cotton, Ludhiana	9	—	9	—	4	1	—	6	2
JCT Fibres, Hoshiarpur	3	—	3	—	2	2	—	—	1
	80	7	70	3		18	10	17	35

Source: Constructed by the author from a list of the names of the chairpersons and the members of the boards of directors of the top corporate companies in Punjab. The list was provided in a report by the Centre for Monitoring Indian Economy (January 1995). The table also appeared in Singh (1999, p. 154).

[1]All Baniyas are Hindus.

Table 11.6. Estimated Value per Enterprise of Fixed Assets, Working Capital, Outstanding Loan, and Turnover of Smaller Trading Enterprises in the Indian Punjab by Caste Group, 1990–91

Caste Group	Enterprises (Number)	(Percent)	Fixed assets (Rs.)	Working Capital (Rs.)	Loans (Rs.)	Turnover (Rs.)
Higher castes	217,468	84.43	24,951.83	38,502.41	4,224.29	306,766.79
Dalits	39,044	15.16	8,844.97	5,065.23	1,064.76	74,486.64
Scheduled tribes	1,028	0.40	9,363.82	28,014.85	11.49	121,350.83
Not reported	32	0.01	130,215.94	37,501.88	0.00	274,495.31
Total	257,572	100.00	22,461.27	33,391.81	3,727.92	270,812.79

Source: Singh (1999, p. 147).
Note: Includes proprietary and partnership enterprises within the same household.

Table 11.7. Estimated Value per Enterprise of Working Capital and Turnover of Smaller Trading Enterprises in Punjab by Caste Group and Location (Rural/Urban), 1990–91

Social Group	Enterprises (percent) Rural	Urban	Working Capital (Rs.) Rural	Urban	Turnover (Rs.) Rural	Urban
Higher castes	74.63	91.47	11,153	54,534	80,217	439,565
Dalits	25.04	8.06	3,444	8,684	45,583	139,003
Scheduled tribes	0.33	0.45	5,738	39,918	68,836	149,411
Not reported	0.00	0.02	16,200	38,922	50,625	289,420
Total	100.00	100.00	9,205	50,770	71,508	414,013

Source: Singh (1999, p. 147).
Note: Includes proprietary and partnership enterprises within the same household.

Table 11.8. Value per Enterprise of Fixed Assets, Working Capital, Outstanding Loans, and Turnover of Smaller Trading Enterprises Run by *Dalits* in Punjab by Location, 1985–86

Location	Estimated Number of Enterprises		Fixed Assets	Working Capital	Loans Outstanding	Turnover (Rs.)
Rural	OATE[1]	106,647	37,294	2,140	1,965	65,388
	Others	913	825	-	-	27,004
Urban	OATE	5,447	5,073	1,801	302	54,780
	Others	306	11,088	9,346	-	90,037

Source: Singh (1999, p. 148).
[1]OATE is an acronym for "own account trading enterprises," referring to enterprises without hired labor.

Table 11.9. Value per Enterprise of Fixed Assets, Working Capital, Outstanding Loans, and Turnover of Smaller Trading Enterprises of All Castes by Location in Punjab, 1985–86

Location		Estimated Number of Enterprises	Fixed Assets	Working Capital	Loans Outstanding	Turnover (Rs.)
Rural	OATE[1]	197,698	22,744	3,472	1,685	57,357
	Others	5,532	30,471	11,824	1,181	311,832
Urban	OATE	117,259	18,389	15,658	1,850	52,670
	Others	23,117	26,129	108,404	20,901	880,537

Source: Singh (1999, p. 148).
[1]OATE is an acronym for "own account trading enterprises," referring to enterprises without hired labor.

social groups or classes differently may lead to a reassertion of social identities and a more marked social differentiation than before. This social differentiation may also be more marked than the two-class labor-versus-capital models suggest. Therefore, rather than breaking down social barriers to development, it may increase the social distance between the classes, which is often reflected in the spatial segregation of classes (Singh, 1993 and 1999). I argue here that this kind of economic growth may have strong implications for the labor market and its mobility and in the making of the new working class as industrialization progresses. I argue that rural-urban labor mobility (which may not always be rural to urban but may even be urban to rural) is unlikely to be a neat two-class (capitalist and pauperized), state-led affair. It will also not be a free movement of labor even if the state leaves it to the market, because the market process is likely to be mediated by the social institutions and identities mentioned above. In fact, the state may even use traditional social institutions to restrict or guide labor mobility, as China has used *Hukou*, the age-old system of household registration kept alive by successive dynasties and regimes to this day.

Social Structure and Labor Mobility

The role that institutions like Hukou and caste play in the industrial transformation of socially segmented economies like China and India needs to be acknowledged and understood. These institutions may also have affected the differential performance of the Chinese and Indian economies in recent times. In China's standard story of reform-led development, focused more on foreign direct investment and international trade, the role of indigenous, local, and traditional institutions is inadequately considered, at least by the economists. In India, the economists have almost completely avoided issues such as caste and religion and have conveniently shielded themselves behind the rhetoric that "caste is class."

Hukou, which can be regarded more as an entrenched social institution than as a mere state instrument, obviously has had a direct bearing on labor mobility in contemporary China. Indeed, it seems to have been primarily used in recent times for regulating labor mobility.

China's is not a simple case of massive migration and massive controls. The way Hukou has been used in China not to restrict but to *guide* labor mobility is striking. The state arranged cheap migrant labor for basic urban sectors like construction and infrastructure and for major manufacturing sectors. It liberalized or practiced Hukou selectively in ways that allowed labor to move whenever and into whichever regions and sectors cheap labor was needed (indeed, labor has actively been encouraged and organized by the state from different regions and provinces). This has been the extent of the liberalization, if that is the proper term, of Hukou. Like the earlier marketization of the grain sector, Hukou is one of those areas of China's reforms where liberalization has taken longer to come. This is similar to the opening up of foreign investment in India—despite policies supporting it and claims to the contrary, foreign investment has not really taken off. However, it is important to note here that in India the state has almost no policies for regulating migrant labor.

China's migrant labor policy successfully maintained huge reserves of labor, thus keeping wages down and creating the country's celebrated low-cost advantage in the manufacturing sector. China even created a huge bureaucracy to guide the movement of migrants. Even recruiting is partly done by state agencies. This guided movement of labor from the rural/agricultural sector to the urban/industrial sector could be seen as an unusual way of primary accumulation from agriculture. With its vibrant foreign investment and exports, China's industrial sector perhaps did not need a financial surplus from agriculture and a home market as much as it needed cheap labor. The Indian economy, on the other hand, has a more inward orientation; for this reason, a financial surplus from agriculture and a home market have been very important in India. China has been successful in mobilizing labor easily and cheaply. This success has probably been helped by a sense of nationalism inspired by the idea of building a new China. In India, industrial labor is comparatively expensive, highly unionized and politically affiliated, and widely seen as an active enemy of reforms.

In China, sectoral and spatial labor transfer is definitely and in a planned way linked with the so called *Xiaokang* project, which aims to create a reasonably well-off society by 2050 and to quadruple the GDP by 2020 from the 2000 level. Project planners have established 7 percent as the target for the annual growth rate and 1 percent as the target for the yearly shift of the labor force from agriculture to the nonagricultural sectors. This does not seem to be impossible, for the Chinese have done it before—in the 20-year period preceding 2000. Interestingly, there are no such targets or targeted policies in India directly related to shifting labor from agriculture. It is *expected* that as agriculture develops and the urban industrial sector expands its employment-generating capacity, labor from agriculture will move out.

Through its use of Hukou in regulating labor mobility in the country, China has forced a particular kind of working class to be formed and kept the peasantry more or less back. (In addition to Hukou, China has accomplished this through "rurbanisation" and a rural industry led by the so-called Township and Village Enterprises, which have, however, grown weaker of late.) Because of these effects, Hukou might have perpetuated, if not sharpened, the deep-rooted rural-urban distinction in a social structure traditionally and historically dominated by the urban gentry. This particular mode of primary accumulation from agriculture might have had a lot to do with social mobility (or immobility) of classes, too, just as caste affects social mobility in India. Rural-urban division itself is very caste-like and extremely deep-rooted both in China and India.

Of course, Hukou and caste are two different things. Yet in some sense, Hukou is caste-like. Both are forms of social exclusion. Both have a hierarchy and an identity aspect. Both eventually control the social mobility of classes. Caste may well be performing Hukou-like functions in restricting or guiding labor mobility. In India, everybody knows who is whom and where people are from (if people don't know these things about others, they try to find out!). The Indians do not have to keep a Hukou to identify and exclude the ruralites or migrants. Name, surname, caste, religion, racial features, and provincial identity give one away. Whereas the *Mingongs* of China can be recognized by their appearance also, in India the migrant identity is mixed with other identities too, such as caste, occupational, provincial, and communal identities. (Note the social invisibility of Mingongs in China: they are hardly noticed in everyday urban life despite their pervasive presence. This is somewhat like the social attitude toward poverty in India.) In India, there are landed and nonlanded castes, menial castes, artisanal castes, merchant castes, and so on, all of whom are identified with different regions. Of course, caste is much more pervasive and far-reaching in its social and economic role than Hukou. However, Hukou may just be one of the many social institutions associated with the divisions and segmentations that exist in Chinese society. It may be that the social class divisions in China are subtler and less visible than in India's caste system. This could be a result of, among other things, the different nature of occupational status in China, the blurred distinction between the state and society, and the scholarly preoccupation with the state and the party.

The traditional urban gentry of China, in whose hands politics, bureaucracy, and even military continue to rest are like the *Brahmins* of the Middle Kingdom. The caste-like distinction between the gentry and commoners in China has persisted through the years regardless of the political regime in power. This distinction may have been perpetuated in recent times by keeping the commoners back, spatially and occupationally, through Hukou and through *Danwei*. The distinction may also have been reinforced through controls on higher education, which have helped form the educated elite. It would be an injustice to the interesting and complex social structure of China to ignore *social* distance between classes and to insist that the division is only between the rich and the poor. This would be akin to the argument that "caste is class" in India.

It is hard to imagine an India with Hukou (more difficult, perhaps, than imagining a China without Hukou). What would Mumbai, Kolkata, or Delhi be if there had been a Hukou to restrict the influx of outsiders? Or what would Delhi be without the in-migration of Bengalis, Punjabis, and Biharis, which are only three of the major groups of "outsiders" who are now numerically strong and comfortably claim to be Delhites. (The migration of these groups to Delhi is similar in ways to the privileged interregional Han movement and large-scale migration into Manchuria from other parts of China during the early twentieth century.) In Delhi's case, Bengalis' in-migration is associated with the early twentieth century shift of the British from Calcutta to Delhi; the British brought along the *Bhadralok* Bengali bureaucracy with them. Punjabis' influx is associated with the Partition of India and the creation of Pakistan in 1947 and later to other sociopolitical factors and movements in Punjab. The case of the Punjabi migration to Delhi is perhaps somewhat different because of the Punjab's physical proximity to Delhi; in fact, Delhi once was a part of the Greater Punjab. The influx of the Biharis is a more recent phenomenon—from the past 20 or 25 years. Occupationally, Punjabis are more likely to be found in the service, industry, and white-collar sectors, whereas Biharis hold a mixture of manual and informal service sector and white-collar jobs. It seems that India has had a much longer and perhaps a more interesting history of market-led internal labor mobility, of all types, including rural-urban. Spurts of economic development in different regions, social upheavals, and catastrophes have also periodically led to large-scale population movements of working people, both blue- and white-collar.

Yet the seeming "free-for-all" labor market in India might be deceptive. Just because there is no Hukou, or household registration system as such, in India, Indian labor is not necessarily free to move. In fact, social structure does restrict or hasten labor movement in India. In addition, factor markets in India (as also in other developing economies such as China) are far from integrated, and the dictum that labor—most obviously manual labor—moves from comparatively less developed areas to the more developed ones holds true in India, as well. Ethnic, religious, caste, cultural, and linguistic divisions and their corresponding identities (market imperfections of their own kind, one could say) may effectively restrict labor movement or even encourage some other kind of movement. Labor from certain areas may be more or less welcome in certain other areas. The state may not interfere directly (as the state in China does) and may uphold the idea of the free market and democracy, yet the demands of social structure would dictate who would leave the countryside and how they would be welcomed or "settled" in the cities (for the mostly poor and lower-caste migrants, survival in the market environment is already disadvantaged). Once in the cities, it is not uncommon in India for migrants to organize themselves around their caste and community identities, as much to seek and protect their rights in the city as to let their community organizations serve as networks for future incoming migrants. (The idea of political rights is apparently meaningless in China. In India, even the poorest of the poor migrants get their voting rights almost immediately upon arrival in the city, and it becomes politically not only incorrect but undesirable to evict them.) No wonder labor in India can be observed to be moving in caste and community groups. That is true as much of agricultural as of nonagricultural labor, of Bihari farm laborers in Punjab or Malayalee[11] Stenos and nurses across the country. The phenomenon is helped by community-based identities and networks on the one hand and by caste and regional discrimination in the job market on the other hand.

It is not surprising that migrant manual labor in Punjab has come from outside and from a distant, impoverished, and itself a violently caste-ridden region like Bihar (and some areas of Eastern Uttar Pradesh near Bihar). Punjab's and Bihar's economies are interesting contrasts. One is

---

[11]Malayalee referes to people from the state of Kerala, who speak Malayalam.

a classic Green-Revolution, rapidly grown economy; the other is "backward." One is known for semi-feudalism and the other for enterprising peasant proprietors. The labor migration that has occurred between them represents the most pronounced and the best-known case of interprovincial rural labor migration in India. The rural laborers from Bihar were economically deprived and were members of the lowest castes; there was hardly demand for them in their own social and economic space. With few opportunities in the neighboring region, these illiterate and socially excluded laborers literally took the train to far-off Punjab, which was the most prosperous and booming province in the country at the time. In the process, they were not just meeting an economic demand for labor in Punjab's agricultural and nonagricultural sectors but they were also filling a social space where local peasants and artisans refused to join the ranks of the proverbial industrial proletariat, contrary to expectations.

The peasants in Punjab have refused to become workers in the factories. Instead, they have aspired to industrial entrepreneurship or white-collar jobs. They have not gotten access to the trade sector, which is in the hands of the traditional business community. Some have clung to their land; some have migrated abroad, legally and illegally. The decisions they have made regarding occupation should be understood not in terms of inflated aspirations or lack of industrial enterprise but in terms of the mobility of social classes. To be poor would still be preferable, or less demeaning, than being *socially* at the bottom of the hierarchy. The Jat Sikhs have been a dominant caste in Punjab. If they become factory workers, they slip down the social ladder. *Sectoral* labor mobility in terms of occupations is closely tied with *social* mobility of classes. The compulsions of social hierarchy may restrict or hasten sectoral, occupational, or spatial mobility.[12]

As a whole, caste and religious discrimination is a fact of life in the Indian labor market. Workers belonging to certain castes or minority communities may not even expect to work for, or may prefer not to work for, nonstate employers of certain other communities or groups. In fact, entrepreneurs themselves go by strong regional, provincial, and

---

[12]Incidentally, Punjab's case also shows that rural-urban labor mobility may not be as straight and simple as it appears. The laborers may traverse a long and complicated path, working in the rural sector or elsewhere before ending up in the urban industrial sector. Punjab attracted migrant labor both in the rural farm sector and in the manufacturing sector. However, a large section of the rural labor has "graduated" to the urban manufacturing sector over a generation. Also, the way migrants in Punjab have come to hold considerable political power in the province because of their numbers shows how considerations of electoral democracy affect internal migration in India.

ethnic identities, such as Marwari, Punjabi, and South Indian. It is not uncommon to find certain social groups flooding particular sectors of the job market, both white- and blue-collar. Certain communities dominate economic sectors such as trade and industry (such as the case of the Malayalee Stenos and nurses across India, as mentioned above, or the case of trade and industry in the hands of different social classes, as shown in the previous section). Labor (also capital) in India has a tendency to move together in their social groups both sectorally and spatially. When rural laborers move to the cities, they are not necessarily taking the jobs that the city dwellers do not want—the so-called leftover or undesirable jobs—as many researchers believe. The job choices they make are more likely to be influenced by the imperatives of the social structure—perhaps only those who have nothing to lose in their social status would be inclined to accept the jobs that no one else wants. Migrants often compete with the locals, and sooner or later some of them succeed. Migrants may work in the informal service sector because this sector may provide an entry point; the formal sector, especially the private sector, may be "protected," with its jobs reserved for particular caste groups and communities. The informal service sector may also be attractive to migrant workers because it has a socially ambiguous status.

It is interesting to note that, despite social and cultural differences, such as those of caste and religion, or maybe because of these differences, India as a whole seems to be more receptive to internal migrant labor. Migrant labor exists on the fringes but is allowed and tolerated. This is true not only because there is no Hukou.

Of course, there are occasional protests in some provinces and cities against "outsiders." In Punjab, certain Sikh groups wanted the rural migrant laborers to leave because they believed that the presence of the migrants, who are Hindu even if largely lower caste, would threaten the Sikhs' numerical dominance in Punjab. In addition, there are periodic outbursts against outsiders in Mumbai for cultural, demographic, and economic reasons.

However, Indian cities seem to be absorbing migrants more permanently, more democratically, and into a wider range of occupations than Chinese cities are doing. Indian cities also give migrants more physical space, too. There are "migrant villages" both in Chinese and Indian cities, but migrants in Indian cities seem to be more spread out. Slums are only one part of the story, although these get more attention. This is not to deny, however, that industrialization projects in both China and India are using forced or hostage labor. The Indian economy has yet to effectively come out of the traditional, socially determined forms of labor organization. This is evident from the remnants of "attached" labor in Indian agriculture ("attached" through caste) and the persistence of "bonded" labor here and there in both rural and urban locations of India.

Bibliography

Andors, Stephen, 1977, *China's Industrial Revolution: Politics, Planning, and Management, 1949 to the Present* (New York: Pantheon Books).

Au, Chun-Chung, and Vernon Henderson, 2002, "How Migration Restrictions Limit Agglomeration and Productivity in China," NBER Working Paper No. 8707 (Cambridge, Massachusetts: National Bureau of Economic Research).

Banerjee, Biswajit, 1983, "Social Networks in the Migration Process: Empirical Evidence on Chain Migration in India," *Journal of Developing Areas*, Vol. 17, pp. 185–96.

Bian, Yanjie, and John Logan, 1996, "Market Transition and the Persistence of Power: The Changing Stratification System in Urban China," *American Sociological Review*, Vol. 61, No. 5.

Cai, Fang, 2000, *China's Migration* (Zhengzhou, China: Henan People's Press).

———, 2001, "Institutional Barriers in Two Processes of Rural Labor Migration in China," Working Paper No. 9 (Beijing: Institute of Population and Labor Economics, Chinese Academy of Social Sciences).

———, 2005, "The Rural-Urban Income Gap and Critical Points of Institutional Change," *Social Sciences in China*, Vol. 26 (Autumn), pp. 93–111.

———, and Meiyan Wang, 2004, "Changing Labor Participation Rates in Urban China and the Policy Implications," *Social Sciences in China*, Vol. 25 (Winter).

Costello, Michael A., 1987, "Slums and Squatter Areas as Entrepots for Rural-Urban Migrants in a Less Developed Society," *Social Forces*, Vol. 66, No. 2, pp. 427–45.

Dewar, Margaret, 1956, *Labour Policy in the USSR, 1917–1928* (London: Royal Institute of International Affairs).

Dong, Xiao-yuan, and Paul Bowles, 2002, "Segmentation and Discrimination in China's Emerging Industrial Labor Market," *China Economic Review*, Vol. 13, No. 2–3, pp. 170–96.

"Don't Let Delhi Go Mumbai Way: SC," 2005, *Times of India*, September 8.

Faure, David, 2002, *Town and Country in China: Identity and Perception* (New York: Palgrave in association with St. Anthony's College, Oxford).

Fei, Hsiao-tung, 1980, *China's Gentry: Essays in Rural-Urban Relations* (Chicago: University of Chicago Press).

Ford Foundation, *Labor Mobility in China, A Review of Ford Foundation Grantmaking 1997–2001* (Beijing: Ford Foundation, undated).

Government of India's National Sample Survey Organisation (NSSO, 1996)

Government of India's National Sample Survey Organisation (NSSO, 1989)

Gu, Chaolin, and Haiyong Liu, 2002, "Social Polarization and Segregation in Beijing," in *The New Chinese City: Globalization and Market Reform*, ed. by John R. Logan (Oxford: Blackwell Publishers).

Guang, Lei, and Lu Zheng, 2005, "Migration as the Second-Best Option: Local Power and Off-Farm Employment," *China Quarterly*, Vol. 181 (March), pp. 22–45.

Harris, John R., and Michael P. Todaro, 1970, "Migration, Unemployment, and Development: A Two-Sector Analysis," *American Economic Review*, Vol. 60, No. 1, pp. 126–42.

Hinton, William, 1990, *The Great Reversal: The Privatization of China, 1978–1989* (New York: Monthly Review Press).

Howe, Christopher, 1971, *Employment and Economic Growth in Urban China 1949–1957* (Cambridge, United Kingdom: Cambridge University Press).

Hugh, Patrick, ed., 1976, *Japanese Industrialization and Its Social Consequences* (Berkeley, California: University of California Press).

Iredale, Robyn, 2000, "China's Labor Migration since 1978," in *Contemporary Developments and Issues in China's Economic Transition*, ed. by Charles Harvie (New York: St. Martin's Press).

Jasny, Naum, 1961, *Soviet Industrialization* (Chicago: University of Chicago Press).

Jie, Fan, and Wolfgang Taubmann, 2002, "Migrant Enclaves in Large Chinese Cities," in *The New Chinese City: Globalization and Market Reform*, ed. by John R. Logan (Oxford: Blackwell Publishers).

Johnson, D. Gale, 2002, "Can Agricultural Labor Adjustment Occur Primarily Through Creation of Rural Non-farm Jobs in China?" *Urban Studies*, Vol. 39, No. 12, pp. 2163–74.

Lewis, A., 1954, "Economic Development with Unlimited Supplies of Labour" (Manchester School of Economic and Social Studies, May).

Lewis, W. Arthur, 1955, *The Theory of Economic Growth* (London: Allen and Unwin).

Lin, Justin, Fang Cai, and Zhou Li, 1996, *The China Miracle: Development Strategy and Economic Reform* (Hong Kong SAR: Chinese University Press).

Mazumdar, Dipak, 1983, "Segmented Labor Markets in LDCs," *American Economic Review, Papers and Proceedings*, Vol. 73 (May), pp. 254–59.

Meng, Xin and Junsen Zhang, 2001, "The Two-Tier Labor Market in Urban China," *Journal of Comparative Economics*, Vol. 29 (September), pp. 485–504.

Moore, Barrington, 1966, *Social Origins of Dictatorship and Democracy: Lord and Peasant in the Making of the Modern World* (Boston: Beacon Press).

Nee, Victor, 1996, "The Emergence of a Market Society: Changing Mechanisms of Stratification in China," *American Journal of Sociology*, Vol. 101, No. 4.

O'Leary, Grey, 2000, "Labor Market Developments," in *Contemporary Developments and Issues in China's Economic Transition*, ed. by Charles Harvie (New York: St. Martin's Press).

Perry, Elizabeth, and Xiabo Lü, eds., 1997, *Danwei: The Changing Chinese Workplace in Historical and Comparative Perspective* (Armonk, New York: M.E. Sharpe).

Ping, Huang, 1996, "Hukou System and Rural-Urban Migration in China," *CERES, the FAO Review.*

———, and Frank N. Pieke, 2003, "China Migration Country Study," paper presented at the Regional Conference on Migration, Development and Pro-Poor Policy Choices in Asia, Dhaka, Bangladesh, June 21–24.

Singh, Arvinder, 1993, "Peasants, Merchants and Accumulation: A Study of the 'Awkward Classes' in the Context of Rapid Agricultural Growth" (Trivandrum, Kerala, India: Centre for Development Studies, April).

———, 1999, "Industrial Transition in an Agricultural Surplus Region: A Study of Punjab" (Ph.D. dissertation; Trivandrum, Kerala, India: Centre for Development Studies, May).

———, 2003a, "China Is Far Ahead: But Did India Run?" (unpublished; Beijing: China Centre for Economic Research, Peking University, January 13).

———, 2003b, "China: One Goal, Two Policies, Three Problems, Four Aspects," *The Financial Express,* New Delhi, June 23.

———, 2003c, "The Xiaokang Pursuit: Will Agriculture Help or Obstruct?" paper presented at an international conference on "China in the 21st Century: Chances and Challenges of Globalization," Institute of Far Eastern Studies, Russian Academy of Sciences, September 23–25.

———, 2004a, "Much to Celebrate, Much to Take Stock," *China Report,* Vol. 40, No. 4, pp. 351–55.

———, 2004b, "Una carrera con China?" *La Vanguardia Dossier,* Vol. 12 (July–September).

———, 2005, "Comparisons Between China and India," *China and the World Economy* (May–June).

Skinner, G. William, 1977, "Urban Development in Imperial China," in *The City in Late Imperial China,* ed. by Skinner (Stanford, California: Stanford University Press).

Srivastava, Ravi S., 2005, "Bonded Labor in India: Its Incidence and Pattern," Working Paper No. 43 (Geneva, International Labour Office, April).

———, and S.K. Sasikumar, 2003, "An Overview of Migration in India, Its Impacts, and Key Issues," paper presented at a Regional Conference on Migration, Development and Pro-Poor Policy Choices in Asia, Dhaka, Bangladesh, June 21–24.

Tawney, R.H., 1935, *Land and Labor in China* (Boston: Beacon Press).

Todaro, M.P., 1969, "A Model of Labor Migration and Urban Unemployment in Less-Developed Countries," *American Economic Review,* Vol. 59, pp. 138–48.

———, 1989, *Economic Development in the Third World* (New York: Longman, 4th ed.).

United Nations Educational Scientific and Cultural Organization (UNESCO), 2004, "Together with Migrants," Research Action Project (Beijing, January).

Wang, Feng, and Xuejin Zuo, 1999, "Inside China's Cities: Institutional Barriers and Opportunities for Urban Migrants," *American Economic Review*, Papers and Proceedings Vol. 89 (May), pp. 276–80.

Weber, Max, 1964, *The Religion of China: Confucianism and Taoism*, trans. and ed. by Hans H. Gerth (New York: MacMillan).

Yang, Martin M.C., 1969, *Chinese Social Structure: A Historical Study* (Taipei: Eurasia Book Co.).

Zhang, Zhongli, 1955, *The Chinese Gentry: Studies on Their Role in Nineteenth-Century Chinese Society* (Seattle: University of Washington Press).

———, 1962, *The Income of the Chinese Gentry* (Seattle: University of Washington Press).

Zhao, Zhong, 2005, "Migration, Labor Market Flexibility, and Wage Determination in China: A Review," *The Developing Economies*, Vol. 43 (June), pp. 285–312.

PART V

INDO-CHINA ECONOMIC
COOPERATION

12

Indian Economic Development and India-China Cooperation

NALIN SURIE*

Relations between India and China have been developing and diversifying in a steady manner over the last five years. During this period there have been a series of high-level visits from both sides that have further helped the process of mutual understanding and laid the foundation for cooperation in a diverse set of sectors. Premier Zhu Rongji visited India in January 2002; Prime Minister Vajpayee visited China in June 2003; and Premier Wen Jiabao was in India in April 2005. Each of these visits has helped improve the quality of the relationship.

As the two most populous developing countries, which are neighbours and ancient civilizations that have had contact to mutual benefit, there is growing realization that our common experiences are very important for furthering the processes of socio-economic development in our respective countries.

The Declaration of June 2003 provides a road map for the development of relations and comprehensive cooperation between India and China. The Joint Declaration of April 2005 demonstrates that bilateral relations have entered a new phase of development. It reflects the consensus that bilateral relations transcend bilateral issues and have acquired a global and strategic perspective.

Both sides have recognized the importance of trade and economic relations for strengthening bilateral relations. Important progress has been

---

*Nalin Surie is India's Ambassador to China.

made in this direction. Bilateral trade has grown at a fast pace, mutual investment is growing as are our links in financial matters, civil aviation, customs cooperation, agriculture, tourism, and so forth. All this while peace and tranquility is maintained in the border areas based on the agreements of 1993, 1996, and 2005.

The leaders of the two countries now meet regularly on the sidelines of regional and multilateral meetings and conferences. Prime Minister Manmohan Singh and President Hu Jintao met on several occasions in 2005.

The Indian model of economic development has become a topic of discussion of late on account of our rather high growth rates particularly in the last two years. Unfortunately, not enough deep analysis has been done in public discourse over why these growth rates have become so high and why they are sustainable. What is perhaps not so well known is that, since 1980–81, India's average real growth rate over the next 20 years was just under 6 percent. This was happening surely but steadily and did not attract attention. Nor did India seek such attention.

The central idea of the Indian model is to unleash the productive capacity and forces of our people, especially their entrepreneurial abilities and ideas. This has been enabled by our democratic political system and market-based economy, that has the benefit of a strong institutional and financial infrastructure, which is rapidly growing and adapting itself to the changing needs of the marketplace and to the requirements of greater accountability and transparency.

The other very important factor is the wave of optimism and confidence in the country's abilities and talents that is gaining strength. That India has been able to compete effectively in the global marketplace not only in knowledge-based industries but also in high tech manufacturing, pharmaceuticals, auto components, and so forth, has added to the feeling of self-belief in the country.

There are several reasons why the economy is doing well. Growth is now well spread across various sectors, and the agricultural sector is picking up. There has been very substantial growth in manufacturing, and, of late, this has begun to lead economic growth. There is improvement in business expectations and confidence, and corporations have accumulated significant internal resources. Investment in the economy now continues to be driven by domestic demand, and global competitiveness is a new factor. The export sector is also beginning to play a more important role.

Rapid growth requires stable financial markets and these have remained generally stable and mature. This has enabled, among other things, efficient allocation of resources.

Over the nine quarters ending in December 2005, the Indian economy grew in real terms at around 8 percent. Our savings rate is around 29 percent, and the investment rate is 31 percent.

Like China, India is a developing country, and there are many factors that inhibit or adversely impact on growth rate. This is true also of developed countries, although factors that inhibit growth in these countries may differ from those in developing countries. The argument over the impact of inefficient government on growth rates is not new, and this is also true of the participation of government in productive activity. The mantra today is that governments should increasingly distance themselves from direct participation in economic activity. In developing countries like ours this argument can now perhaps be made with some justification in many cases because past government participation in economic activity enabled development of the economy, institutions, and the market itself so that the private sector could play a more important and determining role today in economic growth.

There is no doubt that inefficiency, whether in the government or private sectors, will adversely affect growth. We are fully aware of this in India, and efforts are being made to reduce such inefficiency in government. In his recent address to our Parliament on February 16, 2006, the President of India drew attention to several changes that India intends to implement to reduce government inefficiency and improve the quality of governance.

It is true that under-developed infrastructure affects the growth rate of the Indian economy. Yet in spite of this, we have maintained, on a secular basis, high growth rates. We are fully aware of this deficiency, which is now being addressed on a priority basis. Very significant improvements have already taken place in the telecommunications and road sectors and these are being expanded. Indeed, development of these sectors is providing a huge thrust to growth. Simultaneously, inadequacies in power generation, ports, airports, and the railways are being addressed. These issues have also been addressed at some length in the president's parliamentary address (see above). For instance, the government has setup a Special Purpose Vehicle called the India Infrastructure Finance Corporation Limited to provide long-term debt funds to commercially viable projects in the infrastructure sector. The National Highway Development Project envisages a total investment of Rs. 1.75 trillion over the next seven years. The Ministry of Power is facilitating, among other projects, the construction of five major power projects with a capacity of 4,000 megawatts each.

India and China are the two largest developing countries and among the geographically largest countries in the world. They are also the two most populous countries and rapidly growing. Together, we both account for more than one-third of the world's population. Over the next ten years, if we sustain our current growth rates, we will probably become the two largest markets in the world, and will be two of the largest global producers of a whole series of goods and services. As our cooperation increases, our common developmental efforts will benefit not only our countries but the rest of Asia and the world as a whole. This rapid and sustained development of one-third of human kind will, in my estimation, be hugely beneficial to the whole world and influence the future course of events.

If you look at the socio-economic problems identified by the Chinese leadership that need to be addressed—such as unemployment, rural-urban inequalities, regional imbalances, environmental and water problems, needed improvements in health and education, and the status of women—you will find that India's problems are virtually identical.

Take the rural sector as an example. In the president's address to both houses of parliament in February 2006 to mark the opening of the budget session (which is akin in many respects to China's annual NPC session) drew attention to the ambitious schemes that the government intends to put in place to deal with issues such as rural unemployment, development of rural infrastructure, and improvement of health and educational facilities. The present focus in China on the development of the new socialist countryside is similar.

Which is the best example that our two countries should look towards in resolving the problems each faces? Is there another country that faces these problems in the same magnitude and under similar socio-economic circumstances? It is true that our systems of political governance are radically different from each other. But the more we share our developmental experiences, the more commonalities we find both in terms of problems and solutions to those problems.

It is not only in the rural sector that we need to share our experiences and learn from each other. This applies across the board to environmental issues, availability of clean drinking water, manufacturing, education, health, the institutions of the market economy, banking, financial management, employment generation, urban development, and many others. Obviously solutions implemented by one country cannot be automatically applied to the other without any adjustment. But the process of learning from each other has begun and needs, in my view, to be hastened quite substantially.

Competitors or partners? I think China and India will be both, but the important thing is there is space for both countries in a growing world. Is India-China development cooperation a zero-sum game? Not at all. It has positive effects not just for India and China, but also for the Asia-Pacific region and the global economy.

The India-China economic and trade relationship is still a work in progress, but it is headed in the right direction. The discussions at the recently concluded Ministerial-level Joint Economic Group in New Delhi on March 16, 2006, reflected a determination to build on the very impressive development of the bilateral trade and economic relationship over the last five years. The opportunities are enormous and manifold.

Business leaders in both countries are presently engaged in identifying opportunities for productive activity and cooperation with each other. A Joint Study Group, set up by heads of both governments, submitted their report to Manmohan Singh and Wen Jiabao in New Delhi in April 2005. The report identifies potential complementarities between India and China in expanded trade and economic cooperation and has recommended a series of measures that would facilitate trade in goods, services, investments, and other areas.

Our governments have also decided to entrust a group of experts to study the feasibility of and benefits from an India-China regional trading arrangement. This group of experts has begun its work.

Finally, it is likely that bilateral trade will reach US$20 billion (or more) by 2008. India's and China's rediscovery of each other has begun.

13

India-China Economic Cooperation

ARVIND VIRMANI*

The legacy of relations between India and China began to change in the 1980s, with the opening of both economies. As long as their relationship was seen through a geopolitical prism, it was easy for both countries to view it as a zero-sum game. With the shift in both countries from an import substitution to an export promotion strategy during the 1980s, the focus shifted gradually to economics. With the acceleration of globalization during the 1990s, the imperatives of global interdependence and an appreciation of the possibilities of mutual gain have also increased. This is particularly so in China, whose share of world trade is now about eight times that of India; they have similar shares of foreign direct investment (FDI) and capital flows. Starting in 2000 these developments led to the establishment of an India-China Joint Study Group (JSG) on accelerating bilateral economic cooperation, of which I was a member as Director and Chief Executive of the Indian Council for Research on International Economic Relations (ICRIER). ICRIER also did a number of background studies for JSG, covering goods and services. After the presentation of this report to the two governments, the two countries formed an agreement for economic cooperation when Premier Wen Jiabao visited India in April 2005. However, the following discussion has nothing to do with that group or the government; these are my personal views.

*Arvind Virmani is Principal Advisor (Development Policy), Planning Commission, New Delhi, India.

I will first review the trade between the two countries and then briefly mention issues connected with comprehensive economic cooperation and a multilateral context.

India-China Trade

In 2004, India was among China's top 20 trading partners, fifteenth in imports, and eighteenth in exports. China was a much more important trade partner for India in 2004, ranking in the top five, second in imports, and third in exports. The details of India's trade with China, from India's perspective, are shown in Table 13.1.

Trends in the export, import, and trade shares are depicted in Figure 13.1. China's shares in India's overall imports and exports have been rising rapidly over the past six years. It is interesting to note that the gap that opened up between the import share and the export share in the middle of the period has now closed.

Figure 13.2 gives the rate of growth of trade as well as the growth of China's share in India's international trade from 1997–98 to 2004–05. The main point is that normally we look at the growth of trade, which for India is somewhat faster than the rise in the trade share of China. That is because India's trade has been growing quickly over this period. But still the trade share has been rising and accelerating over this period at 3.4 percent per annum, as you can see from the bottom line in the figure.

Figure 13.3 depicts the volatility of exports and imports along with the rate of growth of total trade. The figure shows that there is much less variability in India's imports from China than in India's exports to China. There is much more fluctuation in the rate of growth of the export trade. The precise degree of volatility is shown in the second column of Table 1, which shows that the coefficient of variation of the export growth rate is double that of the import growth rate.

More precisely, the coefficient of variation of exports is 1.2 and that for imports is 0.6. This can bring up a number of hypotheses. One is that India's imports are driven by normal market considerations. In contrast, there is much more implicit or explicit government intervention in China's imports from India; there is an element of government signaling to the socialist/public sector part of the economy. These signals have apparently turned positive over the past few years. This is probably also the reason for the closing of the gap between the import and export shares that had opened up in the middle of the period (Figure 13.1). So perhaps the positive signals from the Chinese government have been partly responsible for this growth in trade.

Table 13.1. India's Trade with China

Year	Mean	CV	1996–97	1997–98	1998–99	1999–2000	2000–01	2001–02	2002–03	2003–04	2004–05
Trade (US$ billion)											
Exports to China			0.6	0.7	0.4	0.5	0.8	1.0	2.0	3.0	5.3
Imports from China			0.8	1.1	1.1	1.3	1.5	2.0	2.8	4.1	6.8
Trade with China			1.4	1.8	1.5	1.8	2.3	3.0	4.8	7.0	12.1
Trade balance	-0.8	-0.5	-0.1	-0.4	-0.7	-0.7	-0.7	-1.1	-0.8	-1.1	-1.4
(percent of trade)	-25%	-0.5	-10%	-22%	-44%	-41%	-29%	-36%	-17%	-16%	-12%
Growth rate											
Export	39%	1.2		17%	-41%	26%	54%	15%	108%	50%	81%
Import	33%	0.6		47%	-1%	17%	17%	36%	37%	45%	67%
Trade	34%	0.8		33%	-17%	20%	28%	28%	60%	47%	73%
Trade share	18%	0.9		27%	-16%	4%	17%	28%	33%	18%	29%
Share in all/total											
Export	2.9%	0.6	1.8%	2.1%	1.3%	1.5%	1.9%	2.2%	3.7%	4.6%	6.6%
Import	3.6%	0.4	1.9%	2.7%	2.6%	2.6%	3.0%	4.0%	4.5%	5.2%	6.2%
Trade	3.3%	0.5	1.9%	2.4%	2.0%	2.1%	2.5%	3.1%	4.2%	4.9%	6.4%

Source: www.dgft.delhi.nic.in, Department of Commerce.

Figure 13.1. China's Share in India's Total Trade
(In percent)

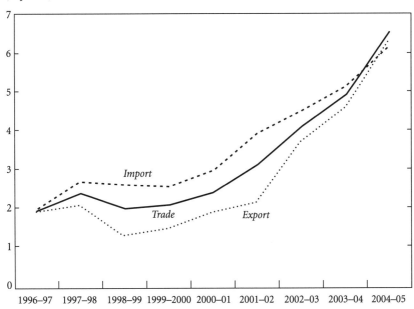

Source: www.dgft.delhi.nic.in, Department of Commerce.

The commodity composition of trade in Table 13.2 lists India's top 10 exports to China and top 10 imports from China. Similarly, Figure 13.4 depicts the concentration ratio for exports and imports at the two-digit level by ordering them from those with the highest to the lowest share and then cumulating the share. So, on the horizontal scale, if we look at the number five and track it to the graph, we get the five-product concentration ratio at the two-digit level.

The bottom line in Figure 13.4 shows the concentration with respect to imports. The concentration is very high: the top five commodities account for almost 70 percent of India's imports from China. The concentration in India's exports to China is even higher. The top five exports account for more than 80 percent of the exports from India to China. Now we return to Table 13.2 to see the list of commodities. The top export from India to China is the two-digit category "ores, slag, and ash" (26) with 52 percent of total export value. The category of salt, sulfur, lime, and cement (25) has another 2.6 percent of export value. So there is a very high concentration of basic raw material exports.

Figure 13.2. Growth Rate of India's Trade in China
(In percent)

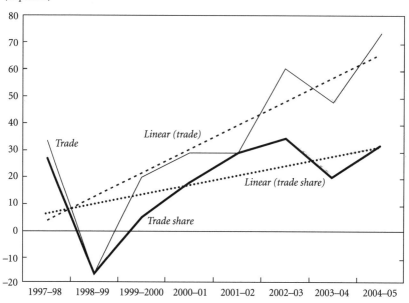

Source: www.dgft.delhi.nic.in, Department of Commerce.

It seems that this has a more general implication beyond India. China is now drawing many raw materials from all over the world—from Latin America, Africa, and Asia. Thailand, for example, is a raw materials exporter to China. Indonesia, another raw materials exporter, has seen a surge in exports to China. I think this is going to be a factor around the world. A theory that was very prominent in Latin American economist literature envisioned countries in the "center" as an exporter of industrial goods and the periphery as an exporter of raw materials. I think some element of that arrangement is emerging with respect to China and other developing countries.

The second noteworthy point is with respect to intermediate goods. The next-largest exports from India to China are iron and steel, followed by plastics. There are a number of undifferentiated products, and this, again, has certain implications for India and for other countries. That is, intermediate goods industries are subject to much cyclical fluctuation. In recent years, the fluctuation has been driven by very high aggregate investment rates in these products. High aggregate investment creates a

Figure 13.3. Growth Rate of India's Trade in China
(In percent)

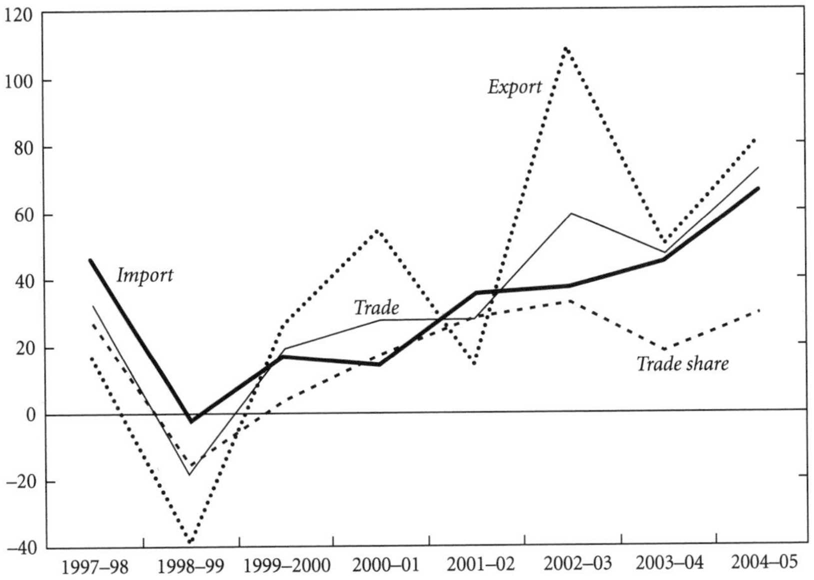

Source: www.dgft.delhi.nic.in, Department of Commerce.

demand for these commodities, which results in a jump in investment in these industries, so the supply rises eventually. Thus, temporary imbalances lead to higher imports, but these are eliminated by higher supply, and could even be followed by exports of the same intermediate goods.

Table 13.2. Composition of India-China Trade

India's Top 10 Exports to China			India's Top 10 Imports from China		
HS	Commodity	Share	HS	Commodity	Share
26	Ores, slag, ash	52.1%	85	Electrical machinery and parts	25.6%
72	Iron and steel	11.5%	84	Nuclear reactors, boilers, machinery	14.8%
39	Plastic and articles	7.4%	27	Mineral fuels, oils, and waxes	12.0%
29	Organic chemicals	6.5%	29	Organic chemicals	11.7%
28	Inorganic chemicals, compounds	3.9%	50	Silk	4.3%
25	Salt, sulphur, lime, cement, etc.	2.6%	71	Pearls, stones, jewelry	2.2%
3	Fish and aquatic invertebrates	1.9%	28	Inorganic chemicals, compounds	2.1%
84	Nuclear reactors, boilers, machinery	1.8%	72	Iron and steel	1.8%
52	Cotton	1.5%	59	Textile fabrics, industrial textiles	1.5%
74	Copper and articles	1.2%	54	Man-made filaments	1.5%

Source: www.dgft.delhi.nic.in, Department of Commerce.

Figure 13.4. India's Import and Export Concentration of Trade with China
(Cumulative share, in percent)

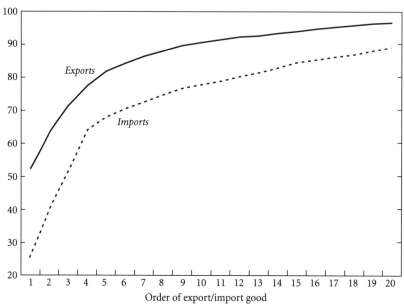

Order of export/import good

Source: www.dgft.delhi.nic.in, Department of Commerce.
Note: Sorted on year 2004–05.

Over time, perhaps during the next 10 years, all countries, including India, may face this fluctuation in intermediate goods trade with China. That is, the net demand for these undifferentiated, intermediate products will sometimes be converted to net excess supply turning to net exports.

Future Potential

Before examining the future potential of India-China trade, it is useful to take stock of the existing position from another perspective. China's trade with India is less than 1.5 percent of its trade with the world, whereas India's trade with China is over 6 percent of its total trade. Consequently, India's exports to China constitute 6.6 percent of its total exports, whereas they make up only 1.4 percent of China's imports. China's exports to India account for 1 percent of its total exports, but constitute 6.2 percent of India's imports. This is simply a reflection of each country's share of world trade, with India's being about 0.8 percent and China's about 6.4 percent.

The bilateral trade potential is very high, given the size and economic dynamism of the two economies. Since 1980, China's average growth rate has been the highest, whereas India's has been the eighth or ninth highest. They are among the 10 largest economies in terms of current exchange rates and among the five largest in terms of purchasing power parity. They are also neighbors sharing a long border, although this border consists of the highest mountain range in the world; and the sea route between the two countries is long. Both countries are signatories of the Bangkok Agreement and already participate in the Asian currency union mechanisms.

More formally, Dr. Amita Batra at ICRIER has built an augmented gravity model that provides quantitative estimates of the gap between actual trade and trade potential between India and other countries. It finds that the potential for trade between India and China is between two and a half times and six times the actual trade in the year for which the model was estimated. The data used were for the year 2002. Some of this potential has already been actualized in the subsequent three years to 2005 and is in the process of being realized more fully.

There are also a few other related studies by Batra that have been published as ICRIER working papers and are available on the ICRIER website (www.icrier.org). These papers, as well as our analysis for the India-China study group, show the scope for intra-industry trade. Both countries are highly diversified economies with very diversified manufacturing structures. Thus, there is considerable scope for intra-industry trade in intermediate manufactured goods. The share of private consumption in India's GDP is relatively high compared with other emerging economies, whereas that of China is perhaps the lowest in the world. As consumer goods grow in importance, there will also be increasing scope for intra-industry trade in differentiated products and intermediate goods specialization.

There are identifiable differences in export specialization in the two countries, based on natural resource endowments, skills, and policy. The most interesting and important resource-based difference is in textiles. Given the abundance of cotton in India, India's exports are heavily concentrated in cotton textiles and garments, whereas China has a commanding position in textiles and garments based on man-made fibers. An ICRIER study some years ago showed that the two countries' exports were largely noncompeting because of this. Among the reasons for this divergence in skill development were a highly rigid labor policy for organized industry, small-scale industry reservations, and exorbitant indirect (excise) taxes on man-made fibers in India. One of the indirect consequences of the rigid labor policy has been a greater use of educated labor and higher value-added niche products in India.

There are also differences in skills, because of either cultural or historical development. In the case of general skills, India has a comparative advantage in the English language and in dealing with multiethnic, multireligious workforces. These strengths could enable a clear advantage in industries such as advertising and entertainment. China has developed a lasting advantage in labor-intensive mass manufacturing, based on the virtual absence of labor laws for the FDI export sectors, the single-party system of government, and the organization and management of the socialist investment system. There are also differences in sector-specific skills. India has developed, over the past half century or more, skills in engineering/automobiles, specialty chemicals, and pharmaceuticals. China, by contrast, has developed over the past 25 years skills in consumer electronics, telecommunications, and other consumer durables. On the other hand, China and India are similar in that the labor force in each country has strong math and science skills.

The ICRIER studies also identified at the two-digit and six-digit levels a list of commodities with the greatest export potential from India to China and vice versa. Among the former are agriculture and allied products, iron and steel and articles thereof, nuclear reactors, boilers and machinery, man-made steel fibers and man-made filament yarns, organic chemicals, and cotton. Among the categories that have potential for exports from China to India are nuclear reactors, boilers and machinery, organic chemicals, silk, and electrical and electronic equipment. Nuclear reactors and boilers and machinery appear in both lists and indicate the potential for intra-industry trade.

Barriers and Constraints

To realize the full potential of India-China trade, remaining barriers and constraints have to be relaxed. These include customs rules and procedures, standards, certification and regulatory practices, nontariff barriers, and rules of origin.

Some of the problems that have arisen with respect to customs valuation are (1) the use of a minimum reference price instead of the World Trade Organization–sanctioned transaction cost method; (2) a variation of customs valuation across ports, resulting in additional costs to exporters; and (3) a lack of clarity in guidelines and procedures relating to imports for exporters. Though some of these things apply to all trade, there are some changes that may be more acute in a bilateral context that would lead to an increase in India-China trade. Thus there is a need to evolve a mutual consensus on customs valuation, clarify guidelines, facilitate uniform documentation across ports, and increase the efficiency of handling at ports and customs. An existing mechanism, the India-China Customs Cooperative Group, can be used for this purpose.

To illustrate, variation across ports creates special problems for small exporters. For a large exporter, like the United States to China, these problems are minor; but if you have many small exporters, as we have in India-China trade, these variations create additional costs for both sides. Similarly, there are problems related to imports for exporters. This may be very simple for, as an example, traders in Taiwan Province of China or Hong Kong SAR, but not for those in India. We need more clarity and guidelines.

Also, there are certain problems related to standards, certification, regulatory practices, rules, and regulations in terms of national treatment and accessibility. The Chinese language poses a problem for Indian traders, because most Indian trade is in English. It is difficult for them to keep up with the Chinese regulations. This situation creates an extra problem for Indian traders that could be easily remedied if the rules and regulations were published and updated regularly, preferably in English, the language of international commerce.

The certification process, including with respect to sanitary and phytosanitary standards (SPS), also involves delays and high costs. SPS requirements generally exceed what is necessary to protect consumer health. India has a great interest in certain agricultural commodities, the standards for which need clarification. Certain other standards related to commodities such as granite are not available. Harmonization of technical and agricultural standards would greatly facilitate India-China trade.

Certain nontariff barriers (NTBs) are also hindering the growth of trade between the two countries. There are problems related to tariff quotas, preshipment inspection, and definitions of rules of origin. For example, there are NTBs on automotive parts and components, and a tariff-quota on agricultural products. These barriers need to be eliminated. A preshipment inspection agreement between the two countries could help reduce NTBs and related barriers. Problems relating to rules of origin can be sorted out by agreeing on clear definitions. This in turn could result in smoother movement of goods between the two countries.

Removal of these constraints and barriers in a spirit of cooperation and mutual accommodation will set the stage for a quantum jump in economic cooperation between the two countries.

Next Steps

Going forward, from a global perspective, everybody knows that China has been the fastest-growing economy, averaging 9.5 percent for the past 25 years, but not many people know that India has been the eighth- or ninth-fastest-growing economy over the past 25 years. This is because many people think that India's reforms started in 1992 and that India has been lagging by about a decade. The fact is that India's reforms started around the same time as China's (1980), but its average growth rate has been slower (Virmani, 2005). The East and Southeast Asian economies that have grown faster than India during the past 25 years are likely to slow during the next decade. India, in contrast, has been on a rising growth rate trend since the reforms of the 1990s. It is therefore likely to be among the five fastest-growing economies (if not among the top three) along with China. It will become one of the primary global growth drivers by the end of the decade along with China. By 2010, it is likely to be the fourth-highest contributor to world GDP growth after the United States, China, and Japan. The possibilities for trade and economic cooperation between China and India will therefore continue to expand.

Once the identified barriers are removed (hopefully in a year or two), we should be in a position to start discussing a comprehensive economic cooperation agreement. Given the high reinvestment, "vent for surplus" approach of the socialist-owned part of China's economy, a free trade agreement is likely to benefit China more than India. So there has to be a trade-off. I think both sides need to recognize that you cannot have these special agreements unless both sides can balance the gains and losses. There are already some special losses to certain manufacturing sectors such as toys. However, India expects some gains in the services sector. The agreement has to be a comprehensive one that includes trade in both goods and services.

Another area of economic cooperation that is very important for the future of Asia is that Indian and Chinese economic cooperation be embedded in an Asian context. India and China have either framework agreements or ongoing discussions for a Free Trade Agreement/Common Economic Partnership Agreement with the Association of Southeast Asian Nations (ASEAN), Japan, and Korea. We have to harmonize these by developing an East Asian community in which ASEAN, China, Japan, and India are equal partners. In December 2005, there was a meeting of the East Asian Economic Community, in which both India and China were involved. China's attitude toward Indian inclusion will be closely watched by people in India and Asia as an example of its general approach to hegemonic competition versus mutually beneficial cooperation.

Bibliography

Batra, Amita, 2004, "India's Global Trade Potential: The Gravity Model Approach," ICRIER Working Paper No. 151 (New Delhi: Indian Council for Research on International Economic Relations, December).

————, and Zeba Khan, 2005, "Revealed Comparative Advantage: An Analysis for India and China," ICRIER Working Paper No. 168 (New Delhi: Indian Council for Research on International Economic Relations, August).

Batra, Amita, and Arvind Virmani, 2004, "Response to East Asian Regionalism and Its Impact—The Indian View," paper presented at the International Conference on East Asian Regionalism and Its Impact, organized by the Institute of Asia-Pacific Studies, Chinese Academy of Social Sciences, Beijing, October 21–22.

————, 2005, "India-China Economic Relations," *Security and Society,* Vol. 1 (Summer), pp. 106–16.

Virmani, Arvind, 2005, "Policy Regimes, Growth and Poverty in India: Lessons of Government Failure and Entrepreneurial Success," ICRIER Working Paper No. 170 (New Delhi: Indian Council for Economic Research, October). Available via the Internet: http://www.icrier.org/WP170GrPov9.pdf.

————, 2006a, "China's Socialist Market Economy: Lessons of Success," ICRIER Working Paper No. 178 (New Delhi: Indian Council for Research on International Economic Relations, January).

————, 2006b, *Propelling India from Socialist Stagnation to Global Power: Growth Process,* Vol. I (New Delhi: Academic Foundation), forthcoming.